# THE VIOLENCE IN OUR BONES

Also by Neera Chandhoke

*State and Civil Society: Explorations in Political Theory*
*The Politics of U.N. Sanctions*
*Beyond Secularism: The Rights of Religious Minorities*
*The Conceits of Civil Society*
*Contested Secessions: Rights, Self-determination, Democracy, and Kashmir*
*Democracy and Revolutionary Politics*
*Rethinking Pluralism, Secularism and Tolerance: Anxieties of Coexistence*

Books co-authored by Neera Chandhoke
*Understanding the Post-Colonial World:*
*Theory and Method* (with Nehru Memorial Museum and Library)
*Reinventing Social Democratic Development: Insights from Indian and Scandinavian*
*Comparisons* (with Olle Tornquist, John Harriss, and Frederik Engelstad)

Books edited by Neera Chandhoke
*Mapping Histories: Essays Presented to Ravinder Kumar*
*Contemporary India: Economy, Society, Politics* (with Praveen Priyadarshi)
*Social Protection Policies in South Asia* (with Sanjay Kumar Agrawal)

# THE VIOLENCE IN OUR BONES

### MAPPING THE DEADLY
### FAULT LINES WITHIN
### INDIAN SOCIETY

## Neera Chandhoke

ALEPH

**ALEPH**

ALEPH BOOK COMPANY
An independent publishing firm
promoted by Rupa Publications India

First published in India in 2021
by Aleph Book Company
7/16 Ansari Road, Daryaganj
New Delhi 110 002

ISBN: 978-93-90652-42-6

1 3 5 7 9 10 8 6 4 2

Printed at Parksons Graphics Pvt. Ltd., Mumbai

# CONTENTS

# REFLECTIONS ON VIOLENCE

*They say my verse is sad: no wonder,*
*Its narrow measure spans,*
*Tears of eternity and sorrow,*
*Not mine, but man's.*[1]

—A. E. Housman

## THE QUESTION

Do 'We, the People of India,' have violence in our bones? This is the question this work seeks to address. The answer is neither a clear yes or no. Any answer to the question of whether violence is in our bones is bound to be ambiguous. In fact, any question that relates to human beings, their desires, their proclivities, their moral judgements, and their tendency to violence cannot but be ambivalent. After all, human beings are complex, contradictory, and entirely unpredictable.

Admittedly, the impulse to violence is a part of individual and collective psyches of, if not all, at least a majority of people. We do not need to carry out large sample surveys to establish the point; observations of how people think and behave are enough. Observers are stunned when they note that individuals can turn on their own neighbours and friends in times of collective violence in the most brutal of ways. Scholars are taken aback at the depravity to which human beings, who are otherwise sane and rational, can descend at moments of crisis. Chapter 1 on Partition violence in India illustrates precisely this conundrum.

What we need to note is that the impulse to violence does not easily convert to violent acts that intend to maim and kill. A number of

---

[1] A. E. Housman, *The Collected Poems of A. E. Housman*, New York: Henry Holt and Co., 1940, p. 155.

factors spark off the transition from despicable thoughts and emotions to ignoble acts of torture and murder. This transition requires a catalyst or a trigger. The catalyst can be provided by an ideological system, such as racism, that motivates and encourages people to inflict bodily and mental harm upon groups and individuals identified as the 'other'. Another ideology which implicitly and explicitly sanctions violence against the so-called lower castes is caste-based discrimination. A third ideological system that induces violent acts is communalism. There are other stimuli to violence: patriarchy, homophobia, and ethnic rivalry, for instance.

Equally, acts that injure, maim, and kill can be triggered off by merchants of hate, or 'entrepreneurs', who seek to foment trouble between communities or groups. It is unwise to make generalizations about the human condition, but common sense points to a considerable distinction between a not-so-nice human impulse to violence, for example, Y's strong desire—'I wish X was dead'—and murder, which is not nice at all. What is the trigger that motivates Y to pick up an axe and actually kill X? Y may, despite his murderous thoughts, be disinclined to take the ultimate step, that of taking a human life, most of the time. But a malevolent character, who knows of Y's somewhat inchoate and unexpressed—or even expressed—craving that he would like to see X dead, can function as the trigger. A malicious person can work on Y's mind, convincing him that X should be killed, or that he needs to be murdered. If Y is malleable, if he is vulnerable to persuasion, or if his anger or resentment overcomes better sense, he might well succumb.

In the hands of clever manipulators and demagogues, an unspoken or even an unrecognized impulse to violence makes the transition to acts of violence. If 'they' can make you believe absurdities, reportedly wrote the French Enlightenment philosopher Voltaire, 'they' can make you commit murder. I use the word 'reportedly' advisedly because Voltaire has been credited with many quotes, some of which were manufactured by others. The exact quote in this context is: 'Truly whosoever is able to make you absurd is able to make you unjust.'[2]

We, as observers of the human condition, or more expressly, the political condition, can sense the terrible impulse to violence hovering

---

[2]Anthony Jay, *The Oxford Dictionary of Political Quotations*, Oxford: Oxford University Press, 2012, p. 323.

over the horizon like a dark shadow. We might resist, we might give in, or we might just rest satisfied by hurling the choicest abuses at our, sometimes, hapless victim. If we give in, we are ready for the move from an unarticulated desire to the dreadful act of murder. Lovers of detective fiction (which the philosopher Bertrand Russell is supposed to have said is the only form of fiction worth reading) will appreciate this point.

Individuals certainly kill if they form part of a crowd intent on murder. At such times, perfectly stable people can be swept away by torrents of hate and unthinking reaction. They abdicate reason and morality and surrender to murderous impulses. People kill if a clever manipulator turns his vile intent to controlling their minds. States notoriously use violence to maintain control over populations. But violence is also a weapon of the last resort, the weapon of the weak, the dispossessed, and the weapon of those who have been subjected to overlapping injustices because power holders simply do not listen. In such cases, violence takes the form of resistance to injustice. Sometimes, all these factors operate in tandem and push people to act in unforeseen ways. At other times, people resist incitements to commit violence.

Violence can often be random, sometimes spontaneous; violence may be organized, and is often an effective but a short-sighted tool of power of the state and of the dominant classes. Violence may exist as part of our individual and collective psyches, but it is not always recognized, and even if recognized, not always realized. Which of us have not been taken aback by our propensity to think of violence? Which of us has not been frightened by our readiness to accept, if not sanction, the sheer brutality or completely inhuman acts of violence in our and other societies?

## THE AGE OF VIOLENCE
Consider our recent history. Life in India has been marked by the rise of vigilantes who maim, murder, and wound in the name of the God, Lord Ram. On 18 June 2019, in Jharkhand, a mob assaulted Tabrez Ansari on suspicion of theft. He was reportedly tied to a pole and lynched while the crowd surrounding him demanded that he repeat the slogan 'Jai Shri Ram'. He did so but the beatings did not stop. The police rescued Ansari, but took him to the police station instead of the hospital. He was admitted in a hospital four days later, where he succumbed to his

injuries.[3] Ansari was twenty-seven years old. A life ended even before it had begun for the young man. And we in the rest of India watched the sorry and the scary theatre of violence silently, unbelievingly but mutely. We should make no mistake; silence is acquiescence.

Indians perhaps have become used to performative acts of violence staged in public spaces for sometimes ridiculous reasons. We have become cynics. Lynching of vulnerable people has become a part of everyday life in India over the last few years. People have been lynched because they transport cows, because WhatsApp messages spread rumours of child-lifters, because people appear suspicious, and simply because they are different—a mentally challenged person here, a disoriented woman there. Between 10 May 2018 and 2 July of the same year, frenzied mobs killed people in sixteen different incidents because unsubstantiated WhatsApp posts warned that they might be child-lifters.[4]

India is the inheritor of the philosophy of non-violence. We live in the land of Mahavira, of Gautama Buddha, of Ashoka, and of M. K. Gandhi. The leader of the Indian independence movement, M. K. Gandhi spoke powerfully and persuasively against violence and for non-violence. We will come to his ideas in the last chapter of this work. The irony is that Gandhi's life was cut short by an act of violence committed by an extremist, Nathuram Godse, who subscribed to the right-wing ideology of Hindutva. Indians should remember that a deep commitment to non-violence runs through various texts that constitute the literary and philosophical tradition of the country. The epic Mahabharata tells us 'Ahimsa Paramo Dharma'—non-violence is our supreme dharma, or an attribute of a normative order. We have to learn this lesson. This very lesson is often forgotten.

One of the stories in the Mahabharata recounts the anecdote of an upper-caste sage, Kaushika, who wanders from place to place searching for wisdom. He ultimately sits at the feet of a low-caste butcher, amidst carcasses of animals in a slaughterhouse, and learns how to balance righteous conduct with tolerance and non-violence. Vrinda Dalmiya

---

[3]Jaideep Deogharia and B. Sridhar, 'Jharkhand lynching: 5 villagers held, 2 cops suspended', *Times of India*, 25 June 2019.

[4]Vrinda Dalmiya, 'Care Ethics and Epistemic Justice: Some Insights from the Mahabharata', in Arindam Chakrabati and Sibaji Bandyopadhyay (eds.), *Mahabharata Now: Narration, Aesthetics, Ethics*, New Delhi: Routledge, 2014, pp. 115–31.

suggests that Kaushika's transformation began when he shamefully confronted his moral fall (his gaze had burnt a crow to cinders because its cawing had disturbed his meditation) and linked it with a cognitive limitation. He realized that whereas he might not know, or only know imperfectly, there can be others, even those who are on the margins of society, who might know more than him about living a life of non-violence. The acknowledgement of imperfectibility can lead to a conversation in which each recognizes the other as a bearer of wisdom. In this case, Kaushika learned of the tradition of non-violence from a seller of meat.[5] Non-violence is one of the basic ways in which Indians represent themselves to the world. Non-violence should have been one of the basic creeds of Indian civilization.

And yet, the biography of our nation is scarred by indescribable acts of individual and collective violence. Headlines of morning newspapers regularly disburse news about the latest incident of often incredible brutality inflicted on the bodies of women, of children, of the lower castes, of minority groups, and of vulnerable others. Violence is executed with deadly precision. At any given day and time, everyday violence ranges from road rage to major destruction that follows brutal and completely amoral terror attacks to crowds that run amuck setting fire to public property to demonstrations that go painfully wrong and lead to death. Some forms of violence are extraordinarily collective, such as communal or caste riots, or civil wars, resulting in thousands of deaths. Some penetrate deep into the body politic and blend into the ordinariness of everyday life, such as violence against women.

## GENDERED VIOLENCE

On 10 January 2018, a horrific tragedy took place in the village of Kathua in Jammu and Kashmir. An eight-year-old girl was repeatedly raped and brutalized by eight men before she was killed. The post-mortem report recorded that her rapists and killers had suffocated her. She died of asphyxia on 14 January. Her body was found abandoned in a field on 17 January.

According to reports, the gang rape and brutalization took place in a temple, the abode of the gods. The villagers wanted the minority

---

[5]Ibid.

community to which this child belonged—the Gujjar–Bakerwal, who are Muslims—to flee the area so that their land could be appropriated. This outrageous act of gang rape was intended to frighten the rest of the community away.

We read the details of the crime in the morning paper with mounting revulsion. The custodian of the temple, Sanjhi Ram, his friend, Parvesh Kumar, and special police officer, Deepak Khajuria had reportedly lured the girl into the sacred place, and lined up to torture, rape, and kill her. On 10 June 2019, a special court in Pathankot sentenced the three perpetrators to life imprisonment. Three police personnel, Assistant Sub-inspector Anand Dutta, Special Police Officer Surendra Verma, and Head Constable Tilak Raj, who had helped the perpetrators of the crime destroy crucial evidence, were sentenced to five years' imprisonment. Sanjhi Ram's son, Vishal Jangotra, was exonerated of the crime. A seventh perpetrator is to be tried in a separate court on the plea that he is a juvenile.

The priest, if he can be called by that title at all, of the temple had allegedly masterminded this horrific crime. He had sedated the girl and rendered her unconscious throughout her captivity, so that she was unable to resist sexual assault and murder. What was even more despicable was that ministers belonging to the Bharatiya Janata Party (BJP), that was then in alliance with the Peoples Democratic Party (PDP) in the state of Jammu and Kashmir, defended the act. More contemptible is the fact that some powerful lawyers reportedly belonging to the Hindutva brigade tried to obstruct the filing of a First Information Report (FIR) in the police station. Other men, who belonged to the right-wing group Hindu Ekta Manch, marched in the streets of Jammu to protest against the arrest of the rapists and murderers.[6] A small child had to pay for an ideology that aims to obliterate the minority community in India, or least frighten it into submission.

This is perhaps the most reprehensible face of violence in contemporary India. Man's inhumanity to man, as Housman writes, brings forth tears of eternity and sorrow. These searing moments of violence not only make for headlines in the morning newspapers. One major indication of the rapid brutalization taking place in the country is the rising incidence of crimes against women: incidents of rapes

---

[6]Asifa Bano, 'The child rape and murder that has Kashmir on edge', *BBC News,* 11 April 2018.

and murders of women have increased over the past few years. On 16 December 2012, the country was shaken by the gang rape and brutal murder of a young woman, Jyoti Singh, who came to be known as Nirbhaya, in a moving bus. Mass protests by students, professionals, and homemakers overwhelmed public places, particularly the lawns of India Gate in New Delhi. The intensity of public anger was so great that demonstrations caught the attention of domestic and global media.

The United Progressive Alliance (UPA) government under Manmohan Singh set up the Justice Verma Committee to investigate the issue. The Criminal Law (Amendment) Act was enacted in 2013. The Sexual Harassment of Women at the Workplace (Prevention, Prohibition and Redressal) Act was foregrounded in the same year. Issues of sexual violence were once again catapulted into the public domain. Protestors carried banners and raised slogans. Some of the slogans carried two messages that occasioned discontent. One, there seemed to be a consensus that castration and/or capital punishment would act as a deterrent. Two, the general belief seemed to be that the greatest danger to women was from strangers in dark streets. Both these inferences have been proved wrong in most parts of the world.

Fortunately, enlightened young men and women managed to transcend these simplistic solutions. They vowed to reclaim the streets and public spaces and make them safe for women. Many groups reiterated the right of a woman to sexual desire, to freedom, and to autonomy in the language of rights. Women held placards that spoke of their freedom to wear what they want and go where they want, without being seen as easy and willing targets. The theme that charged other enlightened sections of the public was 'azadi'—freedom—from patriarchy.

The government of the day passed stricter laws and mandated the creation of fast-track courts for prosecution of cases of rape. Rajasthan, Jammu and Kashmir, Haryana, and Arunachal Pradesh have introduced the death penalty for the rape of minors (children below twelve years of age). The definition of sexual crimes after the Nirbhaya case has expanded to cover stalking, acid attacks, and voyeurism, and threats as well as acts of violence.

Yet, grave crimes against women continue to escalate.

In 2017, it was reported that thirty-four girls were tortured and raped at a government-funded shelter home in Muzaffarpur in Bihar.

The shelter that housed 470 girls was run by a state government-funded non-governmental organization—the Seva Sankalp Evam Vikas Samiti, headed by one Brajesh Kumar Thakur. A report on the shelter home, 'In Muzaffarpur's shelter home a web of silence shielded sexual abuse', revealed that thirty-four young girls had been sexually abused by a network of men, including the owner of the home and government officials responsible for the protection of vulnerable children.

The abuse came to light when Tata Institute of Social Sciences (TISS), Mumbai, conducted an audit for a report on the home. The auditors reported the case to the police and the matter came up before the court. In court, the girls revealed chilling details of being beaten up, confined, drugged, and raped. Speaking to the police after Thakur's arrest, neighbours said that they used to hear the girls' cries at night as if they were being subjected to torture. But 'Brajesh Thakur is of dabang (overpowering) character'—which was why no one dared to ask him about what was going on.[7]

Brajesh Thakur and others were sentenced to life imprisonment by a special court in Delhi on 11 February 2020. 'It is writ large,' said the court, 'that this is not a case of a single solitary incident of rape, but a meticulously planned and ingeniously executed conspiracy wherein the care-givers, the supervisors and the administrators in a state-sponsored children's home themselves turned into predators, perpetrators of crime, and abettors and repeatedly subjected numerous minor girls to atrocious acts of rape and aggravated penetrated sexual assault over an extremely long period of time spanning about four years.'[8] Who will compensate these young girls for their lost innocence, the pain that was inflicted on them, and the trauma they no doubt still grapple with? This story speaks of India's shame, the inability of our government and people to protect little children, both girls and boys, from being subjected to inhuman violence. It is the duty of the state to provide shelter to the homeless and particularly to vulnerable children and adolescents. What has been provided is unthinking funding to organizations that deal in paedophilia and rape of children.

---

[7]Snigdha Poonam, 'In Muzaffarpur's shelter home, a web of silence shielded sexual abuse', *Hindustan Times*, 31 December 2019.

[8]'Brajesh Thakur, 11 others given life terms in shelter home case', *Hindustan Times*, 12 February 2020.

These sorry incidents are but a part of a larger story of discrimination against women. The latest figure available from the National Crime Records Bureau (2014–16) tell us that statistics on the rape of women have gone up by 12 to 15 per cent, and that other crimes against women have risen by 3 to 5 per cent. As many as thirty-nine crimes are reported every hour in the country. The capital of India, Delhi, holds the dubious distinction of being the 'rape' capital of the country, but figures on sexual crimes have also risen in Bengaluru and Pune.[9]

## THE CULTURE OF SILENCE

What is more worrying is the data from the National Family Health Survey, which is a national representative survey, conducted in 2015–16. This data is regarded as the most credible in the country. Detailed questions on physical and sexual violence were asked to a sample of 79,729 women between 2015 and 2016. The survey reported that every third woman since the age of fifteen has faced domestic violence of various forms in the country; 27 per cent of women have confronted physical violence since age fifteen, and this is more common in the rural areas than in urban ones. The report also showed that 99 per cent of the cases go unreported. In most cases, the perpetrator of domestic violence is the husband, or other male relatives of the victim. The average Indian woman, it was reported, is seventeen times more likely to face sexual abuse from her husband than from others. If marital rape and assault is excluded from the statistics on violence against women, only about 15 per cent of sexual violence that is reported to the police is committed by people outside the home. At the same time, the year 2016 saw the lowest conviction rate in trials on violence against women completed by courts.[10]

It is not surprising that international opinion holds that India is the most dangerous country in the world for women. The Thomson Reuters Foundation concluded exactly this after its survey in 2018. The survey measured sexual and non-sexual violence, discrimination, cultural traditions, healthcare, and human trafficking. Three years earlier,

---

[9]Deepanshu Mohan, 'Rising number of crimes against women reflects decay in India's institutions', *The Wire*, 18 April 2018.

[10]Chaitanya Mallapur, 'Crimes against women up 83% but conviction rate hits 10-year low; Delhi reports highest crime rate in India', *Scroll.in,* 12 December 2017.

India ranked third in the grading, by 2018 our country topped the list of countries known for crimes against women, particularly in the field of sexual violence. Ironically, India ranks higher than war-torn Afghanistan and Syria. The conclusions were reached after a number of experts on women's issues were polled.[11] In sum, though more cases of crimes against women are being reported, still, not enough cases are registered due to the involvement of family members, powerful people, and for other reasons.

What exactly does under-reporting of sexual violence against women in India tell us about the state of gender relations in society, or rather, about the fundamentals of our society? One reason for helplessness is under-representation in the workforce. Data shows that women are dropping out of the labour force in the rural sector. Nearly half the number of women who were in the workforce in 2004–05 had dropped out in 2017–18. The sixty-first round of the National Sample Survey Office recorded that 48.5 per cent rural women above the age of fifteen were employed for a major or a subsidiary activity [before 2018] but this number had dropped to 23.7 per cent in the report of the Periodic Labour Force Survey. The drop of women in the labour force is not sudden, this is a trend that began in 2011–12. The decline in urban women's employment is less, dropping from 22.7 per cent in 2004–05 to 18.2 per cent in 2017–18.[12]

The figures are troublesome, because employment is not only a matter of securing an income. Employment, among other factors, enables women to challenge structures of patriarchy. Lack of opportunities to access economic independence intensifies women's vulnerability. This, in turn, increases the stifling grip of a culture of silence. Women are told to be quiet when they are subjected to sexual crimes, either to avoid stigma or to keep the family together, or both. Two, given that substantial parts of the country, as subsequent chapters will discuss, are held together by security forces, and these forces are granted immunity against prosecution by draconian laws, a culture of immunity protects perpetrators of crimes against women. It is not only security forces that are granted immunity, politicians and their minions, police officers,

---

[11]Belinda Goldsmith and Meka Beresford, 'India most dangerous for women with sexual violence rife', Thomson Reuters Foundation, 26 June 2018.

[12]Sonalde Desai, 'Squandering the gender dividend', *The Hindu*, 12 June 2019.

and men who exercise great power manage to get away after they have committed sexual crimes, as do militants in conflict regions.

It follows that institutions, procedures, and agents who are supposed to protect citizens—such as the police—and institutions that dispense justice—such as tribunals, committees, and the courts—are compromised. All governments can be arbitrary and heedless of the interests of their citizens, particularly the most vulnerable sections of society. Such arbitrary exercises of power are kept in check in a democracy by institutions, laws, and civil society organizations. When the capacity of civil society organizations to mount protest against exploitation and sexual abuse of women is neutralized by state power, and when institutions and laws that possess the capacity to protect citizens are subordinated to problematic ideologies such as some abstract notion of national security, the rights of citizens are violated with a degree of impunity. What does the security of the nation mean when the security of its women is at risk? This is the question we should be asking the holders of state power and the dispensers of ideologies that support state power. This culture of impunity percolates to the men of the household. We witness everyday violence that makes life precarious for women.

Political theorists hold that the state, as the condensate of power, sets the framework for all sorts of transactions in the household, in society, in religious groupings, in educational institutions, in the workplace, and even in sites of recreation. If the government is silent when criminals brutalize women and little girls, if it does not attempt to protect the lives of the vulnerable, or when the holders of state power barely blink when terrible things are done to people who are defenceless, they are guilty of complicity in violent acts against women. They are also guilty, as we shall see, of crimes against religious minorities, against the lower castes, against the inhabitants of regions which are termed security threats, and even against those who resist violence against their bodies and minds. When the government is silent, when it is complicit in acts of astounding violence, it gives tacit consent to patriarchy, which sanctions brutality against women in pursuit of the ignoble task of keeping them in their place.

Given the stifling grip of structures of patriarchy, it is scant wonder that the representation of women in legislatures, whether Parliament or state assemblies, is so low. In India, women constitute 48 per cent of the population, but hold hardly 12 per cent of the seats in legislative forums. This results in gross under-representation. In a democracy, all citizens have the right to voice, that is, the right to participate in debates in the public sphere and the right to be represented in decision-making bodies through electoral means. Unfortunately, we cannot be sure that the interests of women in a patriarchal society will be adequately represented in the legislative assembly by male representatives. We also cannot be assured that women in India will be given enough space in the public sphere to express their views. Though representatives who are elected on the basis of geographically delineated constituencies are expected to proxy for all voters, including those who did not vote for them, in societies dominated by patriarchy, adequate representation of women by male members is debatable, and most probably negligible.

Lack of representation in decision-making bodies is worrying because every morning, newspapers tell us of some bestiality inflicted upon the bodies and the psyches of women of all ages. News headlines tell us how women are targeted in perverse ways by mobs. And if women are not represented in legislative bodies or in decision-making institutions, there will be few people to speak up for them. On the other hand, the ideology of patriarchy has drawn enough supporters to either neglect women's interests, or outvote them. Vulnerability is exacerbated if women are further pushed to the margins of society through threats, intimidation, and violence. It is not surprising that vulnerable women are likely to be socially and economically marginalized, politically insignificant in terms of the politics of 'voice' as distinct from the 'vote', humiliated, dismissed, and subjected to intense disrespect in and through the practices of everyday life. This compromises democracy because some citizens do not possess full rights just because they belong to a section of people that has been maligned and denigrated.

In a society dominated by the self-arrogated spokespersons of patriarchy, women are at risk in two ways. One, they continue to be subjected to vicious and perverse stereotyping. Two, if women are diminished in the public eye, they can easily come to harm. All human beings have rights simply because they are human and we need no other justification for the recognition that people have rights. But if individual citizens are denied rights simply because their gender is cast in destructive ways, their rights are violated. Women might not have committed any crime, done anyone an injury, broken the law, or acted in a manner that is considered disorderly. And yet they are harmed bodily, mentally, and economically, and denigrated socially only because they are members of a gender that has been disparaged in language and in action. Therefore, protection for women requires special measures, such as guaranteed representation in Parliament. Special representation is not an exception to the democratic principle, it is a condition for the fulfilment of democracy, notably equality, freedom, and justice.

It is particularly so because entrenched patriarchal structures of thought and sentiment defy legal regulations that prohibit violence against women. Shortly after the Nirbhaya rape case that stirred nationwide outrage and protest, one of the rapists, Mukesh Singh, then in prison, was interviewed for a BBC documentary, *India's Daughter* (2015). He had the temerity to say that a girl is far more responsible for a rape than a boy, because girls are expected to be in the house doing housework. She is not expected to be in the streets, bars, or discos at 9 p.m., wearing the wrong clothes and doing wrong things. If women transgress these rules, according to him, men have a right to teach them a lesson. If the girl had accepted the rape, he said outrageously, we would have dropped her off, she would have survived. Because she fought back we had to kill her. Can we think of anything more depraved than this face of patriarchy in India?

Perhaps he is nothing but a representative of patriarchy that condemns women to unfreedom, perhaps he was justifying rape in an India where some women have increasingly come out of the house, begun to work, defied male norms on how to dress and how to behave, and refused to accept relegation of women to the home. But then, women are not safe at home either. Scholars who have analysed data on crimes against women have recorded that most of these crimes are committed by men who are known to the family and often by the male members of the household. It is clear that women, like other vulnerable communities in India, are subordinated by dominant ideologies that shape the mentalities of both men and women.

The mounting data on violence may have turned us into cynics; we seem to accept that violence is endemic to the project of living together. 'Tum abhi shahr mein kya nae aaye ho/ruk gaye rah mein hadsa dekh kar (You seem to be new to this city/you halted in your tracks when you saw a violent incident)' writes the Urdu poet Bashir Badr.[13] This is a tragic comment on the indifference with which we treat the violence that harms and kills our fellow citizens. How can this happen in a democracy? Why does violence on such a large scale happen? This is the question. Perhaps we can tackle this question only when we map out different kinds of violence in our society. This is what this work attempts—to map out the landscape of violence that has been superimposed on our democracy, our past, our present, and our future.

## DEMOCRACY AND VIOLENCE

It is by now widely acknowledged that democracy has succeeded in a major way in India. This form of government has enabled the participation of groups that had been barred from the world of politics and political contestation among equals for centuries. The political agency of the lower castes had been crippled by sometimes visible, sometimes invisible, but nevertheless highly effective systems of social prohibitions. The Scheduled Tribes (STs) remained outside the boundaries of mainstream India. And other vulnerable groups had inhabited the margins.

The codification of universal adult franchise as the linchpin of Indian democracy has slackened inhibiting social bonds. The predominantly poor, lower-caste women, and rural voters acquired political agency though the ballot box. They now exercise freedom of choice, at least on the day they cast their vote. In the sphere of electoral politics, and in civil society, groups aggressively fight remnants of historical injustice. The fight against discrimination forms part of wider struggles for equal status promised by the Indian Constitution.

The negotiation of caste, gender, and class hierarchies in the electoral domain has marked a significant turning point in the way Indians think of themselves in relation to each other, and in relation to the state. In a society that has been for centuries deeply hierarchical, rigidly stratified, and highly exclusionary, the institutionalization of the norm of universal adult franchise has proved to be nothing short of transformative.

This is remarkable because India was, at Independence, considered an unlikely candidate for democracy. It was widely believed that democracy

---

[13]Translation provided by the author.

requires economic productivity, wealth, literacy, a large middle class, and some degree of well-being. Our country was stamped by poverty, illiteracy, inequality, caste and religious confrontations, and the scars left by Partition. Yet the *idea* of democracy, quite distinct from the institutionalization of democracy, has proved durable. Over the years, we see the consolidation of a body politic shaped by democratic imaginings and aspirations and inspired by equality of political status. India, in short, has proved an exception to the rule that theorists of Western democracy had till now carved in stone, i.e., that democracy demands 'these' and not 'those' preconditions.

Our country's record in maintaining democracy is undeniably impressive. But we also cannot deny that the face of Indian democracy has been deeply scarred by violence. Large parts of the country are rocked by 'low-intensity' operations undertaken by security forces. The phrase 'low-intensity conflict', just below the threshold of conventional war, involves armed confrontation between state and non-state actors. This stretches from skirmishes on India's borders with neighbours to insurgencies to secessionist struggles to regions wracked by internal disturbances to ideological battles. Unconventional battles fought between non-state armed groups and security forces are one feature of violence amidst democracy.

We also have on our collective conscience both memories and forecasts of ugly violence in society: caste violence; communal riots, predominantly between Hindus and Muslims; ethnic strife; and terrible viciousness against women and children, against the lower castes, against the transgender community and, increasingly, against the Muslim population, which forms a minority in society. The reasons why some groups adopt violent means to deal with opponents, often imagined, sometimes real, range from trifling issues such as transport of cattle to claims for regional autonomy and secession.

Perhaps we should not be so surprised at the scale of violence we find in the country. The vast size of India, a highly differentiated population, uneven economic development, linguistic differentiation, regional imbalances, class and caste hierarchies, politicization of religious identities, appropriation of tribal lands, agrarian distress, joblessness, poverty, and deep inequality breed frustration. We see frustration at the subhuman quality of life led by a majority of our people, and anger at the non-performance of various governments. The disjunction between electoral and social and economic democracy hangs low and heavy over our heads. Anxiety about the precarious nature of people's lives breeds dissatisfaction and anger. Discontent and anger spills over into the streets. It sometimes takes on perverse forms: instead of targeting policies and the government, the discontented, egged on by cynical politicians, target their own people by constructing them as the 'other'. But we cannot underestimate at the same time the power of ideologies of hate, and the role played by merchants of hate and their cadres. The political economy of inequality is itself shaped by perverse ideas and even more perverse actions.

Notably, violence does not hurt the powerful, who barricade themselves against their fellow citizens with iron fences and security guards. It does not harm politicians, who use security forces to protect themselves against the very citizens who have elected them into power. Violence harms ordinary people. People die in bomb blasts on buses and trains, they die because they are lynched by mobs, they perish in communal and caste riots, they die of hunger, they die when floods come roaring in and sweep away their livelihoods because of environmental devastation, they die when earthquakes ravage their homes and workplaces, and they die begging on the streets of the metropolis, often in front of showy malls whose shops offer glittering goods for consumption. Patriarchy has taken the lives of many women and children. Above all, they die because violence has become the accepted way of doing politics, both for the government and for some groups of citizens. The innocents are helplessly caught between different purveyors of violence and devastating acts of violence.

On reflection, political violence, or violence deployed in the cause of political gain, from special concessions from the state to communal and caste violence to struggles for a state of our own, appears to be an anomaly in a democracy. Why should groups pick up weapons, or support those who do so, when they have the democratic right to question injustice and renegotiate justice, in and through campaigns and movements in civil society and through their representatives in Parliament? Civil society in India is messy and chaotic, but it has on occasions proved creative. In democracies, protest can be challenged through democratic and constitutional means. The draconian laws passed by the BJP in its second term such as the Citizenship Amendment Act (CAA) has, after all, been challenged by citizens in innovative, peaceful, and constitutional ways since 15 December 2019.

By contrast, the route that violence takes is unpredictable and dangerous. It leads to harm, bears consequences that may well be unintended, such as deaths of innocent bystanders. It generates fear and resentment, loses out on the sympathy quotient, invites retaliation, and sweeps up the perpetrator, the victim, and innocent bystanders in a vicious spiral of merciless destruction and impairment. 'Each new morn,' says Macduff of war in Shakespeare's *Macbeth*, 'New widows howl, new orphans cry, new sorrows Strike heaven in the face, that it resounds.'[14] And yet in our democracy, the government, powerful groups, or even the victims of injustice and resentment opt for 'new sorrows' that strike heaven in the face.

Despite the fact that democracy and violence are antithetical concepts, they manage to coexist with each other in India, not very happily but not that uneasily either. This is the plain and unvarnished truth. Can we overlook the fact that violence has become a routine way of doing politics in India? That it has become a routine way of doing things is not the subject of great speculation. There is a large body of literature on the successes of Indian democracy, and an equally large one on violence, whether spontaneous, episodic or organized.

Yet studies, analysis, acclamation, condemnation, and critical engagement with both concepts tend to wend their own literary, polemical, analytical, and descriptive way with little prospect of intersection. Indian democracy forms a subset of understanding of democracy, and studies of violence fall within the scholarly field of insurgencies, security, conflict studies, conflict resolution, strategic studies, terrorism, and, in the case of Kashmir, India-Pakistan relations. It is almost as if it has been ordained that democracy and violence shall not meet. Whether it has been ordained by the logic of democracy, or by the logic of violence, or both, is an open question.

What is clear is that violence is found at every site of social and political interaction, from the violence of everyday life to political violence that is deployed to make claims upon the state or to resist

---

[14]William Shakespeare, *Macbeth*, Robert Maynard Hutchins (ed.), *Great Books of the Western World*, Vol. 2, Chicago: William Benton, 1952, pp. 284–310.

injustice. This compromises India's credentials to democracy. Consider our recent history. India elected a new government in 2014. The BJP-led National Democratic Alliance (NDA) came to power at the centre and was re-elected in 2019. In the first five years under BJP rule, India's ranking in the global index of democracy slid rapidly.

According to the 2017 Global Democracy Index published in January 2018, India had slipped from the 32nd to the 42nd place. The Global Democracy Index ranks 167 countries across 60 criteria clubbed under 5 broad categories. These categories are electoral process and pluralism, functioning of government, political participation, democratic political culture, and civil liberties. India ranked below the United States, Italy, France, and South Africa. The report stated that this decline was due to the rise of conservative religious ideologies in an otherwise secular country, increases in vigilantism, and violence against minorities, particularly Muslims and dissenting voices. The media is but partially free, journalists are at risk from the government, military and non-state actors and radical groups, and the threat of violence has a chilling effect on media coverage. India has become a more dangerous place for journalists, especially in the central state of Chhattisgarh and in Jammu and Kashmir. Authorities in these states have restricted freedom of the press, closed down several newspapers, and heavily controlled mobile internet services. Several journalists were murdered in India in 2017 as in the previous year, concluded the report. The report placed India in the category of a flawed democracy.[15]

According to the 2018 Global Democracy Index compiled by the Economist Intelligence Unit and published in January 2019, India was placed in a better position. Though Prime Minister Narendra Modi was, according to the report, popular with the middle classes, the BJP had used coercive measures to acquire power.[16] In the 2019 report, the position of the country compared to the 2018 index improved by one position from 42 to 41.

In the Global Democracy Index report made public on 23 January 2020, India slipped ten places in the 2019 ranking to 51st place. The

---

[15]PTI, 'India slips to 42nd place on EIU Democracy Index; US at 21st', *Livemint*, 31 January 2018.

[16]Zaheer Ajmal, 'Modi's India slips in Democracy Index from 27th rank in 2014 to 41 now', *National Herald*, 18 January 2019.

report attributes the primary cause of democratic regression to an erosion of civil liberties in the country. The report focused on the repeal of Article 370 and 35A in Kashmir, the deployment of a large number of troops in Jammu and Kashmir, the arrest of the political leadership, the internet ban, and other security related measures that suspended civil liberties in the state. The NRC (National Register of Citizens) exercise in Assam led to the identification of 1.9 million citizens as non-citizens. Above all, the CAA, which ties acquisition of citizenship by refugees to religious considerations, specifically non-Muslim, has aroused the fears of large numbers of Muslim citizens, stoked communal tensions, and led to protests across the country. (All forms of communication were blocked in Jammu and Kashmir in August 2019, the state was reduced to the status of two union territories, and a complete lockdown of the state ensued. Connectivity of mobile phones was restored only in the second week of October of the same year.) India continues to be categorized as a flawed democracy.[17]

The conclusions of the reports are not misplaced. We just have to dwell on the diverse and intricate ways in which violence is produced and reproduced in our body politic to realize that violence, as a specific form of politics, is neither an aberration nor outside the provenance of democracy. We also recognize with distress that violence is not an unwelcome visitor, or an uninvited stranger who has strayed into our otherwise harmonious world, but whose prolonged stay can be ended only if we, in a determined fashion, refuse to extend hospitality. We can no longer say that a democratic social order has no place for violence.

History tells us that the beast of violence lurks on the boundaries and in the crevices of any society. It can enter centre stage at the proverbial drop of a hat. The trick is to ensure that the beast remains confined to the margins. On balance, we have to accept that violence is part of our everyday individual and collective lives. Violence may or may not course through our bones. But no matter how democratic a society may be, violence lurks on the sidelines, waiting for a cue to enter and wreck a carefully and painfully constructed democratic world where people see themselves as equal members of a political

---

[17]Saira Aslam, 'India drops 10 ranks in Democracy Index', *The Hindu*, 23 January 2020.

community. Intelligent societies led by statesmen keep the beast at bay; short-visioned leaders who subscribe to right-wing populist democracy invite violence into the public forum.

A democratic government should make every effort to keep violence at bay. It should recognize the significance of the primary task of politics: to ensure security of life and liberty. Violence has to be kept outside the boundaries of a society through democratic, responsive, just, and responsible governments. But if governments prove unresponsive to the needs and the demands of the people, if politicians prise open fault lines of a society, and if groups try to assert power over others, the politics of the affirmation of power and resistance to power takes the form of violence.

History also tells us that when corridors of communication and interaction between citizens and governments are blocked off; when we cannot access our own representatives, when politicians who hold, jealously guard, and exercise power are overcome by hubris; and when representatives fail the people, violence bursts forth and tears the seams of the national fabric. It can erupt against the state and against other citizens.

The most sickening form of violence is state violence used by people in power to suppress aspirations. Violence is not the root problem, it is a symbol of a democratic deficit, of unrepresentative and unresponsive democracies, of injustice, of the failure of the state to control dominant groups, and of the readiness of the state to use violence against its own people. The tale of power-seeking, cynical and amoral politics is best told in the words of poet Baban Londhe, in the *Shroud*.

> Acting innocuous, they would eat
> the marrow of our bones
> Days passed by
> Darkness pressed from all sides
> We battled against sunshine and rain
> And like fools awaiting salvation
> we have stood our ground
> and are sunk to the neck in mire
> But now they say plans are worked out
> for our salvation
> —covering our wasted tombs

in a new shroud
What munificence?[18]

'They would eat the marrow of our bones', writes the poet. Poetic and literary modes of protest are powerful and damning indictments of the many lapses in India's democracy. That is why this work relies on poetic and literary imaginations to tell the sorry tale of violence and narrate the courageous tale of resistance. Poetry and literature tell us harrowing stories of violence; and political theorists inspired by the literary imagination have to reflect on broader themes and causal structures such as practices of discrimination, breaking of contracts, poverty, and historical memory.

Whatever be the task of the political theorist, the unhappy coexistence of democracy and violence cannot be wished away by neglecting either the context of violence that is democracy or ignoring the pervasiveness of violence in Indian democracy. Whatever be the trigger, we can no longer see violence as an aberration or see democracy as a gigantic fraud that is perpetuated upon political innocents. Our democracy is deeply flawed, even though we have several achievements to our credit. Unless we wish to engage in the time-consuming and ultimately thankless task of constructing binary opposites: violent democracy versus democracy where violence is but an aberration, we have to accept it as a part of bad politics. Today, violence has crept out from the borders of our society; we see with fear and dread an ugly beast with a cavernous mouth, ready to consume our own people.

The prevalence of violence in democratic politics might well compel us to acknowledge that democracy and violence inhabit the same political space. To repeat, the argument is not that democracy is embedded in violence. But it is not too distant from violence either. The relationship is not external, the links that bind democracy and violence together have to do with the exercise of power and the will to extreme power both by the state and by groups in society. If democracy cannot limit assertions of power, control groups that use violence to dominate and suppress, mitigate discrimination, remedy broken promises, and deliver justice, it cannot neutralize violence.

---

[18]Baban Londhe, 'Shroud', in Arjun Dangle (ed.), *Poisoned Bread: Translations from Modern Marathi Dalit Literature*, Hyderabad: Orient Blackswan, 2009, pp. 59–60.

The assumption behind the mapping out of violence in this work is that the phenomenon is not a matter only for conflict theorists, or for strategic and/or security studies; it is a matter for those who study and value democracy. Something must have gone wrong somewhere. We have to come to terms with the flaws in our democracy, the lapses in democratic life, and the imperfectability of democratic justice. We have to come to terms with violence in Indian democracy. This we can best do by charting out the terrain of violence in the country. Before that, however, we must be clear in what sense the term 'violence' is deployed in this work.

## WHAT IS VIOLENCE?

Before we begin to map out violence in India, we must pause and ask what we speak of when we speak of violence. Words are tricky things and we can never be certain that we have used the right word to express or convey what we wanted to say. An interesting exchange between Alice and Humpty Dumpty in *Through the Looking Glass* might illustrate what I am trying to say.

> 'I don't know what you mean by "glory,"' Alice said.
>
> Humpty Dumpty smiled contemptuously. Of course you don't— till I tell you. I meant "there's a nice knock-down argument for you?"
>
> 'But "glory" doesn't mean "a nice knock-down argument,"' Alice objected.
>
> 'When I use a word,' Humpty Dumpty said, in rather a scornful tone, 'it means just what I choose it to mean—neither more nor less.'
>
> 'The question is,' said Alice, 'whether you can make words mean so many different things.'
>
> 'The question is,' said Humpty Dumpty, 'which is to be master— that's all.'[19]

Lewis Carroll, mathematician and logician, excelled in the subtle art of satire and wordplay. Coded in this exchange between Alice and Humpty Dumpty, which appears to be a piece of delightful literary nonsense at

---

[19] *Lewis Carroll, Alice's Adventures in Wonderland And Through The Looking Glass, and What Alice Found There*. Edited with an Introduction and Notes by High Haughton, London: Penguin, p. 186.

first sight, is a message. The search for unequivocal meaning, Carroll seems to tell us, is doomed. Speakers assume that their words mean more or less what they want them to mean. But readers or listeners interpret these words/sentences/paragraphs through their own prism of understanding. Within a given range, the term 'violence' can be infused with any one of the several meanings the author/speaker wishes to attribute to the term, ranging from intimidation, abuse, brutality, force, and coercion to harassment.

But we dwell too much on this point, and for this particular argument the point is relatively minor. We tend to use extensively and often unnecessarily the term 'violence' in everyday speech. But this is hardly a matter of immense significance. In the hands of a skilled speaker who is inclined towards extravagant propositions and fulsome overstatements, the substitution of violence for other words can be used tellingly and to dramatic effect. Violence is, after all, a high-impact word. There is absolutely nothing wrong here. We seldom choose the words we use with care and after considerable deliberation. That would prove fatal for whatever spontaneity or conversational skills we possess. Instinctively, though, we seem to know which word sounds better, or more effective, in a sequence of words.

The problem is that through overuse, the *concept* of violence becomes a stand-in for other concepts or terms. These other terms might be infinitely more suitable simply because they illustrate precisely what we are speaking of, and what the implications of the use of those terms are. For example, we often use the term violence to indicate rude behaviour. Ram, we tell a friend, used violent language. We might actually mean rude, or uncivil, or abusive language. But violence is a convenient word, ready at hand to condemn something we disapprove of. It has been subjected to overuse perhaps for this very reason.

It is a sad reflection on the present state of political science, wrote the great German Jewish philosopher Hannah Arendt, that our terminological language does not distinguish between key terms such as power, strength, force, authority, and violence. All of these refer to distinct and different phenomena. Otherwise, these words would hardly exist. To use them as synonyms, suggested Arendt, indicates not only a certain deafness to linguistic meaning, it also results in blindness with respect to the realities they correspond to.

Arendt's essay on violence published in 1970 bore the stamp of the time—the Cold War, the nuclear arms race, American intervention in Vietnam, campus and worker revolts in Europe and the United States, and the Naxalite movement in India. The late 1960s and the early 1970s witnessed substantial outpourings of philosophical literature as political philosophers attempted to think through what violence means and what it stands for. And this was the urgent need of the day, for large numbers of students, activists, and workers had revolted against the system and opted for violence.

Revolutionary romanticism and a passionate desire for a new order that could deliver justice and eliminate injustice exploded across the globe at this point in time, inspiring minds and sparking off imagination. Campus revolts broke out in the late 1960s in the USA, Germany, France, Italy, Japan, Mexico, and other countries. Young people rejected the ideas, the institutions, and the visions of a liberal capitalist order that had been forged in the aftermath of the Second World War.

In France, in May and June 1968, a crisis of unprecedented magnitude overpowered society as students revolted against poor educational conditions and authoritarian administrations. They demanded free access to universities and more personal and political freedoms. Workers demanded power. The police crackdown resulted in injuries and arrests of scores of students. Demonstrations in Paris and other cities against police brutality swelled, and a general strike paralysed the country as workers joined students in solidarity. In May 1968, 10 million French workers went on strike and occupied factories. Ultimately, the French government headed by Charles de Gaulle was forced to capitulate and resign.

In the United States, campus revolts against American involvement in the Vietnam War gave voice to a generalized ethos of rebellion against the established order. Civil liberties movements, gender struggles for equality, the struggle for the right to sexual preferences, and rebellions in the ghettos of American cities inhabited by African Americans dissipated expectations that the American way of life, summed up in the image of the melting pot, provided an exemplary model for the rest of the world to follow. Hundreds of thousands of African Americans participated in urban protests and mounted a formidable challenge to practices of discrimination and racism, as well as poor housing, dismal schooling, unemployment, and police brutality.

Revolts and popular discontent across the world challenged the precepts of not only liberal democracy and the market order, but also state communism that had been institutionalized in the Soviet Union. Old Soviet style communism was denounced and dismissed as moribund, as unable to offer any solution whatsoever, and indeed as part of the problem. It was Mao Zedong of China, and his philosophy of the autonomy of politics, who became the inspiration for youth in rebellion. In India, an ideologically grounded armed struggle of the dispossessed and the rural poor took on the might of the Indian state. It is not as if the tribal, the landless, and the peasant had not revolted against injustice in India earlier. But in 1967, these isolated and often random outbursts of violence were consolidated and strengthened by the ideology and strategy of guerrilla war fashioned by Mao Zedong. Many of these protests, opting as they did for piecemeal strategies of violence, and lacking a sustained leadership and coherent and focused ideology, quickly dissipated, or were sternly repressed.

## THE MAXIMALIST TAKE ON VIOLENCE

Hannah Arendt, writing against this background, set out to distinguish power from violence. Power, she argued, exerts moral force and cannot be conflated with violence. To make this point, she warned against the practice of using violence either as a catch-all term or as a synonym for other more apt concepts. We cannot reduce, she argued, public affairs to dominion.[20] Arendt raised a significant point. We must know what we speak of when we speak of violence, simply because the concept has become a hot favourite of a number of influential theorists. In the process, it has been subjected to some degree of overuse. It has simply imploded. We no longer seem to know the difference between torture in the police stations of Delhi and little babies dying of malnutrition in remote areas of India.

Take the concept of structural violence, which periodically renews itself in the academic domain. The anthropologist Akhil Gupta, in his work on the arbitrariness and the randomness with which the lower bureaucracy treats groups targeted by poverty eradication programmes,

---

[20]Hannah Arendt, *On Violence*, London: Allen Lane and Penguin, 1970, pp. 43–56.

argues that structural violence is responsible for the paradox of Indian politics. The paradox is that huge numbers of Indians remain mired in poverty despite a plethora of anti-poverty programmes. Gupta relies heavily on the Norwegian sociologist Johan Galtung's notion of structural violence.

In 1969, amidst a profusion of writings on violence, the concept of structural violence had been popularized by Galtung. He was interested in violence because he was interested in peace. Basically, he expanded the concept of violence to include injustice. A society in which no one physically harms another human is peaceful, but only in a negative sense. Positive peace can be obtained when structural violence, embedded in unjust social and political institutions and practices, is banished.

Structural violence does not involve the use of force to cause harm to another person. However, the net impact of structural violence or injustice is the same as that of intentional violence.[21] Both forms of violence cause harm because they impede the realization of human capacities. Since the outcome of structural and intentional violence is the same, both forms can be placed in the same category.

The identification of two different concepts is a little puzzling. We can easily argue that peace or the absence of violence is a precondition for justice. No government can launch projects of affirmative action, for instance, if the country is wracked by civil war. Alternatively, we can suggest that justice gives us peace and dispenses with violence. Why should justice and peace be conflated? Gupta, who follows Galtung, suggests that we find invisible forms of violence in India. One such form of violence is poverty that leads to the death of millions of poor, especially women, girls and lower-caste and indigenous people. Poverty is crippling because it prevents people from doing what they should be doing, or what they want to do. It can, therefore, be seen as a case of structural violence.

The debate on structural violence centres around precisely this proposition. If P takes up an axe and attacks Q, Q is harmed. But Q is also harmed if her life is stalked by hunger and poverty. Structural violence, it is argued, produces victims and triggers suffering. This is not the result of an intentional act of violence. Everyone who profits from

---

[21]Johan Galtung, 'Violence, Peace and Peace Research', *Journal of Peace Research*, Vol. 6, No. 3, 1969, pp. 167–91.

an unjust system is the perpetrator of violence, and anyone who is badly affected is the victim. All those who tolerate suffering are complicit in this violence. The poor, the oppressed, the vulnerable are victims, and all those who are not poor are purveyors of violence.

The proposition is bound to take lovers of detective fiction aback. In the genre of British classical detective fiction ranging from Agatha Christie to Ruth Rendell to Colin Dexter to P. D. James, a murder most foul has been committed. The task of the detective through intricate processes of reflection and some investigation is to discover who has murdered and for reason. The story goes thus. P commits a murder and Y is killed. Why P murdered Y is the stuff of detective fiction, which is at the same time an exploration of social relations, of the mentalities of the people who were associated with the victim, and of police procedures. Murder is intentional, though in some cases it might be accidental. But no detective, from Sherlock Holmes to Hercule Poirot to Miss Marple to Adam Dalgliesh will set out to investigate death by starvation. Death through starvation is an avoidable tragedy, but we hardly identify it with murder.

The currently fashionable concept of structural violence is both theatrical and imprecise. As an expansive notion of violence, it can mean anything. It can mean the production of violence by social orders. And it can mean the production of social orders by violence. Violence does not have a beginning, a midpoint, or an end. It is a part of institutions, practices, and culture, embedded in the very woodwork that frames the life of the social collective.

Certainly, the ascription of violence to the intricate and confusing movement of capital produces an argument that is both appealing and persuasive. Why should we only see police brutality as an instance of violence that is attended by great harm, but not see artificially created food shortages that cripple little children, or harm expectant and lactating mothers as violence? All too often, cases of direct and transparent violence get precedence in news reports, and malnutrition is seen as the product of a malfunctioning system. The idea that capitalism and violence are synonymous carries a distinct appeal, and has converted many radicals to the terminology and the imaginaries produced by the concept of structural violence.

Yet, doubts remain, simply because the expansion of a concept beyond recognizable boundaries can also loosen it out to an alarming degree. Nuclear war that kills millions and irremediably scars generations to come represents a straightforward case of violence. This is clear. Do great divergences in income also represent a case of structural violence, or do they properly belong to another category, say inequality and injustice? There is a qualitative distinction between the two.

Consider the case of a government that has taken on the responsibility of providing reasonably priced food to poor citizens. But food just does not reach this segment of the population. Failure to ensure that people have assured access to food will almost certainly lead to starvation and premature deaths. Before rushing to condemn this government of inflicting violence on hapless and vulnerable citizens and of causing harm, we would do well to ponder why the government lapsed on its responsibilities. For instance, citizens living in a particular region may not get the food allotted to them because of poor administration, inadequate infrastructure, unseasonal rains which lead to losses of food stocks, corruption in the distribution of food, imperfect mapping of target populations, and general insensitivity and cynicism. Irrespective of the exact combination of reasons why food has not been delivered, people have been harmed. This is indisputable.

Now consider a government that intentionally denies food to the poor in the same region mentioned above, simply because it is inhabited by a religious or caste group that did not vote for the present government in the last election. The elected government decides to reward its supporters and penalize its opponents, even though it has announced a food aid programme to help the poor, and a majority of the poor live in this region.

Can we equate the two cases of failure to provide food? Surely not. In the first case, hunger and starvation is the outcome of a host of processes that might well belong to happenstance; for example, a tornado might devastate the region. Or the government may be unable to extend help to people in need because road robbers, mercenaries, or insurgents routinely hijack the convoy of trucks carrying food. In the second case, the government decides not to provide food to citizens and *can* be held responsible for hunger related deaths. In this case, harm has been caused by the intentional denial of basic rights of citizens.

Theorists of structural violence rule out intentions as central to violence and focus on harm. Harm is produced through a complex of processes that are difficult to unravel and, moreover, seem to be produced unintentionally. Consider now the implications of this formulation. The argument is that our roles in a society are produced and reproduced by violence, and are predestined, or so it appears. We are fated to be either the vendors or the addressees of violence. It depends on the social class we are born into. This practically rules out the capacity to act according to our judgements. We cannot, ever, be trapped in Hamlet's classic dilemma—to 'be' or not to 'be' violent.

There is more. If Raju intentionally injures Rati through acts of violence, he is morally responsible. We can only allot moral responsibility for harm if we are convinced that Raju had set out deliberately to injure someone. Recollect that criminal law distinguishes between premeditated murder and extenuating circumstances such as diminished responsibility. If Raju has infringed the right of Rati not to be harmed, and in the process violated his own duty not to cause harm, he must be prepared to take responsibility for the act. This may range from imprisonment, paying of compensation to the victim of violence and/or her family, or community service. But if injury is caused unintentionally, or because Raju is the bearer of roles that structures have laid down for him, can we demand that he take on responsibility?

When it comes to the state and its personnel, the detachment of harm from intention and responsibility bears serious implications. State officials are practically liberated from complicity, and, thereby, responsibility. And targets of violence have no one to fix blame on. They cannot, after all, demand redress or compensation from impersonal structures. Nor can they drag these structures to the bar from which justice is dispensed. The addresses of violence are, as a result, denied agency. Structural violence theories cannot really explain this aspect of human behaviour.

The proposition made by votaries of structural violence, that the state is nothing but a condensate of power and illegitimate violence, and that societies are governed by the relentless impulse to violence, or that violence runs rife, is frankly trite or, more precisely, banal. All states and all societies exhibit a relentless will to power. Our modern democratic state, backed as it is by weapons of mass destruction, is embedded in violence and engaged in a constant effort to subdue citizens. This is well known; it is even a given. But the modern democratic state also speaks the language of entitlements and rights, of representation and participation, of accountability and responsibility. Therefore, the state is, for many political groups, a field of expectations. It naturally becomes the target of collective protest when these expectations are betrayed. Protests against the state spill over into protests against symbolic or material power wielded by 'big men' in society. Where democracies have not been institutionalized, or where the army or the dictator rule, the idea of democracy inspires people to fight for their right to liberty against the state and authoritarian societies. Where democracies have been inadequately institutionalized, protests demand the rollback of injustice and realization of the democratic idea.

Institutions of democracy often falter, and falter seriously. This is particularly true of Indian democracy, which is but imperfectly realized. What is important is that the idea of democracy has inspired marginal groups to fight for what is right, and what is their right both in state and in society. Some groups act and some do not. But structural violence underplays crucial factors of intention, responsibility, and agency. The concept cannot come to terms with the fact that yesterday's victims have today revealed enormous capacity both to speak back to histories not of their making, and to make their own histories. These histories may not be the ones they wanted to make in the first instance, but this is politically not all that significant. None of us make history in conditions of our own choice, as Karl Marx reminded us. What is important is that people want to make the transition to actors. It is this crucial factor of deliberate intention that often goes missing in theories of structural violence.

I do not mean to dismiss the concept of structural violence. It undeniably articulates the sense of frustration and anger at the high degree of tolerance society exhibits towards poverty, deprivation, and exploitation. But when we draw attention to these features, we *castigate* the kind of society we live in. We do not *conceptualize* violence. Arguably, theories of structural violence should be able to explain why I bear moral responsibility for something I did not do to another person who has been harmed, or if I did not intend that harm should be caused to another through my actions. This has to be explained and clarified. But it is precisely this aspect that theorists of structural violence do not explain.

If we need to know of what we speak when we speak of violence because we want to clarify processes that lead to political judgement, we should try not to extend the concept, overload it, or use it as a handy synonym for other concepts. This route leads nowhere except to considerable conceptual muddles.

## THE DISCRETE VIRTUES OF A MINIMALIST THEORY OF VIOLENCE

It is possible that the overextension of a concept can lead to its implosion; a coherent and *political* concept of violence must necessarily be economical *if* we want to know what we speak of when we speak of violence. For this, we need to distinguish the characteristics of violence, and figure out which of these features *define* violence.

The most obvious feature of violence is the use of force. In the English language, the etymological origin of violence can be traced to two terms, of which the first is 'violentus': this term captures the property of an act. For example, we could describe Raju's act in shutting the door of his car with great force as violent. All that we mean to indicate is that Raju shut the car door with more force than was required, or that he slammed the door shut by using excessive force. Here, 'violent' is used purely descriptively. We can, of course, push the implication of the statement further, and suggest that the act told us in graphic detail about the state of Raju's mind. He was either furious or desperate, either frustrated or threatened, or he might just have been in a hurry to keep an appointment because he was running late. What is incontrovertible is that the term 'violence' captures the dominant property of an act, or that it is used evocatively. Doors are opened and shut at fairly regular intervals and we hardly register this empirical fact. It is the insertion of 'violent' as a prefix to the act of shutting the car door that marks the act as worthy of note.

Note that as of now, Raju's act in slamming the door shut with excessive force did not hurt anyone, or infringe anyone's right not to be harmed. Matters would be qualitatively different if his action had injured Rati who, exiting the car from the rear door, had her hand on the doorjamb at the exact moment that Raju slammed the door shut. The description of an act that harmed someone because it was performed with more force than needed as violence corresponds to the word 'violare', or violation of the right not to be harmed.

This brings us to harm as the second component of violence. But before we discuss harm, let us dwell on force a little more. Force is, arguably, a generic feature of violent acts. Is force the *distinguishing* feature of violence? Perhaps not, for it is possible to distinguish between force and violence. One, force can be used to protect someone. Rati has to use some degree of force if she wants to prevent her child from running into a crowded road. Rati has used force, and the use of force causes injury. But it also prevents greater harm. Two, in games such as soccer or boxing, the players use a great deal of force and often injure each other. We describe these sports as violent. Three, actions can involve force but this does not harm anyone. Raju, as we have seen, slammed a door shut with great force, but he did not harm anyone. Here, again, violence is used descriptively.

Conversely, people can be harmed without being subjected to excessive force. Think of sophisticated modes of torture that leave no trace on the corporeal body. Someone can be drugged before he is killed, or she can be put to death by administering highly sophisticated forms of poisoning that do not cause convulsions such as frothing at the mouth or savage biting of the tongue.

The strange story of the death of the Sphinx who guarded the doors of Thebes comes to mind in this context. Wandering through the land after he had visited the Oracle at Delphi, Oedipus confronts the Sphinx. This creature, half-human and half-animal, had been sent by the gods to Thebes to punish the inhabitants for the sins committed by King Laius of Thebes. Many moons ago, a soothsayer had warned Laius and his wife, Jocasta, that their son would kill his father and marry his own mother, and thus commit both incest and parricide.

A panic-stricken Laius ordered that the feet of his newly born son should be pierced and bound together, and that the baby should be abandoned on Mount Cithaeron to perish. Fate had a different future in store for the infant. Overcome by compassion, the servant handed over the infant to a shepherd who tended the sheep of King Polybus of Corinth. The baby, christened Oedipus because the injury to his ankles had led to swollen feet, was adopted by King Polybus and his queen. In due course, Oedipus, rendered distraught by the rumour that he had been adopted, trekked to Delphi to consult the Oracle. Terrible news awaited him—that he was fated to kill his father and wed his mother.

Determined to sidestep these twin scourges, Oedipus took the road away from Corinth. On the way, he got into an altercation with a group of attendants carrying an elderly gentleman in a palanquin. During the ensuing scuffle our benighted hero struck the elderly gentleman with his stick. The gentleman, who was King Laius, was killed on the spot. Completely oblivious to the fact that he had, after all, committed the grave sin of parricide exactly as a malevolent fate had ordained, Oedipus fled the spot. He subsequently came across the Sphinx who sat astride the gates of Thebes.

From this strategic perch, the Sphinx allowed people to enter the city only if they could solve a riddle she posed to them. A dreadful fate awaited people who could not answer: they were devoured by the Sphinx. The Sphinx, who had been anointed by the gods to slowly but surely ruin Thebes, cut the city-state off from the rest of the world. Oedipus proved a saviour because, much to the astonishment of the Sphinx, he was able to solve the riddle. The Sphinx was so taken aback by his sharp intelligence that she threw herself off the cliff either in shock, or utter desperation, or both. The fall put a violent end to the gatekeeper of Thebes. This must be the only case in history of a death brought on by a person who, in our world, would be hailed as an expert at quizzing. In sum, the use of force may be used to prevent harm, it may not harm anyone, and harm can be produced by factors other than force. Force is a component of violence, but it is not its defining feature.

Is then harm the constitutive aspect of violence? Despite major disagreements, theorists of violence generally accept that harm is central to the concept. But this is not the end of the story because harm can be caused intentionally or unintentionally. There is a finite difference between intentional and unintentional harm. To illustrate this point, let us revisit our earlier example. Raju shut the car door with some force, and in the process hurt Rati whose hand was on the doorjamb. But Raju might not have meant to hurt Rati at all. He simply may not have noticed that the latter was also exiting the car. Can we seriously hold him responsible for injuring his passenger? He acted thoughtlessly, we can conclude with some justification, and this thoughtlessness, or absent-mindedness, or whatever his state of mind might have been at that time, caused distress.

Can we, in all honesty, blame him quite as much as we would have if he had shut the door on Rati's hand intentionally, in full knowledge that she had placed her hand on the doorjamb? As suggested above, we cannot but acknowledge the difference between a government that fails to reach food to its citizens because trucks carrying food were hijacked and a government that intentionally holds back food from one section of citizens. In both cases citizens suffer but the moral responsibility of the government towards these citizens is surely greater in the second case than in the first. The distinction between knowing and not knowing, or intention and happenstance, has important implications for any judgement on violence. According to a theorist of structural violence who focuses on harm, every time I fail to contribute to a charity that I know provides poor children education, food or literacy or healing, I perform an act of violence. But surely there is a qualitative difference between not contributing to a charity because I forgot, and injuring someone directly by knifing her?

If I set out to injure, say, Rati, I am culpable and therefore morally responsible. Will I be culpable if I fail to save Rati from harm? Certainly, the failure to avert harm is morally condemnable. If I watch someone assaulting Rati and do not intervene, I am, rightly speaking, a coward. Does cowardice imply that I am *responsible* for Rati's injuries? Negligence and cowardice are significant insofar as they are undesirable attributes of the human condition, but surely intention is even more significant.

The belief that intention defines violence presumes voluntary action insofar as I had a choice between doing and not doing harm. I, or you, the state or non-state actor, choose to do harm, and this makes each of us morally responsible. Consider, again, the distinction between two sorts of acts. A car driver causes an accident and injures people, not intentionally but because he had a cardiac attack while at the wheel. Compare this incident with the case of a car driver, who, under the influence of alcohol, runs over people sleeping on the pavements of Delhi. Who is morally culpable and responsible, and who should compensate the victims of violence: the person who had no choice or someone who had a choice and chose badly? It is the factor of choice that distinguishes the concept of violence from descriptions of an act as violent, because it allows us to make judgements.

Let me wrap up the argument above. Central to the concept of violence is intention. This naturally excludes natural disasters that cause massive harm from the category of violence. For example, a storm wrecks everything in its path and leads to immense harm. People are uprooted, dislocated, and killed, property destroyed, and the environment devastated. Storms or 'acts of God' cause harm, but can we place this incident within the conceptual category of violence? Properly we cannot, because in this case we can neither discover a purposeful agent, or an identifiable victim whom our agent intended to harm. Harm has been caused, and *descriptively* the storm that caused harm can certainly be termed violent.

Conceptually, matters are different because violence does not belong to happenstance, or something that is an unintended by-product of processes independent of human volition, or something that is because it cannot be otherwise. Intention implies that an agent, whether a non-state actor or the state, or both, choose to inflict violence on others. If they choose to inflict violence, they must bear responsibility for these acts, be punished and/or be forced to compensate for harm. If we are heedless of poverty, we can be called indifferent, callous, selfish, and blameworthy. Are we violent? The problem should be clear by now. Because the concept of violence has been subjected to indiscriminate expansion, it has become a stand-in concept, or an easy synonym for other concepts.

For example, if the owner of a textile unit makes his workers labour for long hours without adequate remuneration, this particular form of injustice is properly called exploitation. When millions of Scheduled Castes (SCs) and Scheduled Tribes (STs) in poverty-stricken areas in central and eastern parts of India suffer from avoidable harm, eke out a bare existence, continue to be subjected to rank indignities, and die premature deaths, their situation is best conceptualized as social injustice. When the security forces of the state fire upon them without any justification, and when this leads to injuries and death, this is best conceptualized as violence. Violence and injustice are wrongs but in different ways. Violence infringes our right to bodily and mental integrity; injustice denies people a fair share in the benefits and the burdens of their society. Both harm but in distinctive ways.

Certainly, violence as part of political rhetoric plays a powerful role in arousing outrage, but we might fail to understand what is so distinctive about particular ways of causing harm. There is arguably a substantive distinction between being denied social and economic rights and unmarked graves, encounter deaths, mutilation, rape, stabbings, strangulation, decapitating, burning, and drowning. The concept of violence is best reserved for the latter category of cases. Why should we carry out this differentiation in any case? In a democracy, injustice is as much a cause for anger, resentment, and protest as violence. If we use the two concepts as synonyms, not only are our political vocabularies reduced and we become alarmingly monolingual; we can no longer distinguish between the ills of the human condition, the causes of these ills, or indeed the remedies for these maladies.

## ORGANIZING THE DISCUSSION ON VIOLENCE

This work is organized in the following way. In the first chapter, the argument holds that the founding moment of the Indian Republic was deeply embedded in tremendous violence. Even before the Partition of India had been announced, violence had broken out in northern India, especially Punjab. Bengal, the other province that was partitioned, witnessed horrendous violence in 1946. In August 1947, the violence that erupted between the Hindus, Sikhs, and Muslims in Punjab acquired unprecedented proportions. Arson, destruction, loss of lives, gang rapes, and brutal sexual violence marked the month of India's independence and the rest of the year in 1947.

The second chapter focuses on communal violence. The violence that erupted in India during the Partition was not a new development even though the scale was new. The years before the country was partitioned witnessed immense violence between Hindus and Muslims. This left its imprint upon the body politic. The politicization of religion, the making and the unmaking of religious identities, and the confrontation between politicized identities has been produced and reproduced in different forms till today.

The third chapter dwells on the violence engendered and nourished by caste discrimination. In India, attempts to repair complex forms of historical injustice, specifically 'untouchability', have produced unanticipated outcomes. Whereas economic deprivation has been addressed, somewhat, and while former 'untouchables' or Dalits have wrested the right to voice from the closed fists of recalcitrant elites, a major part of the community is still denied respect and is subjected to gross forms of humiliation as covert violence and overt violence. Sometimes, this violence is inflicted because Dalits are vulnerable, sometimes because they aspire to equality, which is their right, and sometimes because they have done better than other castes in education and in the professions. Despite constitutional guarantees, Dalits continue to be discriminated against.

The argument in the fourth chapter takes up the vexed issue of violence in Jammu and Kashmir and particularly in the Kashmir valley, a region that has been stalked by violence since 1989. Despite the insistent and massive erosion of the special status of Jammu and Kashmir right up till the late 1980s, few political analysts could predict that the valley would be overwhelmed by religious fundamentalism and violence. In August 2019, the state of Jammu and Kashmir was stripped of its special status that had been constitutionally guaranteed; the state itself was downgraded and split to form two union territories and the people subjected to an unprecedented lockdown. We still do not know whether violence will abate as a result of the coercive measures imposed against the region by the central government.

The discussion in the fifth chapter considers violence in the Northeast of India. One of the most conflict-ridden regions of India, the Northeast has witnessed immense violence, sometimes in the form of insurgency and crackdowns by the security forces and sometimes in the form of interethnic strife. The militarization of the region has been paralleled by the rise of insurgent groups fighting the Indian government as well as their own people.

The sixth chapter deals with what has been called 'red terror', waged by the Maoists in the central and eastern parts of India. The Maoists have let loose a fury of violence on innocent citizens who travel in trains that are blown up, who inadvertently walk or drive over landmines placed by guerrilla bands of the party, who are caught fatally in the crossfire between the armed guerrillas and the security forces of the state, and who, inhabiting the region the Maoists have made their base, live in constant fear that they will be targeted as informers or police agents, and executed by kangaroo courts. Coercion, intimidation, and strong-arm tactics are outrageous and condemnable. These acts violate our basic moral sensibilities and violate deeply held convictions that the least that is due to human beings is respect for the right to life, howsoever stark that life may be.

The concluding chapter focuses on the Gandhian response to violence in his times. His argument holds relevance for us till today. Violence is counterproductive, it causes bodily injuries, maims minds, and diminishes personalities. It affects both the perpetrator and the victim. There are good reasons why we should avoid the route to violence and destruction. Gandhi shows us not only that violence should be avoided but also why it should be avoided.

## CONCLUSION

The mapping out of violence in India for this volume has not been easy. Violence brings us face to face with some very unpalatable dimensions of the human condition. Whatever be the trigger that sparks off violence, that excavates violence from its habitation in the dark shadowed minds of individuals and collectives, the consequences are serious. It leaves societies with bruised bodies, scars both physical and mental and diminished human beings. We need to find a way out of the sometimes senseless violence that has overwhelmed our country. We have to go back to Gandhi and see how he responded to violence in the first decades of the twentieth century. Today, at a time when our belief that democracy would tame violence has been belied, there is no reason to suppose that we cannot find a way out even though we realize that we might just have violence in our bones. I wish it were otherwise.

## Chapter 1

# INDIA'S PARTITION

*The bus braked suddenly and Tara awoke with a start. She smelled a nauseating stench. On the side of the road lay scattered half-eaten corpses, some desiccated by the sun, others rotted by the rain. Vultures were perched on and near them, scavenging, jostling for space, and picking at the bodies. The charred remains of half-burnt buses were scattered here and there.*

—Yashpal, *Jhootha Sach* [1]

## INTRODUCTION: THE FOUNDING MOMENT OF THE REPUBLIC

Let us begin the discomforting and disorienting story of violence in India with the Partition of the country. For most people, 15 August 1947 signifies Independence; for others, the date signifies Partition. We celebrate Independence with great enthusiasm, but people in parts of the country also recollect and mourn the tremendous violence that was unleashed. They retell harrowing stories first narrated by their parents and grandparents; they grieve at the loss of their ancestral home and the merciless way in which people were torn away from a land that was the repository of their memories, locus of their traditions, centre of their loyalties, and the main anchor of their imaginations. How can they forget that the days preceding and following the moment of independence were scarred by large-scale and brutal riots between individuals belonging to three groups: Hindus, Sikhs, and Muslims in the regions of Punjab, North West Frontier Province, Jammu, the Kashmir Valley, Sindh, and Bengal?

The division of India into two countries—Pakistan and the Republic

---

[1]Yashpal, *This Is Not That Dawn (Jhootha Sach),* translated by Anand, New Delhi: Penguin, 2010, p. 478.

of India—was the outcome of a political agreement between leaders. The covenant was not based on the agreement or the consensus of the inhabitants of the regions that were going to be affected. Nor were people happy when the decision was announced. How could they be? They were wracked by fear and anxiety. Insecurity about the present and the future sparked off a train of cruelty, sadism, and terrible abuse that was unprecedented in history. Remembrance of the horrors of Partition continues to hang over our collective heads. We experience revulsion when we think of the dreadfulness that attended the division of the country. Above all, we realize in great pain that the founding moment of the Republic of India was embedded in terrible violence. Has violence been handed down as the heritage of this great republic? Perhaps.

In order to understand how we arrived at the present moment, we have to understand the paths we followed and did not follow.

In effect, we cannot make sense of the massive and large-scale violence that swept parts of the country in 1947 unless we locate it in history. We cannot reconcile with the fact that neighbours turned on neighbours, friends on friends, acquaintances on acquaintances in perverse and brutal ways unless we bring historical imagination to bear upon this issue. Still, few people can make sense of the violence that took place during the territorial Partition of India. The Hindi poet Sachchidananda Hirananda Vatsyayan 'Agyeya' was witness to the insane bloodletting in Punjab. Overcome by regret and disbelief, he wrote a series of anguished poems titled *Sharanarthi* between 12 October and 12 November of the same year.

Sitting in waiting rooms, on the benches, or among piles of luggage on platforms of railway stations, he scripted a testimony of the large-scale and mind-numbing violence unleashed in Punjab. On 24 October 1947 he wrote: 'aaj jaane kis hinshr dar ne/desh ko bekhabri mein das liya/sanskriti ki chetna murjha gayi/mrigi ka daura pada/ichashakti bujh gayi.' (Who knows which violent dread has stunned the country. Awareness of our common culture and of our great civilization has withered. An epileptic fit has extinguished the autonomy of our will.)

Punjab could only have been overcome by an epileptic fit—there was no other explanation. People attacked each other with weapons sharpened on the touchstone of hate and bloodlust. Ethnic cleansing of entire districts was carried out with the precision of a skilled surgeon's knife. Historians tell us that in 1947, confrontations were scripted by well-organized groups from all communities. But we also have to recognize that violence, once it is sparked off, takes on a life of its own. It multiplies. It reproduces like the amoeba. It sweeps up an entire people and mercilessly crushes their sensibilities.

The trigger that extricated violence from the realm of the unconscious and the unimagined and brought it into the public sphere of uneasy performances and theatres of blood was the division of territory. Entrepreneurs of hate profited from this. Resultantly, newly drawn boundaries that included some but excluded others turned homelands into alien, arid, destroyed, and desolate spaces. Homes were wrecked and burnt to the ground, families were torn apart, and mosques, temples, and gurudwaras were desecrated and demolished. Even if violence was planned and executed by ganglords and organized right-wing groups, it escalated into unplanned acts of extreme and insane sadism and cruelty. This is what happens when communities confront each other as members of a religious group that considers other groups as the enemy. This is what communalism does to people. It turns them into victims but also executioners, the tortured as well as the torturer, the persecuted as well as the persecutor. During prolonged phases of mindless violence, it becomes difficult to distinguish between perpetrators of violence and those who are annihilated by extreme forms of cruelty.

The sadness is that the ability of violence to numb moral judgement and evoke brutality unfolded in regions where people had lived together, worshipped at roadside shrines of Sufi saints, and shared a language, music, folk tales, rituals, and memories. The experience was heart-rending. Few, writes Alex von Tunzelmann, can grasp how it might feel to have their fathers barricaded in their houses and burnt alive; their mothers beaten and thrown off speeding trains; their daughters torn away, raped, and branded; their sons held down in full view, screaming and pleading while a mob armed with rough knives hacked off their hands and feet.[2] We hear of what happened in 1947 from historians, tellers of tales, our parents, and grandparents. We are profoundly shaken. Can we ever know how people felt, or even imagine what they suffered in that period?

---

[2]Alex von Tunzelmann, *Indian Summer: The Secret History of the End of an Empire,* London: Simon and Schuster, 2007, pp. 266–67.

Can we even begin to understand the way our society was pitchforked into the deepest slough of barbarity?

A question bothers—or should—the collective psyche. How is it that in 1947 people aligned themselves with their religious identity, forgot other social relations, marginalized solidarities, and swept aside shared histories? Why did they turn on each other in vicious ways, killing, burning, maiming, desecrating bodies, and scarring minds? Generations will continue to ask throughout the history of the subcontinent: why Partition? And ask we must—what drove people to such savagery? We ask these questions exactly as young people in today's Germany ask: how did their grandparents participate in the butchery of six million of the Jewish community, supervised by Adolf Hitler and his henchmen? For present generations, the extent and the seriousness of the violence is unimaginable. But it happened, and it is our duty to chronicle Partition violence for the sake of our future. This must never happen again. A society that cannot learn from history is condemned to, as George Santayana famously said, repeat it. Therefore, we need to understand why Partition happened before we recount the painful way in which it happened.

It is difficult to isolate one or even a cluster of factors that resulted in the Partition of the country. The territorial division of India was the outcome of a complex mix of factors. Volumes have been authored on this theme. We can only focus on a few of these. They might be significant because these factors continue to impact life in India even today, in the form of communal violence, hate against minorities, the mixing up of the fate of our own people with that of Pakistan's, and the uneasy tension which permeates our lives during periods of communal disharmony.

## THE ORIGINS OF THE PARTITION OF INDIA

To repeat the question asked above: at which point of history did the fearful idea of Partition begin to dominate political imaginations? On balance, historians trace the origins of the Partition to the epoch of colonialism. We have to understand that British colonialism was unlike any other form of rule that Indians had experienced earlier. Pre-modern rulers taxed non-believers and converted individuals to the religion of the power elite, they practised violence and subjugated populations by the power of the sword. But they seldom tried to regulate the minds and the personal lives of their subjects on the scale that modern states do. British colonialism, as a proto-modern state, set out to shape and control not only the political and the economic destiny of Indians, not only the way they interpreted the past, but also modes of thinking about the future. The impact of colonialism extended far beyond the economic loot of the country and the appropriation of political power. It permeated and shaped intellects, perspectives, understanding of the past, expectations of the future, and more importantly, the answer to the question—who are the people of India? It continues to do so today.

There was only one way to accomplish this task. Colonialists set out to shape modern India through educational policies. They proceeded to interpret Indian laws and scriptures in light of their own sensibilities, beliefs, and prejudices. European Indologists, Orientalists, missionaries, administrative officers of the East India Company, as well as intellectuals in prominent European universities began to investigate the culture and the belief system of Indians. Agents of colonialism set out to decipher a complex civilization, unravel the plural and convulsed threads of its dominant religion—Hinduism, translate religious texts, and homogenize and codify plural traditions of law. In order to govern a plural and complex society, the colonialist had to understand and, more importantly, change the way the governed thought of themselves historically, legally, and culturally. In sum, the colonial power initiated a system of cultural and intellectual domination.

S. N. Mukherjee suggests, in his work, on the administrator and Indologist Sir William Jones that different projects of understanding India were bound together by an underlying unity. Men, he suggested, came to the country for a variety of reasons: to make money, for adventure, and for a step up the social ladder in England. A majority were driven by a missionary zeal to shape the future of the country. Though the subsequent transformation of India was produced by a variety of factors, these ideas, which set British administrators to the task of reforming the administrative system, left a definite mark upon Indian society.[3]

One of the ways the British set out to reform the administrative system was by translating and codifying complex systems of belief

---

[3]S. N. Mukherjee, *Sir William Jones: A Study in Eighteenth-century British Attitudes to India,* Cambridge: Cambridge University Press, 1968, p. 2.

and allegiance. Colonial officials, in other words, tried to reduce the bewildering intricacies of Hinduism to manageable proportions. The first move towards homogenization was the standardization of, in A. K. Ramanujan's terminology, 'context-dependent'[4] laws into a uniform legal code. Administrators of the East India Company and colonial courts played an active role in shaping this project. Aided by knowledgeable Indians familiar with traditions of law and jurisprudence, and with the languages in which these laws were written—Sanskrit and Persian—administrators began to select and systematize a range of Hindu and Islamic laws.

In 1786, in a letter to the viceroy, Lord Cornwallis, William Jones suggested that the former should commission a project to compile a digest of Hindu and Muslim Law. Civil law, he advised, ought to be in accordance with native practices enshrined in the 1781 Act of Settlement. Towards this end, the multiplicity of laws had to be collapsed and collated. Indian law must possess the consistency and the certainty of English law. This would, he hoped, make the task of English judges easier. Copies of the proposed Digest of Laws, he further suggested, should be deposited in the proper offices of Sadr Diwani Adalat and the supreme court. This had to be done if the British government had to give the natives what Justinian gave to his Greek and Roman subjects—justice.[5]

The difficulty, admitted Jones, is that these laws were written in Sanskrit and Arabic. They had to be translated. He added a word of caution at precisely this point: the pandits and maulvis who familiarized the colonial power with the relevant law could not be trusted. 'I can no longer bear to be at the mercy of our Pundits, who deal out Hindu law as they please and make it at reasonable rates, when they cannot find it readymade.'[6] Administrators had to learn the language and take on the task themselves. The writ of the colonial hand ran over an impressive range of laws, accomplishing nothing less than the homogenization of a plural and context-dependent tradition of jurisprudence. This continued even after the British government took over the empire from the East India Company.

---

[4]A. K. Ramanujan, 'Is There an Indian Way of Thinking?' in McCim Marriott (ed.), *India through Hindu Categories,* Delhi: Sage Publications, pp. 41–58.
[5]Mukherjee, *Sir William Jones,* pp. 130–31.
[6]Ibid., pp. 128–29.

The second legacy of colonialism, a legacy that continues to profile waves of political mobilization and strategies in the present, was the standardization of the plural traditions of Hinduism. This proved momentous because throughout history, Hinduism had a fluid biography. In pre-colonial India, people tended to identify themselves as members of a jati, of a caste, of a linguistic group, and/or as the residents of a region. Etymologically, Hinduism stems from a Persian term 'Hind', or 'Al-hind' in Arabic, first used by the Achaemenid Persians to indicate people who lived beyond the river Indus (Sindhu) in the region of Hind. References to this term are found in the inscriptions of Darius I and other rulers of ancient Persia from sixth century BCE. The term 'Hindu' was used by Persian scholar Al-Biruni to refer to Brahmanical Hinduism. Three centuries later, Ziauddin Barani (of the Delhi Sultanate) made frequent references to the 'Hindu' in his history of India. In his hands, the term denoted a politico-administrative as well as a religious category.

Harjot Singh Oberoi, in his *The Constructions of Religious Boundaries*, argued that the defining religious texts of the Hindus do not employ the word 'Hindu'. It was not until colonial times that the term 'Hinduism' was coined and acquired wide currency. The term covered a wide variety of religious communities, some of them with distinct traditions and opposing practices.[7] The historian Romila Thapar points out that the evolution of Hinduism is not a linear progression from a founder through an organizational system. 'It is rather the mosaic of distinct cults, deities, sects and ideas and the adjusting, juxtaposing or distancing of these to existing ones, the placement drawing not only on belief and ideas but also on the socio-economic reality.'[8]

During the colonial period, Hinduism was standardized and given a definite meaning—metaphysical, upper caste, Sanskritized, and abstract. This process also created a dominant identity that became an anchor for the freedom struggle. The politicization of Islam followed in rapid succession. A fertile ground was created for the competitive politicization of religion, a process that had little to do with religion as faith.

---

[7]Harjot Singh Oberoi, *The Construction of Religious Boundaries*, Chicago: University of Chicago Press, 1994, p. 16.
[8]Romila Thapar, 'Imagined Religious Communities? Ancient History and the Modern Search for Hindu Identity', in *History and Beyond*, New Delhi: Oxford University Press, 2010, pp. 60–88.

Surprisingly, leaders of the freedom struggle accepted Orientalist acclaims of a rich and sophisticated Vedic tradition without acknowledging its adverse impact upon society: that is, the consolidation of Brahmanical superiority and caste discrimination. The identification of Hinduism with a metaphysical and spiritual tradition was complete. The philosopher Bimal Matilal reminds us that Western scholars were fascinated by the highly speculative metaphysical system that occupied the overlap between religion and philosophy. And Indian intellectuals, after centuries of foreign domination, were looking for an identity that could help them assert themselves. Some national leaders sought an escape in the mythical aura of Indian spirituality. As a result, philosophy remained identified with mysticism, and was regarded as inseparable from religion.[9] This version of Hinduism was elevated to a public ethic that inspired and informed the freedom struggle.

A factor that contributed significantly to the creation of an overarching religious identity was the census. The census proceeded to group Indians into categories defined by religion. The historian Dipesh Chakrabarty wrote that census administrators were highly influenced by eighteenth-century understandings of Indian society. According to them, Indian society had been weakened by internal divisions into various castes and religious groups. At every census, Indians were asked to state their religion. This was a question, incidentally, that the British government never asked its own citizens in the United Kingdom. England had, after all, been wracked by a civil war on the issue of religion. But in India the task of categorizing Indians, who possessed multiple identities of region and language, was piloted by the belief that in India religion makes the world go around.

The process of statistically registering Indians according to religion bore a grim harvest. The last decades of the nineteenth century proved decisive in this respect. 'By the 1890s, Hindu and Muslim leaders were quoting census figures at each other to prove whether or not they had received their legitimate share of benefits from British rule (such as employment and education).'[10] In a short period of time, the politics

---

[9]Bimal Krishna Matilal, in Jonardon Ganeri (ed.), *Epistemology, Logic, and Grammar in Indian Philosophical Analysis,* New Delhi: Oxford University Press, 2005, pp. xii–xiii.

[10]Dipesh Chakrabarty, 'Modernity and Ethnicity in India', in John McGuire, Peter D. Reeves and Howard V. Brasted (eds.), *Politics of Violence: From Ayodhya to Behrampada,* New Delhi: Sage Publications, 1996, pp. 207–18.

of demographic majorities and minorities culminated in competitive nationalism. At some point of time, nationalists begin to seek a state of their own. In history, this search has led to major human tragedies— from ethnic cleansing to genocide to territorial partitions. India could not escape these processes and their consequences.

Undeniably, the reports of census commissioners were to herald a mischievous and sinister turn in intercommunity relations. For instance, in 1891, M. J. C. O'Donnell, Census Commissioner for Bengal, proceeded to calculate the number of years it would take the Hindus to altogether disappear from Bengal if Muslim increase went on at the rate at which it was doing.[11] The report as well as subsequent reports fed into tensions between Hindus and Muslims. The ideas in the 1891 report continue to influence the ideology of the right wing in the country.

Colonial descriptions of Hindus and Muslims as fiercely opposed to each other, interpretations of every clash as communal war, and census reports accomplished two political tasks. One, they made people aware of their religious community that was wider than regional and caste allegiances allowed for. Members of these complex communities were either called Hindus or Muslims. The census also made people aware of their numerical strength or the lack thereof. The majority-minority distinction continues to rock India to date. Two, people became conscious that their access to opportunities depended not only on what group they belonged to, but also on what the strengths and advantages of the other group were. Over time, we see the eruption of competitive nation state projects confronting each other in deadly ways.

History proves that anti-colonial nationalism seldom erupts on to the stage of history fully fashioned like the Greek goddess Aphrodite.[12] The processes by which a territorially bound community begins to view itself as a nation and generate the ideology of anti-colonial nationalism is multiple, complex, contradictory, and complementary. The transformation of an otherwise fragmented, hierarchical, and divided society into a nation that demands the right to determine its own future involves

---

[11]Ibid.

[12]Strictly, Aphrodite's birth was also the outcome of a series of developments. According to Greek legend, Cronus, the leader of the Titans, at the behest of his mother, Gaia, the Goddess of the Earth, committed parricide by killing his father, Uranus. Subsequently, Cronus threw his father's genitals into the sea. Out of the sea foam, or aphros, emerged Aphrodite.

parallel and sometimes interlocking processes. The polarization of Indian society through politicization of religion was to bear bitter consequences. Counting of heads and categorizing them under the banner of this or that religion was to result in competitive nation state projects and, ultimately, communal violence.

The opening decades of the twentieth century witnessed the onset of numerous communal riots. This aspect of Indian politics is discussed in the next chapter on communalism. Here, let us note that by the 1930s, a noted poet and Muslim intellectual, Muhammad Iqbal, began to speak of two nations. He proposed that the differences between the two were so deep that the only way forward was a separate Muslim region within the country. Interestingly, the logic of Partition was fully enunciated by someone who was more or less unknown to the mainstream national movement—Choudhry Rahmat Ali, a Punjabi. Then a student at the University of Cambridge, he coined the term 'Pakistan' in 1933 sitting on the top deck of a London bus. He subsequently disseminated the idea in a political pamphlet. Reportedly, he tended to shower political pamphlets on random people. The term 'Pakistan', for Rahmat Ali, was an acronym for five regions—Punjab, North West Frontier Province, Kashmir, Sind, and Baluchistan. Initially, the idea did not catch on. Rahmat Ali was regarded as a bit of an oddball by other groups.

Within ten years, the notion of independence from the British as well as from the Hindus overwhelmed the political imagination of Muslims. They were bound to be in a minority in an independent state dominated by the Hindus. Historians tell us that over time Muhammad Ali Jinnah, an archetypical English gentleman, came to believe that Muslims were not only in a minority, they were in fact a nation. On 23 March 1940, the Lahore Resolution was passed by the Muslim League. It demanded that the areas in which the Muslims were numerically in a majority, i.e., the north-western and eastern zones of India should be grouped, with some territorial adjustments, to form independent states in which the constituent units will be independent and sovereign.

The Delhi Resolution of April 1946 established that Muslim majority zones should be constituted into a sovereign independent state. This meant, writes Patrick French, that East Pakistan would be controlled from West Pakistan, a disastrous proposal which in a short period of time was to lead to the partition of Pakistan in 1971.[13] The Lahore Resolution, continues French, was not detailed enough to spell out the contours of a new Muslim state, and Jinnah was careful to maintain uncertainty. Questions relating to boundaries, population shifts, administration, rights of minorities, and the core issue of whether the political aspirations of the Muslim community could be accommodated within a federal structure were not spelled out. Some historians have argued that Jinnah was not serious about a separate state and wanted to use the proposal to bargain for a better deal. His reputation was that of a man who was not favourably inclined towards religion and religious identities; he was westernized, suave, and savvy. But as French writes, this man, 'whom Motilal Nehru had once said was showing the way to "Hindu-Muslim unity" became the prophet and founder of a Muslim homeland'.[14] No one foresaw the communal conflagration that would result from the splitting up of the country, no one anticipated the wholesale transfer of populations; it was assumed that people would continue to live where they were, and that the presence of Hindus in the new state would safeguard the lives of Muslims who continued to stay back in India.

The repeated bursts of communal violence in the first four decades of the twentieth century prompted India's tallest leader, Jawaharlal Nehru, to write in his diary while in prison in 1935: 'What a disgustingly savage people we are…politics, progress, socialism, communism, science—where are they before this black religious savagery?' His biographer, Sarvepalli Gopal, concluded that Nehru was extremely impatient with religion. It might be an anchor for some, but he did not seek harbourage in this way. 'I prefer the open sea,' wrote Nehru, 'with all its storms and tempests.'[15]

Nehru was to change his mind after the communal fury that accompanied the Partition of India. Gopal cites a letter written to Jinnah by Nehru, in which he expressed extreme discomfort with the great role played by religion in the lives of people: 'I have lost confidence and the last few years have had a powerful effect on me. My own mind moves

---

[13]Patrick French, *Liberty or Death: India's Journey to Independence and Division*, London: Flamingo, 1998, p. 124.
[14]Ibid., p. 125.
[15]Cited in Sarvepalli Gopal, 'Nehru and Minorities', *Economic and Political Weekly*, Special Issue, Vol. 23, Nos. 45–47, November 1988, pp. 2, 466.

in a different plane and most of my interests lie in other directions.... However,' he continued, 'I have given much thought to the problem, and understand much of its implications. But I feel like an "outsider", and "alien in spirit".'[16]

In short, distrust between Hindus and Muslims, which was built up and sharpened by the politicization of religion and divisive colonial policies, led inexorably to the Ppartition of the country. The seeds of the division of the country had been sown early on, when colonial documents began to chronicle the history of Indians as the histories of Hindus and Muslims who could never live together, when every clash was interpreted as a communal clash, when India was told that it was inhabited not by one but by two nations, and when nationalists who did not believe in Partition began to conceptualize Hinduism and Islam as internally homogenous and as the anchors of a political identity and nation that had the right to its own state.

There are many interpretations of the Partition of India. However, the development of a schism between religion as faith and religion as power politics that could not accommodate other aspirations proved both effective and lasting. We still feel the effects of this construction. Both in India and in Pakistan, political groups and their leaders continue to understand their society much as the colonialist understood undivided India, as predominantly religious. This is even though they know that colonial practices of categorizing, defining, and interpreting identities and interests in religious terms inaugurated the two-nation theory.

The two-nation theory is fallacious as well as dangerous. It is fallacious because very quickly Pakistan, that had been designed as a homeland for South Asia's Muslims, was further subdivided on the basis of language, leading to the formation of Bangladesh in 1971. It is dangerous because rulers use it to divide their citizens. In the process, religion has been vulgarized because it was and continues to be reduced to strategy to win elections and forge constituencies. Politics becomes status quoist, conservative, partisan, and vicious, with the infusion of religious vocabularies. The politics of religion, we should know by now, curtails imaginations, truncates solidarities, and impoverishes politics. We only have to recollect the terror of the latter part of 1947 to appreciate this point.

---

[16]Ibid.

## THE ONSET OF PARTITION VIOLENCE

The rocky path to extreme violence was carved into the soil of the northern and eastern parts of India when Hindus and Muslims, charged by rumours over which part of Bengal would go to Pakistan and which would remain in India, clashed in Calcutta in August 1946. The riots left 5,000 dead and 10,000 to 15,000 injured in what came to be known as the Great Calcutta Killings.[17] The Muslim League had declared 16 August 1946 a public holiday to celebrate the party's withdrawal from the Congress-dominated interim government. Jinnah, the fiery leader of the League, called 16 August Direct Action Day. However, neither he nor the premier of Bengal, Huseyn Shaheed Suhrawardy, specified what exactly was meant by the phrase 'direct action'. The lack of clarity led to disaster. Unruly mobs in Calcutta were encouraged to take the term as a sanction for violence. It took the administration ten days to restore order.

As rumours that India was going to be partitioned spread, mobs started attacking those they perceived as the enemy. On 16 August, gangs roamed the streets of Calcutta, looting, raping, and killing. Tunzelmann draws on the memories of journalist and writer Nirad C. Chaudhuri, who recounted what a Hindu mob did to a fourteen-year-old boy in the Great Calcutta Killings. A horde of men stripped this young boy, checked his genitals, made certain that he was a Muslim, and threw him into a pond. Attackers held his head under water with bamboo poles till the time he died. A Bengali engineer, educated in England, noted the time the boy took to die on his Rolex wristwatch. He wondered aloud how tough a Muslim 'bastard' was.[18] For more than a week, gangs spread terror in the streets. And violence relentlessly spread through Bengal, Assam, Punjab, and the North West Frontier Province.

The journalist and editor Nikhil Chakravarty confessed that he had never seen such devastation. Hundreds of festering corpses were piled up on the streets, and a stomach-churning putrid stench overpowered the city in the terrible August heat. Mass murder of the 'other' community was conceptualized and executed in an alarmingly efficient manner, much as Hitler's professional gas chambers killed thousands of German citizens who had been typed as the alien.

---

[17] Barney White-Spunner, Partition: *The Story of Indian Independence and the Creation of Pakistan in 1947*, London: Simon and Schuster, 2017, p. 10.

[18] Tunzelmann, *Indian Summer*, p. 143.

White-Spunner recounts that one of the most feared Hindu gangs in Calcutta was led by a man called Gopal P. Mukherjee. The BBC journalist Andrew Whitehead recalled that Mukherjee's 800-strong gang murdered hundreds of Muslims. If one Hindu was murdered, he had instructed his goons, ten Muslims should be murdered. The fear that Bengal would form part of a future Pakistan propelled anxiety, and resulted in vicious brutality that would swamp large parts of the country for years to come. According to reports charted out in White-Spunner's volume on the Partition, Gopal Mukherjee seemed to believe that if only Bengal was rid of its Muslim population, partition would never come to the land.

In retrospect, the unbridled savagery with which 'homicidal maniacs' were let loose to kill, maim, and burn was shocking, wrote General Sir Francis Tuker, who bore witness to much of the violence in 1946. The worst butchery was in the south of the city. When troops moved in, they had to remove 150 bodies from the crossroads so that vehicles could pass. In one basti, or slum, they found a house with fifteen bodies in one room and twelve in the second. They came across a rickshaw in which the passengers and also the rickshaw puller had been cut down; many bodies were horribly mutilated. People of both communities were massacred in the hundreds.[19]

The historian Suranjan Das analysed that the mob was not made up of subordinate social groups; it was a mixture of upper- as well as lower-social classes. August 1946 saw the first large-scale participation of upper-class Hindu and Muslim Bengalis in communal riots. Political leaders incited the crowds to commit arson. Wealthy businessmen, influential merchants, artists, and shopkeepers were arrested on charges of rioting.[20] Violence bred violence, and violence fetched violence.

In the same year, communal violence moved to rural areas of Chittagong, Tippera, and Noakhali in Eastern Bengal. Muslim gangs under the leadership of Ghulam Sarwar went around Hindu villages. They demanded that Hindus convert to Islam and butchered those who refused. Among the attackers were people whom the victims had known all their lives. This was a pattern that was replicated in different

---

[19]White-Spunner, p. 11.

[20]Suranjan Das, *Communal Riots in Bengal 1905-1947,* New Delhi: Oxford University Press, 1993, p. 209.

parts of India in times to come. Many people jumped into ponds to hide behind the water hyacinths. They were killed by spear-wielding attackers. In the weeks that followed, Hindu men were forced to offer namaz and adopt Muslim names. An ageing Gandhi came to the area on a peace pilgrimage to try and restore some modicum of order. But the fate of India had already been written and sealed, inscribed in the blood of people who had been inhabitants of the same cities, the same villages, the same towns, and the same bastis. The Great Calcutta Killings presaged the outbreak of the worst forms of torture, brutality, rape, mutilation, and killings that India was to witness.

## THE MOMENT OF INDEPENDENCE; THE MOMENT OF PARTITION
As the midnight of 14/15 August 1947 approached, members of the new ministry headed by Jawaharlal Nehru came together in the hall of the Constituent Assembly. The moment was politically significant and wildly euphoric. It could not be otherwise; India was finally free! Hundreds of people began to assemble in the streets outside. However, the atmosphere in Delhi was mixed. Thousands of refugees had poured into the city and were living in refugee camps or camping on the roads.

Still, as the time of Independence came nearer, crowds began to cheer Nehru and Gandhi. Gandhi was not in Delhi at the time, and he did not take part in the celebrations. He was in Calcutta, fighting bravely in his own way for the restoration of sanity. He continued to pray and appeal for harmony between Hindus and Muslims. Quite oblivious to the fact that the country was celebrating Independence, for the Mahatma, the night of 14 and the dawn of 15 August represented Partition, which he had struggled against. It symbolized the high point of religious enmity between two communities, perhaps even the point of no return.

Other sensitive souls shared his agony. The greatest Urdu poet of the twentieth century, Faiz Ahmad Faiz, wrote in torment on the pain of Partition violence: ' Yeh daagh daagh ujaala, yeh shab gazida seher/ woh intezar tha jiska, yeh woh seher to nahin/Yeh woh seher to nahin, jis ki aarzoo lekar/Chale the yaar ki mil jaayegi kahin na kahin/Falak ke dasht mein taaron ki aakhri manzil/Kahin to hoga shabe-sust mauj ka saahil/Kahin to jaa ke ruke gaa safinaa-e-gham-e-dil.' (This [blood-] dappled dawn, this dawn still drowned in darkness of the night. This is not the dawn we waited for, this is not the dawn towards which we had begun our hopeful journey, this is not the dawn we yearned to find in the stars of heaven. We had hoped that somewhere we would find the end of our journey, the shore where we could rest our grief-stricken hearts. This is not that dawn.[21])

In Delhi, in the Constituent Assembly, Nehru spoke just before midnight. The famous 'tryst with destiny' speech, delivered in his usual elegant style and beautiful language, has come to be one of the most famous speeches in the world. His words exuded a sense of excitement and hope as he welcomed the advent of Independence for which generations had aspired and fought for. On the other side of the celebrations, the dark underbelly of Independence was the violence that had erupted even before the tricolour replaced the flag of the Empire.

The irony is that until Independence, no one knew which part of the country would remain with India and which would go to Pakistan. The colonial government announced on 3 June 1947 that India would be partitioned, but the boundaries of the two countries were still to be specified. On 8 July 1947, a British jurist who hardly had any knowledge about India and its people landed in Delhi. He had been charged with the task of dividing the borders of India, and marking out the territory of a new country: Pakistan.

Sir Cyril Radcliffe had been appointed the chairman of the Boundary Commission. The specific mandate of the commission was to divide geographically contiguous Muslim majority from non-Muslim majority territories in Punjab and Bengal. Radcliffe was not familiar with the diversity of the people of India, their languages, their customs, the ways they coexisted, on what they differed, the overlaps, and the schisms. He was asked to partition a country unknown to him; to forge a divide between people—their cities, villages, fields and farms, shops, sacred places, and sites of memory—within the time stipulated for the transfer of power.

The moment they heard about the Boundaries Commission, the Sikh community was up in arms, protesting against any proposal that would geographically alienate their places of worship and their lands. The governor of Punjab, Sir Evan Jenkins, was witness to the violence

---

[21]Translation provided by the author.

triggered off by the mere suggestion that the sacred lands of Punjab would be handed over to another religious community. He warned against any decision that might shake the foundations of the province. Groups armed with weapons had already begun to instil fear in the other community and engage in ethnic cleansing, even if they were not quite sure which part of the region would rest with them, and which part would be given to the other side.Vicious rumours successfully partitioned the people of Punjab even before the boundaries were announced.

The decision of Sir Cyril Radcliffe who chaired the three Boundary Commissions on Punjab, Bengal, and the Sylhet district of Assam was made known only on 17 August 1947 when the three awards were gazetted.This was three days after Pakistan had celebrated its independence, and two days after India had celebrated hers. Lord Mountbatten had presided over a meeting to discuss the award on 16 August 1947. The meeting was attended by the leaders of the Indian National Congress and the Muslim League. The award generated considerable acrimony particularly because Chittagong Hill Tracts had been given to Pakistan, and Darjeeling and Jalpaiguri districts remained with India in the east. The award was, however, accepted. On 22 July 1947, Lord Mountbatten had managed to extract an agreement from the leaders that they would accept the award, howsoever illogical the division might seem to them.

The Boundary Commission announced that Gujarat would remain with India and that Sindh would be a part of Pakistan. Bengal and Punjab were divided. Even as the north–south line between the twin cities of Amritsar and Lahore split Punjab into two, an estimated 17 million Muslims, Sikhs, and Hindus were cut off from their homes, partitioned by a stroke of Radcliffe's pen.They became refugees in their own land; their neighbours became foreigners, inhabitants of another land.

Bashabi Fraser details the tragic impact of new geographic boundaries on human relations in Bengal. In the last paragraph of her poem, 'This Border', she writes:

> This border that cuts like a knife
> Through the waters of our life
> Slicing fluid rivers with
> The absurdity of a new myth
> That denies centuries
> Of friendship and families

This border that now decrees
One shared past with two histories
This border that now decrees
The sky between us as two skies
This border born of blood spilt free
Makes *you* my friend, my enemy.[22]

Anger was nurtured against the background of tremendous insecurity. People torn from their homes and accepted ways of life had hardly any emotional resource with which to meet this sudden rupture. A knee-jerk reaction to the overpowering bewilderment was to lash out violently. Each side blamed the other and vowed to extract vengeance for harm done.

## PARTITION: SPARKING OFF VIOLENCE

Hindus, Sikhs, and Muslims had lived together for centuries. We can only imagine the dread and hopelessness that dominated the minds of people who were forced to leave the familiar and migrate to what had become another country. In a short period of time, the great divide ripened and burst to sunder lives and impact psyches. Driven relentlessly to an almost predestined end, the divide was to poison the minds and memories of entire populations, and stamp the bodies of generations with ineradicable welts.

Take Bengal, which has been partitioned twice in history. In 1905, the partition had been carried out for the instrumental and cynical considerations of the viceroy, Lord Curzon. The act had to be reversed because of a vigorous movement against the partition of Bengal that swept throughout India. In 1947, Bengal was partitioned for the second time. This time, 3.6 million people from East Bengal moved into what had become West Bengal and 7 million Muslims left for East Pakistan.

In September, in Calcutta, which had till then staved off violence because of the presence of Gandhi, neighbourhoods began assaulting each other. In Beliaghata, a Hindu threw a bomb killing Muslim women and children, and this act led expectedly to riots. By early morning of 2 September, 500 people had been killed. Gandhi sent out Hindu volunteers to Muslim mohallas to restore peace and warned Hindus

---

[22]Bashabi Fraser (ed.), *Bengal Partition Stories: An Undisclosed Chapter*, London: Anthem, p. 594.

who were poised to attack their neighbours that he would hold them personally responsible. He subsequently went on a protest fast. Gurkha troops were brought in and curfew was imposed with orders to shoot anyone who broke the curfew.

Fearing Partition, Hindus and Muslims in northern and eastern parts of India left their homes and moved into ghettos. And then they were forced to move from these ghettos into a land that had been a part of undivided India till recently, but which for them was practically another country. As processions slowly and hesitatingly moved across the newly minted and arbitrarily decided borders, casualties and mayhem followed. Dead bodies had already lined the streets of Delhi when Jawaharlal Nehru made his 'tryst with destiny' speech in the Constituent Assembly. Lahore was ablaze with injured Sikhs clustered in gurudwaras.

Patrick French writes of the Punjab Boundary Force that was hurriedly put together to guard 38,000 miles of territory in Punjab, including 17,000 villages, many of which were not linked by road. But the force was helpless. It could not confront the scale of organized communal slaughter that took place in the second half of 1947. It was hopelessly under-equipped and undermanned for the task that lay before it. On 14 August, members of the force discovered the bodies of thirty-five Sikhs who had been knifed at Lahore Railway Station. That night, while Muslim police officers looked on, members of the force tried to prevent a mob from burning down a gurudwara in Lahore which sheltered hundreds of Sikhs. The next day, they rushed to Amritsar to pre empt retaliation. Most of the city's police force had deserted the city. By the time the Boundary Force arrived, many Muslim women had been dragged from their homes and paraded naked outside the Golden Temple. They were subsequently raped and hacked to death.

In Jalandhar, people on every street used long poles with burning rags tied to the top as deadly instruments of mass extermination. The Boundary Force split apart along communal lines on 1 September. It had been created, writes French, with soldiers of the British Indian Empire, but now they were either Indians or Pakistanis. By the end of August 1947, any semblance of law and order collapsed in Punjab.[23]

---

[23]French, *Liberty or Death*, pp. 347–48.

The region was destroyed, its people harmed beyond belief, the project of living together had collapsed.

Amidst the sort of violence that had seldom been seen earlier, the governments of India and Pakistan were rendered as impotent and helpless as the protagonist in Manto's short story 'Thanda Gosht' (Cold Meat). In this short story, Manto writes of the unholy fate of a Sikh man who slung the inert body of a Muslim woman on his shoulder after he had killed six Muslim men crouched for safety in a room. He carried her to a copse, threw her on the ground, tried to rape her, and realized with horror that she was dead—so much cold mutton. The experience of near necrophilia renders him impotent; he is no longer able to respond to his wife, with whom he had once shared passion.

## THE FATE OF PUNJAB

The region that was worst hit was Punjab, the most productive agricultural region of undivided India. It was this province that Jinnah had identified as the cornerstone of Pakistan. Punjab had provided the Indian army with huge numbers of soldiers and officers. It was the granary of the country. The capital of the province, Lahore—one of the most cosmopolitan cities in the subcontinent—was the centre of intellectual life and of the film industry. In January 1947, Punjab was ruled by a coalition unionist government headed by Malik Khizar Hayat Tiwana, which had blocked the Muslim League from power. The government had rejected Partition. But it could not rebuff a malign destiny.

A miasma of uncertainty hung over Punjab as Independence drew nearer. Nobody knew which part of the province would be allotted to which country. Violence swept through Punjab in the months preceding and following August 1947. The conflict affected, in particular, twelve districts on the border. Reportedly, large gangs of men motivated others to loot and murder, assault, and torture. Once fighting began the numbers swelled. As people moved from West to East Punjab, Muslim gangs attacked Hindus and Sikhs as they fled, raping, killing, raiding, and forcibly converting those who were spared. In East Punjab, the pattern was reversed; Muslims fled pursued by Sikh jathas amidst scenes of sickening medieval violence and wanton barbarity.

Until mid-August, the worst of the violence flared up in the cities of Punjab, where it was most visible. Arson was so widespread that the fire brigade became irrelevant; Lahore, Amritsar, Jalandhar, and Ferozepur were the worst affected. Muslim and Sikh leaders tried to intervene and negotiate, but by 21 August the violence moved into the countryside.

In the end, approximately 8 million Hindus and Sikhs moved from what is now Pakistan to India, and 6 to 7 million Muslims from India migrated to Pakistan between 1947 and 1951. About 1 million people were killed in bloody massacres; half of this number in Punjab alone. The violence was organized but also spontaneous, some people were aware that doom was near and others were caught unawares. In every case, Partition left the dead and the maimed in its wake, with trauma haunting the lives of the raped, the brutalized, and families of the dead. Homes and workplaces, recreational spaces, temples, mosques, and gurudwaras were desecrated and destroyed beyond repair.

## POLITICAL INTERVENTION

The scale of the bloodbath shocked the Government of India and the new Government of Pakistan. On the afternoon of 16 August, Sir Claude Auchinleck, the supreme commander of the Indian and the Pakistani armed forces reported to Lord Mountbatten that India was already in the midst of a civil war. On 17 August, Nehru rushed to Punjab to meet Liaquat Ali Khan, the prime minister of Pakistan, and both leaders appealed for peace through public appearances and speeches. Their appeals had little impact on the rioters.

Nehru was in the killing fields of Punjab and Delhi, persuading people to desist from violence, assuring Muslims of their safety, and appealing to Muslims who had left for Pakistan to return. But violence escaped the efforts of the interim prime minister of independent India. It swallowed up collective life. The saga of violence in Punjab shook the foundations of our newly independent country, even as its territory and people were rearranged in a purely arbitrary manner.

The historian Ian Talbot suggests that violence unfolded in Punjab in three phases. The first was sparked off by the resignation of the coalition ministry headed by Khizar Hayat Tiwana in March 1947. This phase was inaugurated by the outbreak of violence in Lahore on 4 March 1947, and serious rioting in Multan and Amritsar. Non-Muslims were massacred in Rawalpindi, Attock, and Jhelum districts of Rawalpindi division. Violence occurred in Amritsar between 11 and 13 April, and this sparked off further disturbances in Lahore, but order was eventually restored. The second phase began on 10 May and was termed by the British governor, Sir Evan Jenkins, as a communal war of succession. Serious incidents of arson, stabbing, and bombing took place in Lahore and Amritsar. The night of 18 May witnessed arson attacks on the neighbourhoods of Chuna Mandi, Kucha Kagzian, and Pipal Vehra in Lahore.

Jawaharlal Nehru called the army to restore order in the city. A month later, a great fire gutted hundreds of non-Muslim shops, homes, and offices of the Shah Almi area of Lahore. On 24 May, a highly planned attack by Sikh jathas on the suburb of Risalpur, where Muslims had fled for safety, involved the use of bombs and grenades. The final bout of violence followed British departure from India in the border districts of Punjab.[24]

On the night of 25 August, in a small town of Sheikhupura near Lahore which had a population of 10,000 Muslims and 10,000 Sikhs and Hindus, a massive battle exploded between communities. Twenty-four hours later several thousand people, mainly Sikhs and Hindus, had been murdered in a frenzy of violence. Parts of the town were on fire. No attempt was made to quell the violence, and the police backed the Muslim mobs. A journalist wrote that Sikhs were afraid to go to the hospital and preferred to take shelter in the gurudwara.

The sight was appalling; hands and feet of men and women had been cut off and their forearms were reduced to black putrescent fly-covered stumps. Babies and children had been cut and slashed with knives. When Nehru visited days later, he found himself sick with horror at the sight; the stink of blood and burnt flesh was inescapable. He wrote to Mountbatten in deep depression, 'I suppose I am not directly responsible for what is taking place in the Punjab.... But in any event I cannot and do not wish to shed responsibility for my people. If I cannot discharge the responsibility effectively then I begin to doubt whether I have any business to be where I am.'[25]

By 26 August, Ludhiana was in flames and Lahore was described

---

[24]Ian Talbot and Darshan Singh Tatla (eds.), *Epicentres of Violence: Partition Voices and Memories from Amritsar,* Ranikhet: Permanent Black, pp. 6–7.

[25]Tunzelmann, *Indian Summer,* p. 225.

as the city of the dead. The famous main street of Lahore, The Mall, was deserted; shopkeepers had downed the shutters of their shops, and the only vehicles on the roads were army jeeps and trucks. Refugees brought with them stories of thousands shot by the police and the army in the neighbouring towns. Sixteen thousand were holed up in camps without food. Nehru felt that the leaders of India and Pakistan should come together to put an end to the violence.

Within a month of the Partition, on 14 September 1947, Prime Minister Liaquat Ali Khan addressed a Muslim League Council in Lahore and accused India of fomenting riots in the Indian part of Punjab and targeting Muslims. He alleged that Pakistan was surrounded by forces who wanted to destroy it. These forces, he said feared that with the consolidation of Pakistan their cherished dream to rule all over the subcontinent of India [would] not be realized.[26]

He gave this speech on the very day he had met Nehru and discussed measures to deal with the violence on both sides of the region. Two days later, the Pakistani foreign minister Muhammad Zafarullah Khan threatened to lodge a formal complaint with the United Nations unless the Indian government took steps to stop the massacres of Muslims. If this was not done, he stated, the Government of Pakistan would resort to direct measures.[27]

The allegation was unwarranted because Nehru had personally toured violence-affected regions and tried to control the riots. He had also tried to persuade the Muslims not to leave their homes and appealed to those who had left to come back to India because security would be provided to them. He stated publicly that once the Congress had accepted Partition, the leadership had done its best to implement the obligations that followed. He also hoped that once peace had been restored the two dominions may, by the free will of their respective people, unite.[28]

On 19 September, Nehru and Liaquat Ali met again in New Delhi to carry forth the Lahore discussion to restore communal peace and harmony and stem the riots. In a memorandum to Liaquat, Nehru recounted the measures taken by the Government of India to control

---

[26]A. S Bhasin, *India and Pakistan: Neighbours at Odds,* Delhi: Bloomsbury, 2018, pp. 2–3.

[27]Ibid., p. 3.

[28]Ibid., p. 3.

the violence, and also recapped speeches of the Indian leadership that sought to stem the violence. This was in sharp contrast to the provocative speeches and editorials by Pakistani leaders and newspapers, openly asking mobs to extract vengeance from Hindus and Sikhs. Nehru also condemned Jinnah's statements denouncing only the violence in the Indian part of Punjab, when far worse incidents of violence had taken part in Pakistani Punjab. [29]

Liaquat Ali sent a message to the British Prime Minister Clement Attlee to convene a meeting of the representatives of the Commonwealth Dominions to consider measures to control the riots and appoint a commission to investigate them. This was unacceptable to Nehru. He was rapidly disenchanted with Liaquat Ali's continuous references to the many brutalities on the Indian side of the border. Nehru was exasperated because he had been stating publicly that India wanted a secure and stable Pakistan on its borders. Any enquiry into the massivxe violence that had erupted in India and in Pakistan was thus foreclosed. [30]

At one point of time, India was known as the country that welcomed people from all parts of the world. The poet Firaq Gorakhpuri had famously written, 'Sar Zamine-e-Hind par aqwame-e-alam ke Firaq/ Kafile baste gaye/Hindostan banta gaya.' India was created as a plural society, wrote the poet, by successive waves of migration. People came in caravans and settled here. But in 1947, a society that had been fashioned by a groundswell of travellers deciding to settle in its territory witnessed processions of bedraggled and dispossessed people. Violence carried great costs. Before Partition, the Muslim population in Punjab numbered 100 million; the community had a slight majority over Hindus and Sikhs. On balance, Muslims constituted one-fourth of the population of undivided India. Forty million Muslims stayed back in India after 1947. Except for two districts, the whole of Indian Punjab experienced complete ethnic cleansing. The first town is Kadian, located 20 kilometres from Gurdaspur. This is the headquarters of the Ahmadiyya community. The second town is that of Malerkotla which neighbours Patiala. Interestingly, Malerkotla has never had a communal riot even though 92 per cent of its population is Muslim, and even though it borders Patiala, which was the worst hit by Partition violence.

---

[29] Ibid., p. 4.
[30] Bhasin, *India and Pakistan*, p. 4.

No one has been able to precisely estimate how many Punjabis lost their lives. The administration had collapsed, floods had ravaged the region, and individuals were hired by whatever remained of the administration and the police for mass disposal of bodies. Violence drowned entire villages and neighbourhoods, trains and crossings. Processions of refugees walking painfully with their pitiful belongings strapped onto their heads took days to reach their destinations, if they managed to do so unscathed. As processions of Indians and Pakistanis crossed, people began to attack each other.

The left-wing author Yashpal recounts a searing tale of one of the many massacres through the eyes of the protagonist, a Mr Puri. The morning was well advanced, narrates Puri, when the train halted at Sirhind station; the platform was deserted with some soldiers standing on guard with bayonets. An ominous stillness pervaded every nook and cranny. On one side of the station, behind the fence, lay several corpses. The train left the station and went only a short distance when the wheels of the train ground to a halt with a metallic screech. Sounds of gunshots came from close by, and bullets hit the sides of the carriages. A group of people with swords, spears, machetes, and guns in their hands jumped over the barbed wires and charged towards the train.

The attackers climbed on the running boards outside the carriages, swinging machetes that cut through people crowded near the entrance, and hurling spears through doors and windows. They pulled at passengers who stood nearest the entrance and threw them outside by the railway track. Three young men, two carrying swords and one holding a spear entered, struck randomly at passengers, and pushed them out of the compartment. 'The man armed with a spear moved his weapon to his left hand, grabbed the young woman by the hair, dragged her towards the door and kicked her out. The spear rose, and came down on the mouth of the older woman open in a scream, its blade piercing her gullet and coming out from behind.' Nearly half the compartment had been emptied out, and no one had the courage to fight back. Puri wondered in agony what had happened to human beings—where had this lust to kill, maul, and destroy come from?[31]

---

[31]Yashpal, *This Is Not That Dawn*, pp. 419–20.

## THE IMPRINT OF VIOLENCE

Where did this lust to kill come from? It is a difficult question. Any answer to this troubled question is unsettling. Perhaps violence occupies the deepest recesses of our psyche; perhaps it lies inert, for the most part, in our bones. It can, however, be ignited by a spark and it can blow up into a conflagration. Some killings were planned and others were haphazard. Violence outstripped the intentions and plans of its perpetrators and spilled over into avenues one would have thought are both unimagined and unimaginable. Killers driven mad by bloodlust often targeted their own community. One of Manto's short stories tells us of a man who slid a knife into the groin of another. The knife sliced the pyjama cord into two and exposed the genitals of the victim. He was not a Muslim. 'Tch tch,' exclaimed the murderer, 'I have made a "mishtake".' Many such 'mishtakes' were made in the heat of bloodshed and rued later.

It is impossible to read accounts of Partition violence without cringing, without despair, and without deeply regretting the loss of a shared history. Violence is not new to Indian society; it is not new to any society. But in Punjab in 1947, the scale and intensity of violence transcended every limit imposed by humanity. The repetitiveness of violent acts never fails to astonish humanity. Hannah Arendt had written that leaders who had masterminded the holocaust in Nazi Germany were not unusual people, they were ordinary people who had lost the ability to think from the perspective of others. They could command the execution of immense violence with a clear conscience.

In 1963, Arendt authored a controversial book titled *Eichmann in Jerusalem: A Report on the Banality of Evil*. The argument was based on the trial of a Nazi officer, Eichmann, who, obeying orders given by his superiors, masterminded the killing of several thousand Jews in a concentration camp. His problem, wrote Arendt, was not that he was evil, or a sadist who delighted in causing harm to others, but that he was thoughtless. He carried out his duties without thought or reflection. The evil that he dished out did not have any roots in his psyche, nor was it deeply enshrined in his body. The mechanical efficiency with which he carried out his assigned job, without once thinking it or its consequences, was banal. Banal because the violence was performed without reflection or any estimation of how recipients can be scarred beyond repair. This was banal violence.

Perpetrators who also became victims of violence during Partition did not stop to think from the perspective of the other. Caught up in frenzy, driven insane by savagery that surrounded them, people became both the hunter and the hunted. The unthinking violence with which mobs mowed down people who had been once their own contributed to the production and reproduction of banal violence. This is what Partition meant for India.

Sometimes, participants in the theatre of violence did stop and think. And this was the undoing of their own sense of self. There is a searing short story by Intizar Hussain which tells us of this. The protagonist tells us: 'Soon I reached another strange place. There the crowd was continuously swelling. People were playing drums of victory.... I asked what this place was, and someone whispered in my ear, this is the age of decadence and this is where everyone is taught a lesson. And who is that man on whose face someone has just spat? The man looked at me bitterly and asked: Don't you recognize him? No. O disfigured one, you are that man. Me? I was shocked into silence. Yes, you. When I looked at the face of that man carefully, my eyes opened with surprise. I was really that man. I recognized myself and died.'[32]

For some sensitive souls who reflected on what they had done, it was just not possible to speak of what they had gone through. A short story by 'Agyeya' painfully recounts this dilemma. In a train compartment, an elderly Sikh gentleman was travelling with someone bent on recounting instances of bloodshed and sexual assault that marked the lives of people during those terrible months of 1947. How can you, asked our Sikh gentleman, even begin to understand my anguish when in the very same breath you speak of the Delhi happenings with such heartlessness? If you had been capable of giving me sympathy 'your tongue would have stuck to the roof of your mouth, it would have frozen with shame before you could utter one syllable regarding the things you were so keen to gossip about—your head would have bowed with shame.'[33]

---

[32]Intizar Hussain, 'The City of Sorrow', in Alok Bhalla (ed.), translated from the Urdu by Vishwamitter Adil and Alok Bhalla, *Stories about the Partition of India*, Vol. 2, New Delhi: Indus, 1994, pp. 85–100.

[33]S. H. Vatsayan 'Agyeya', 'Getting Even', Bhalla (ed.), *Stories about the Partition of India*, Vol. 1, New Delhi: Manohar Publishers, 2012, pp. 119–26.

Consider the tragic irony. People who had no say in the drawing of borders, who were not considered worthy of being consulted, and whose interests were simply not taken into consideration attacked each other in frustrated and frenzied acts of revenge. Khushwant Singh's famous novel *A Train to Pakistan* depicted in blood-curdling detail the arrival of a ghost train full of corpses. Punjab and Punjabis must have been overcome by, in the poet's words, a fit of epilepsy which forecloses rational thought for the time being. But there was also intentional killing and ethnic cleansing carried out by groups who successfully sanitized their districts and their villages of those newly identified as the enemy.

At what point does planned violence take on a life of its own? It is difficult to answer this question, but generally crowd frenzy infects human beings to an alarming degree. This is what the study of violence tells us. How can we subject intentions, actions, and reactions of people who were forced to migrate, who were tracked by murderers and whose lives were extinguished by death, to rational and sane explanations or interpretations? The German critical theorist Theodor W. Adorno had famously declared that there can be no poetry after Auschwitz. Perhaps it is only poets, with their sweeps of imaginaries and their ability to reach into the depths of human consciousness, and writers, with dexterous deployment of searing idioms and phrases, who can capture the intensity and the violence of human emotions and the impact of Partition on the lives of ordinary people.

The experience of Bengal was similar and yet different to that of Punjab. This is encapsulated in the different sort of short stories that were written on the Partition of India. The writers are consumed by memories of loss of homes, of splits in the syncretic culture, and sorrow at the spirit of suspicion that began to hover over the heads of a linguistic community that had great pride in its shared culture. But as writers tell us in Bengal, unlike the massive exchange of populations in Punjab in 1947–48, the influx of refugees across the border has not stopped till date. At times it swells and at other times dwindles to a trickle. It has never dried up. The migrations across the borders in 1950 gave way to a one-sided migration from East Pakistan to West Bengal, Assam, Tripura, and Bihar. The unending flow of people remains an everyday reality in Bengal's porous border. The violence is of a different kind, it is attached to a protracted struggle to survive.[34]

## VIOLENCE AGAINST WOMEN

In order to remind ourselves of what happens when violence outstrips all bounds, we ought to read the novels of Yashpal, whose epic two-part novel *Jhootha Sach* has been compared to Tolstoy's *War and Peace* for its range and vivid depictions of Indian politics. The first part of the novel—*Vatan aur Desh* (Nation and Country) appeared in 1958, while the second part appeared in 1960 as *Desh ka Bhavishya* (The Future of the Country). Yashpal focuses on gender inequality in general and, in particular, the fate of women who were harmed during Partition.

In August 1947, women were subjected to inconceivable brutalities, stripped, paraded naked, gang raped, mutilated, and murdered. Their bodies were tattooed with political slogans with the dates and names of those who had raped them. About 100,000 women were abducted. Feminists writing on gendered violence graphically describe the way breasts were amputated, wombs knifed open, and foetuses killed. The lives of women who had undergone such horrors were irrevocably altered by events over which they had no control. Yet, some of them established a home with their rapists and abductors.

Subsequently, an Inter-Dominion Treaty of 6 December 1947 signed by both the governments initiated the Central Recovery Operation to rescue abducted women. The two sovereign states were bent on establishing their dominion over their subjects. Abducted women were part of the subjects who had to be brought under the umbrella of a sovereign nation. Women who had established homes with their abductors, and who had borne them children, were once again torn from their new homes.

The recovery of these women was deemed necessary to restore an ethical social order. The recovery bred as many tragedies as abductions. Most families refused to accept women who had been abducted and lived with other men, others changed their attitudes towards women of their own family irrevocably. Whoever had survived the killing fields of Punjab in 1947 had few choices. The dislocations and the disturbances of the time had been stamped on their present and their future. They

---

[34]Fraser (ed.), 'Introduction', *Bengal Partition Stories*, pp. 1–56.

were abducted but matters did not improve when they were returned to their homes; many families were disinclined to accept their own daughters or wives.

Women who survived the violence were dispossessed in every sense of the term, rejected by their families, rendered homeless, and forced to live out a bare and forlorn existence in a country that claimed them as its own. Feminist historiography has brought to the fore the way women were tortured and the way they died. Ironically, those who stayed alive also faced great challenges.

This double tragedy is vividly brought out in the short story authored by Rajinder Singh Bedi titled 'Lajwanti'. Lajwanti is abducted during Partition. In time, she is restored to her home and husband. Her husband, in the meanwhile, has become an enthusiastic supporter of the campaign to accept abducted women back into family homes. He took part in processions and urged families to take back their own kin. But once Lajwanti returned to her home, he could no longer see her as his wife. Now he insisted on seeing her as a goddess.

'[Lajwanti] withdrew into herself and stared at her body for the longest time, a body which after the Partition was no longer hers, but that of a goddess…. She wanted to be the same old Laaju once again, the one who would quarrel over trifles and then make up in no time at all. Now though there was no possibility of even a quarrel. Sunder Lal had convinced her that she was in fact a Lajwanti, a glass object too fragile to withstand the merest touch. Laaju would look at herself in the mirror and after thinking long and hard would feel that she could be many things but she could never hope to be the old Laaju ever again. Yes, she had been rehabilitated but she had also been ruined.'[35]

## CONCLUSION

The year 1947 changed the lives of Indians in many ways. Colonial India became a sovereign state and subjects became citizens. The price the country paid for Independence was Partition. The Partition of India impacted individual and collective psyches, and its memories evoke anguish and disbelief till date. Ismat Chughtai summed up this grief-stricken dilemma when she wrote of the 'flood of communal violence

---

[35]Rajinder Singh Bedi, 'Lajwanti', *The Greatest Urdu Stories Ever Told,* Selected and translated by Muhummad Umar Memon, New Delhi: Aleph Book Company, 2007, p. 89.

[that] came and went with all its evils, but it left a pile of living, dead and gasping corpses in its wake. It wasn't only that the country was split into two, bodies and minds were also divided. Moral beliefs were tossed aside and humanity was in shreds, government officers and clerks along with their chairs, pens and inkpots, were distributed like the spoils of war.... Those whose bodies were whole had hearts that were splintered. Families were torn apart.... The bond of relationships was in tatters, and in the end many souls remained behind in Hindustan while their bodies started off for Pakistan.'[36]

Succeeding generations of Indians have taken the independence of the country in which they were born for granted. Today, young people are simply not familiar with the freedom struggle and leaders who strode like colossuses across the theatre of Indian history. Nor perhaps do they feel the need to do so. But there is no way anyone, particularly in North India, can forget Partition. Memories of this event continue to deface the body politic, the wounds inflicted during the latter half of 1947 cannot be healed. They continue to fester, to catapult images of arson, carnage, and terror in the minds of succeeding generations who have been brought up on tales of a home which is now in another country.

Sadly, these memories also shape in perverse ways the perspective of some Indians towards our own people, the Muslims who chose to stay on in India and acquire citizenship. Partition violence provides the frame for many different sorts of violence in postcolonial India; it is almost as if we have become inured to the violence we began our postcolonial life with.

On the fiftieth year of India's independence, scholars began to revisit 1947 and tell us that our society must come to terms with history in order to move forward. We cannot continue to be stuck in a past of violence, in memories of what our own people did to each other. It is important to come to terms with history and admit that terrible things were done on both sides of the newly drawn border, and that any sane society will forswear such brutality in the future. It seems, however, that we have not learnt anything. For more important than memory or the art of remembering is judgement, is the skill in knowing how we remember, and what we can do with that memory. We must take

---

[36]Ismat Chughtai, *My Friend, My Enemy: Essays, Reminiscences, Portraits,* translated and introduced by Tahira Naqvi, New Delhi: Women Unlimited, p. 3.

care to historically locate and contextualize what we recollect. But we must also know what lessons history holds for the present. We must learn from history, not repeat it.

We, however, forget three lessons we have learnt from the blood-spattered history of Partition. One, when we invoke religion to justify 'this' or 'that' act, we commit a serious mistake. When politicized religion, or religion as political ideology, is unleashed on the body politic, it proves uncontrollable. Religion takes on a trajectory of its own. It becomes the master not the instrument of human ambitions for power, land, and resources. When religion justifies ugly revenge, it outstrips both intentions and control.

The central theme of Agyeya's poetic collection *Samanantar Saanp* (Parallel Snakes), is the tale of two interlocked serpents (competing communalism) that caught Indians in their grip and spread their venom far and wide. Hatred oozed out of their eyes and people ran for cover because if they stopped they would die. 'Ham ek lamba saap hain/jo badh raha ha aiththa khulta, sarakta, rengtha,/mein na sir hoon (aankh toh hoon hi nahi)/dum bhi nai hoon/aur na mein hoon daanth zehreele/mein us saanp ki gunjlak mein uljha hua-sa/ek bekas jeev hoon/ bagal se guzre chale tum ja rahe ho/sir jhukaye, peeth par gathri sambhale.' (I am a long snake, which, moving forward, flexes, constricts, opens out, slithers, and stings, I am not its head, nor am I its eyes, nor its tail, and nor am I its poisonous teeth, I am helplessly caught in the coils of the snake. Nearby you pass with bowed heads, laden with bundles on your back.)

Most states are founded by violence, civil wars, wars of independence, and bloody coups. We now have to come to terms with the fact that the postcolonial life of the largest democracy in the world is framed in and stained by blood. Some call August 1947 the month of freedom, others call it the high point of an epoch of violence. And violence continues to constrain freedom of the individual, of the community, of the collective, and even of the nation.

Two, we should learn that the splitting up of a country is a tragedy, but violent ruptures between people who could have lived together as citizens of two sovereign states is a tragedy of epic proportions. Partitions herald the closing in of boundaries and lead to constricted minds and truncated imaginations. India lost not only territory and people in

Partition, other losses were incalculable. We have lost what was called
the Ganga-Jamuna syncretic culture, or tehzeeb, we have lost much of
the language of love and longing that is Urdu, except by courtesy of
song writers of the Bombay film industry. Above all, we seem to have
misplaced the art of reaching out to people who might speak a different
language and worship different gods, but who are quintessentially human
like us. Looming like a shadow over the Indian subcontinent is a saga
of loss—loss of workplace solidarity, loss of friendships and love forged
despite taboos, loss of the art of compromise—and the anxiety and
sorrow that this has bred. We are unable to reach across borders and
speak to each other except in exceptional times when governments of
the two countries regain sanity. The governments of India and Pakistan
are often caught in a situation of undeclared war. Yet, many Indians who
are from what is now Pakistan yearn to see their ancestral homes. And
many Pakistanis we know feel the same. As the poet Gulzar writes with
some poignancy: 'Tumhe aziz hai apna watan/main jaanta hoon/mujhe
bhi us se mohabbat hai/tum yakeen kar lo/zara sa pharak hai gar tum
samajh sako isko/ki tum wahin ke ho aur main wahin se hoon.' (I know
your nation is dear to you, I also love it, believe me. The difference if
you understand is this. You belong there and I am from there.)[37]

Three, we should realize that the division of the country and its
people is not a once-in-a-lifetime event, the painful memories of which
can be acknowledged, accepted, and safely locked away in a collectively
owned closet containing remnants of things that have passed. These
remembrances, centred around grotesque performances of terrible injuries
on the bodies of mainly women, but also men and children, continue
to lacerate our collective imagination, and inhibit the establishment of
lasting civility with our geographical neighbour. History has a lot to
teach us, such as how not to let ourselves descend into the trough of
violence. But it appears that we have not learnt anything from our
history, as the next chapter shows.

Literary figures, perhaps, have a better understanding of sorrow
and destruction than anyone else. They captured the horror of the
events in Punjab, one of the vilest episodes in the whole of history, a
devastating illustration of the worst excesses to which human beings

---

[37]Gulzar, *Footprints on Zero Line: Writings on the Partition,* translated by Rakhshanda Jalil, New
Delhi: Harper Perennial, 2017, p. 51. Translation provided by the author.

can succumb. Violence is the epigraph written for the partition of a country that came under colonialism, saw the eruption of competitive nation state-making projects, and the victory of these projects over progressive politics. Competitive communalism and the desire for a state of one's own unremittingly drove the country to Partition. And now we have to ask the question—how many Partitions? How many times will communalism partition hearts and minds? For how long? How can we put aside the legacies of colonial rule that gave to us essentialist categories of Hindu and Muslim, and of the hate between them to divide people and to rule people? Is it not time to do so?

## Chapter 2

# THE LEGACY OF COMMUNAL CONFLICT

*Phir giri gardan, sar katne lage/Log bat te hi, khuda batne lagey/
Naam jo poochey koi…dar lagta hai/Ab kise pooje koi…dar lagta
hai/Kitni baar sooli par mujhe tanga hai chand logon ne.*

—Gulzar[1]

*Once again necks have fallen, heads have been hacked off/People
have been divided, now Gods are also divided/If someone asks me my
name…I am petrified/Who should I worship now?…I am frightened/
How many times will a handful of people nail me to a stake?*

## INTRODUCTION: THE SPECTRE OF COMMUNAL CONFLICT

Ahmedabad (1969), Belchi (1977), Delhi (1984), Bombay (1992–93),
Gujarat (2002), Khairlanji (2006), Dharmapuri (2012), Muzaffarnagar
(2013). These markers guide our attention to the sordid biography of
communal violence in India. History will tell a blood-soaked story of
shameful incidents that took place in India after Independence, of brutal
acts performed on the body of one human being by another for reasons
outside the former's control, such as birth into a religious community
that has been labelled by the other in perverse ways.

Communal violence, or violence between two religious communities,
mainly Hindus and Muslims in India, throws up uncomfortable issues.
One such issue is how we deal with the past.

The processes that led to the Partition of India formally ended
in 1947, but the tremors of the division continue to impact our lives.
India has a large Muslim minority, which comprises over 14 per cent
of the population. Christians form 2.3 per cent of the population, Sikhs

---

[1]Gulzar, '"Faith is trapped in the teeth of fire": Two poems by Gulzar on India today', translated
by Rakhshanda Jalil, *Scroll.in*, 2 Dec 2020. This translation is by the author.

1.7 per cent, and Buddhists and Jains constitute a small percentage of the Indian people. Hindus form an overwhelming majority; over 79.8 per cent. But it is the Muslim community which has been targeted for reasons that defy the very principles of a decent society.

India has evolved as a multireligious society and people could have learned to live together in peace after the horrors of Partition. Sadly, however, societies which have internalized destructive stereotypes about other communities do not bother to learn from history. Violence between Hindus and Muslims has been a prominent feature of our history since the turn of the twentieth century. The partition of the country does not appear to have resolved the issue. The situation of simmering violence confronts us with a grim question: How can people who subscribe to different faiths, speak different languages, and worship in different ways learn to live together in civility and peace?

There is no easy answer to this question. The proposition that India is a plural society does not automatically translate into us valuing the concept of pluralism. We have to build bridges between the two propositions. Indian thinkers and leaders have tried to build these bridges by privileging secularism, pluralism, and tolerance.[2] Yet, the history of our plural—albeit divided—society continues to be punctuated by communal riots that leave nothing but chaos and destruction in their wake.

Was there a time when Indians believed that murderous riots between religious communities constituted exceptions to normal ways of being? Perhaps. The general feeling could have been that during riots the codes of civility—which otherwise earmark (or should earmark) practices of everyday life—are suspended, and that norms and boundaries that govern social transactions are transgressed. We would have had good reasons to subscribe to this point of view. Some very insightful work in historical interpretation has told us that riots constitute a departure from the norm. Elias Canetti, focusing on destructive collective behaviour during the 1789 French Revolution in his *Crowds and Power*, suggests that such crowd violence transgresses generally established and universally valid distances and boundaries. It destroys a hierarchy that is no longer recognized as binding.[3]

---

[2]Neera Chandhoke, *Rethinking Pluralism, Secularism and Tolerance: Anxieties of Living Together,* New Delhi: Sage Publications, 2019, p. 8.
[3]Elias Canetti, *Crowds and Power*, New York: Farrar, Strauss and Giroux, 1984, p. 19.

There might have been a political moment when we thought that riots constitute episodic and spasmodic events in the biography of a society. However, this breakdown in social codes is not permanent; the rules of civil interaction are merely suspended for a time. They are restored when normalcy returns to the body politic. Riots have a short time span, and when the psychic and physical high that is generated during the course of the riot is spent, people return to living with each other, and limits on human behaviour are re-established. Riots, we could have said, somewhat comfortably at one point in our history, take place in a no man's land where neither the past nor the future is of any import. They occur in a time warp that mindlessly and meaninglessly constitutes a present, a present that is caught up in a vicious but nevertheless terminable spiral of violence. This was a reassuring thought, for then we could, with some ease, dismiss the riot as a contingent event marked by unreasonable crowd behaviour. On such occasions, we could have consoled ourselves, otherwise thinking individuals descend to irrationality and momentary insanity.

The problem is if we think of riots in this fashion, we type them as abnormalities or as departures from the norm. Do they really have nothing to do with history or the present, with social and political representations that are the stuff of everyday life, with political economy, or with tensions that arise out of the project of living together? These tensions permeate neighbourhoods, workplaces, and public spaces. And it is precisely here that we need to pause, reflect, and ask: Do riots really signify isolated instances in human history that are abstracted both from the past and from the present? How do we, in short, interpret the communal riot?

## UNDERSTANDING COMMUNAL VIOLENCE

One answer to the question of how we understand communal violence has been given by the instrumentalist school. Politicians cynically use religion as a weapon to engender a communal riot. In India, irresponsible rumours that a sacred book has been desecrated, or that a piece of pork has been thrown into the courtyard of a mosque, or a piece of beef has been hurled into the courtyard of a temple can result in a communal riot. The closing in of communities and perceived enmity with other religious groups creates ready constituencies for amoral politicians. In other words, these politicians deliberately polarize society in order to augment their own power.[4]

The argument of the instrumentalist school challenges what can be called the primordialist school. The argument of the latter school is best exemplified by the thesis of the colonial government. As discussed in the previous chapter, historians believe that colonial rule created categories of mutual distrust, by recording the belief that Hindus and Muslims are unable to live together. People who are born into a religion cannot tolerate other religious persuasions. The dissemination of the two-nation theory led to mutual suspicion between the two communities and ultimately the partition of the country.

Nationalist accounts and critical analysis of colonial domination of a multireligious society challenge this view. For instance, in 1931, a riot in the industrial town of Kanpur left 400 dead, parts of the city were destroyed, mosques and temples were damaged, and houses burnt. A miasma of devastation and gloom hung over the city. In the aftermath of the riot, the Indian National Congress established an inquiry commission to explore the reasons for the violence. A small committee of prominent Congressmen—Purushottam Das Tandon, Khwaja Abdul Majid, T. A. K. Sherwani, Zaraful Mulk, Pandit Sunderlal, and Bhagwan Das—authored a report. The detailed report interpreted communal riots as a product of colonial stereotypes. Communal riots are an outcome, the report concluded, of certain historical and social processes that have been introduced by colonial rule. The argument overturned the assumption, widely disseminated by the colonial government, that Hindu-Muslim enmity is part of the social fabric. The colonial government had deployed this argument to justify its rule.

Historians tell us that the pejorative term 'communal' was practically invented by the colonial government. The Indian National Congress uncritically accepted the term 'communal', but held that it was the British policy of divide and rule that was responsible for communal violence, loss of lives, and devastation. The official Congress position was that India was home to both Hindus and Muslims, and that it was possible to put an end to the conflict. For this minorities had to be reassured that their rights to religion and culture would be given full

---

[4]The instrumentalist school is best represented in the work of Paul R. Brass, *The Production of Hindu-Muslim Violence in Contemporary India,* Seattle: University of Washington Press, 2003.

protection in an independent India.[5]

In the shadow of the Kanpur riot, the Congress drafted the Karachi Resolution on Fundamental Rights. The Declaration emphasized the right to religion and the freedom to profess and practice any religion. Another addition to the list of minority rights that was part of the 1928 Motilal Nehru Constitutional Draft was the right to cultural autonomy and equal access to educational facilities. On 31 March 1931, M. K. Gandhi, moving the resolution on fundamental rights in the open session of the Congress at Karachi, spoke on the issue. Though Islamic and Aryan cultures are not mutually exclusive, he said, we must recognize that Mussalmans look upon Islamic culture as distinct from Aryan culture. Let us therefore cultivate tolerance. Religious neutrality is another important provision, he continued. Swaraj will favour Hinduism no more than Islam, nor Islam more than Hinduism. Let us from now on, he concluded, adopt the principle of state neutrality in our daily affairs.[6] For Gandhi, the route of toleration led straight to religious neutrality of the state. And religious neutrality is the first principle of secularism.

Three features distinguish the official position of the Congress on communal violence from interpretations of Hindu-Muslim animosity by colonial officials. One, leaders accepted that the Hindu community was as guilty of communal sentiments and violence as the Muslim. Two, the state had to be neutral towards religions. Three, group rights for minorities were not only an essential precondition for individual rights, but important in themselves. In other words, religion was seen as a significant good to which all people had a right. In a society where the Hindu community had the advantage of numbers, minorities had to be protected against the onslaught of majoritarianism. It is this notion of secularism, a notion that includes the right of minorities to protection, that has been abandoned time and again by murderous mobs intent on obliterating the existence of other groups through violence. The picture is more complex than just the amoral use of religion as a mobilizational device either by the government or by ambitious political leaders. We should understand this from our own history that resulted in the Partition of India.

---

[5]Chandhoke, *Rethinking Pluralism, Secularism and Tolerance,* pp. 124–25.
[6]M. K. Gandhi, 'Speech on Fundamental Rights', *Collected Works of Mahatma Gandhi,* Vol. 45, New Delhi: Ministry of Information and Broadcasting, Publications Division, 1971, pp. 372–74.

Religion cannot be understood only as a resource, or merely as an instrumentalist strategy for the mobilization of a constituency and the building up of a larger movement that poses itself against the other community. If a political movement is successful in tapping deep structures of sentiment in a society, arguably these sentiments must already be there, lurking under the skin of a shallow modernity that is expected to usher in a secular age. Religion cannot be harnessed to the cause of violence until it has a grip on people's minds and psyches.

On the other hand, we can subscribe to a distinct set of religious beliefs, but this does not indicate that we ritually murder others who subscribe to a different set of beliefs. People who subscribe to various faiths and have diverse conceptions of good can live together in a country in different ways. Some individuals may or may not be inclined to religiosity and yet abide by social norms when it comes to dining together and inter-community marriage. At the same time, these individuals do not feel the need to attack another set of beliefs, because people have a good reason for believing in their own faith. In liberal theory, we call this attitude tolerance. In India this is best summed up in the adage: 'Tum Ram kaho, hum Rahim kahe, matlab to usiki prakriti se hai.' The translation runs somewhat like this, 'You may call God Ram and we may call our revered one Rahim, both pertain to the nature of the divine.'

We can worship different gods in different ways, and yet live together in some civility. At the same time, the desire to be seen as distinct from others inevitably leads to the construction of boundaries, mainly symbolic, between the collective self and others. This can happen even if there are significant overlaps such as language, region, common memories, traditions, heroes and villains, Bollywood and cricket. But at precisely this point of the argument we must pause. The bracketing-off of identities is a sociological phenomenon. Despite these social and often intangible cultural barriers, forms of cooperation can and do arise in the workplace, in and through social and political organizations, social and political movements, associational life, friendships, love affairs, and through the lost value of solidarity.

However, the moment these identities begin to be used as weapons in pursuit of political, symbolic, and material gain, a sociological phenomenon translates into a political movement that lays claims upon material resources, political power, and symbols of self-representation. Multiple identities are thinned down, one identity dominates, commonalities are diminished, and singularities dominate. The politicization of identities is invariably an outcome of ruthless competition for all sorts of power, often at the cost of human lives. We witnessed this in pre-independence India, when right-wing Hindu and Muslim groups internalized the dangerous constructs of colonialism: that India is divided into Hindus and Muslims. And we see this in independent India.

We must note that the translation of often hidden animosities into violence involves a trigger. This trigger is usually provided by communal organizations that can be found in practically all communities, and/ or entrepreneurs, and merchants of hate who excel in excavating often hidden sentiments of resentment against other communities and in exaggerating incidents that otherwise can be passed off as minor. These entrepreneurs might not belong to any specific community, they may express no loyalty to anyone, and they might, more often than not, be mercenaries up for sale to the highest bidder. But when the trigger is pulled, it stokes the hellfire of hatred, causing devastating violence.

Since the turn of the twentieth century, communal organizations have fostered the creation of divides, exacerbated hitherto muted schisms, and created new ones. The translation of a sociological phenomenon into a political one encouraged leaders to adopt, flourish, and use their religious identity as a weapon, lay claim to a monopoly of power, and to a state of their own. Alternatively, they seek to deny power and resources to members of other communities on the same grounds. This is not religion as faith; this is religion as politics. The transformation of religion as faith into religion as politics distances communal movements from religious beliefs. We have to recognize crucial distinctions between the two processes.

The first distinction is between the community as a social category and the community as a political category laying claim to a monopoly of resources. The second distinction is between religion and politicized religion. Religion as politics in quest of power is quite distinct from religion as faith. Religion as faith is soothing and calming, religion as politics is violent; it calls for violence and for the shedding of blood. Those who search for faith search for harmony; those who use religion as politics intentionally and ruthlessly sow the seeds of terrible discord. The Urdu poet Saghar Khayyami writes of the way leaders of the latter variant have corrupted religion, 'Aisi koi missal zamaane ne paayi ho/ Hindu ke ghar mein aag khuda ne lagaayi ho/Basti kisi ki Ram ne yaaro jaalayi ho/Nanak ne sirf raah sikhon ko dikhayi ho/Ram-Raheem-o-Nanak-o/Eesa toh narm hai/chamchon ko dekhiye toh pateeli se garm hai.'[7] (Can anyone give us an example where God set fire to Hindu homes? Has anyone witnessed Lord Ram burning a settlement? Can anyone believe that Nanak showed the right path only to Sikhs? Ram, Raheem, Nanak, and Isa are gentle, but their courtiers are constantly on the boil. They burn more than a scorching pot.) The consequences can be disastrous.

A number of investigations into the aftermath of riots report that religion as faith transmits to religion as an instrument of power when political leaders, land sharks, and other purveyors of violence who feed off human tragedies provide a trigger and propel violence. Triggers can include hate speech, the labour of cadres who subscribe to an ideological persuasion, provocative slogans, and related catalysts. Other agents can also be involved, ranging from the makers and distributors of small arms, those who loot shops and homes, hearths and workplaces, those who specialize in fomenting hate between communities for perverse reasons to political leaders trying to form a constituency by demonizing another community. Communal violence is nothing but power politics in particularly ugly forms.

Take an incident elaborated later in this chapter. The movement to demolish the Babri Masjid in the town of Ayodhya and build, at the site, a temple dedicated to Lord Ram swept India in the 1980s and the early years of the 1990s. In the 1984 elections parliamentary elections, the BJP won just two seats. The Congress party, riding a massive wave of sympathy after Indira Gandhi's assassination, swept the polls. By the time the 1989 elections came around, the BJP had included the rebuilding of the Ram temple in Ayodhya in its manifesto. L. K Advani took out a Rath Yatra across major parts of the country to mobilize people on the issue. The election was fought on the plank of Mandir versus Mandal. The latter referred to the report of the Mandal Commission that recommended 27 per cent reservations for the backward castes. This was implemented by the then prime minster V. P. Singh. The BJP won

---

[7]Saif Mahmood, 'The secular agenda of humorist Urdu poetry', *Sabrang India*, 1 April 2016, available at <http://sabrangindia.in>. Translation provided by the author.

85 seats in the elections. From that time, the rebuilding of the temple has formed an integral part of the party's manifesto.[8] According to a compilation by the Institute of Peace and Conflict Studies under Nagrik Mancha by B. Rajeshwari, in the wake of the Rath Yatra, nearly 1,800 people died across the country between April and December 1990.[9] An equal number of people died in the post-demolition phase of the Babri Masjid. For the purpose of augmenting political power, collective memories were cynically excavated and relationships with neighbours and co-workers, friends and lovers heartlessly disrupted. The need to achieve political power through complete domination over symbolic representations of the nation was paramount. This had to be done even if the cost of the project was the physical displacement of a minority community from where its members lived and worked, by injuring them, and by desecrating their symbols of faith.

The communal riot, we have come to know, is not an isolated incident. It is preceded by hate speech targeting the other community, vilification, processions, meetings, and other spectacles enacted in the public sphere.[10] The message is clear. When we speak of Hindu or Muslim or Christian or Sikh fundamentalists, we do not speak of religion, we speak of people who exploit religion for their own ends and objectives, for the narrow purpose of securing control over power. Leaders who manipulate emotions and faith do disservice to their society and they do disservice to their religion, that is, if they have a religion.

It is not necessary that religious fundamentalists are religious. Moreover, the moment a conflict breaks out, mercenaries rush to fill their coffers. They pit one group against another through the construction and manipulation of a mob. When people form a part of a mob, the first things that they lose control over are moral judgement and autonomy of will. Leaders who foment communal hate forge shackles that constrict the ability to think independently of what the mob decrees. This destroys political imagination. When politicized religious identity lights a conflagration, it leads to the death of thousands of people, devastates

[8]Sai Manish, 'Babri Demolition, 25 years on: BJP's transition from Ram to reform to Ram', *Business Standard*, 6 August 2019.

[9]Ghazala Jamil, 'Night of Terror: The Dust Kicked Up Before the Babri Masjid Demolition', *The Wire*, 9 August 2020.

[10]Stanley J. Tambiah, *Leveling Crowds: Ethnonationalist Conflicts and Collective Violence in South Asia,* Berkeley: University of California Press, 1997.

settlements, wrecks livelihoods, and leaves nothing but ruin in its wake. Ordinary citizens are left with shattered neighbourhoods and workplaces, ruined relationships, derelict lives, deaths, and the deep vulgarization of religion. But people hungry for power persist in this ignoble project. They seek power at any cost. They drive Faustian bargains on their own behalf; the country's soul in exchange for pelf, gain, and power. And what is worse is that they seek monopoly over power at the cost of lives. We do not need to be a soothsayer to forecast that the tying of religion to cynical and amoral politics causes multiple tragedies.

In sum, the conversion of 'religion as faith' into 'religion as politics' to 'communal violence' as the lowest common denominator that binds humanity together is not inevitable. The movement from one to another moment requires a catalyst. The transition from religion as identity and faith to religion as politics that brings power to a few cynical leaders through violence is intentional. The cost to society is incalculable. When leaders of politicized religious identities compete for the same spatial and material resources, inerasable injuries are inscribed on the corporeal bodies of citizens. They scar the symbolic body of the polity.

We cannot argue that Indians are not inspired by religious sentiments, nor can we deny that they are wary of other religious groups as much as they are wary of other caste groups. But we also cannot accept that our people go around killing members of the other community who are identified as the other at the drop of the proverbial hat.

## DISCRIMINATION AND COMMUNAL VIOLENCE

Most people, we can safely presume, wish to live in peace, for peace is the basic precondition for living a life worth living. Yet, mischief makers continue to mar the body politic with their own deadly projects meant to divide society. It is these projects that form the background for the big communal riot. We are repeatedly told that since 2013, a year that witnessed the communal riot in Muzaffarnagar in Uttar Pradesh, no large-scale riot has erupted in India. This does not mean that there is no communal violence in the country, or that minorities have not been systematically targeted and killed in the most brutal ways possible. On 23 June 2019, *The Hindu* reported that the US Secretary of State released the 2018 Report on International Religious Freedom to the American Congress. It was released shortly after the

BJP came to power for a second term in May 2019 with a massive majority in Parliament. The chapter on India in the report detailed mob-related violence, conversions of minorities, threats to their legal status, and destructive government policies. The Government of India, the report stated, has taken steps to challenge the legal status of minority educational institutions in the Supreme Court. As a matter of right, minority educational institutions have the freedom to hire faculty and design their own curricula. Now things are different because the right-wing government seeks to interfere and regulate these institutions. Cities with Muslim names have been renamed, for example, Allahabad has been renamed as Prayagraj. The contribution of the Muslim community to India's art, literature, architecture, painting, and music is sought to be erased. This, the report continued, has led to intensified tension between communities.

The report highlighted religiously motivated killings, assaults, riots, discrimination, vandalism, and restriction on the rights of citizens to practise their own religious beliefs and proselytize. Authorities have failed to penalize perpetrators of killings in the name of cow protection. Reportedly, the government failed to act when it came to mob violence against religious minorities. The ruling party has marginalized communities and critics of the government. Senior officials of the BJP have made inflammatory remarks on the Muslim community. Authorities have protected speakers of abuse from prosecution. As of November 2018, there have been eighteen such attacks. Eight people had been killed during the year, stated the report.[11]

The BJP in its response slammed the US for bias against the Modi government. In most such cases, the spokesperson stated, these instances are the result of local disputes and criminal mindsets against minorities and weaker sections of the society. The minister for minority affairs Mukhtar Abbas Naqvi dismissed the report as prejudiced and stated that 'Religious Freedom is in India's DNA and we don't need from a certificate from anyone'.[12] When the minister speaks of religious tolerance, he perhaps ignores reports on violence against minorities.

---

[11]Shriram Lakshman, 'U. S. report expressed concern on communal violence in India', *The Hindu*, 23 June 2019.

[12]'US has "no locus standi" to comment on religious freedom in India: MEA on report alleging attacks by Hindu groups on minorities', *FirstPost*, 23 June 2019.

More significantly, when the minister declares that lynchings have nothing to do with religious animosities, he only engages in sophistry. He ignores a remarkable coincidence in our public life. Hate speech and crimes against minorities have reportedly risen since 2014, when the BJP came to power. In July 2017, newspaper reports chronicled that Muslims were the target of 51 per cent of violence related to the cow from 2010–17. Out of 28 Indians killed in 63 incidents, 24 were Muslims, forming 86 per cent of the victims of violence. The website *IndiaSpend* had carried out a content analysis of the English media on cow-related deaths. Ninety-seven attacks over bovine issues were reported after the BJP government came to power in 2014, and half of cow-related violence, that is, 32 of 63 cases, came from states governed by the BJP. More than 124 people were injured in these attacks. More than half the attacks were based on rumours.[13]

Muslims have been attacked in trains, on the road while legally transporting cattle, in fields, and even in their homes on the mere suspicion of carrying or storing meat. They have been publicly lynched and brutally killed. Lynchings continued in 2019 after the BJP government returned to power. Muslims are threatened with violence even when they perform their duties as citizens of India. In Kasganj, Western UP, on Republic Day 2018, gangs of thugs mounted on motorbikes roared into the flag-hoisting area and attacked the residents. The neighbourhood is inhabited predominantly by Muslims. In the violence that followed, a twenty-two-year old youth, Chandan Gupta, was killed when he was hit by a stray bullet.[14]

Lynching of Muslims merely on the suspicion that they are engaged in transporting cattle has initiated a new trend of unspeakable intimidation and violence in Indian politics. Death by lynching in a public place where people stand around and watch, or worse, film the despicable event on their phones and upload it on social media, is the new normal. Violence has become a spectator sport, rivalling ancient Rome, which had devised unique ways of putting men to death in public forums to storms of applause from the audience. In contemporary India, the

---

[13]Delna Abraham and Ojaswi Rao, '86% killed in cow related violence since 2010 are Muslims, 97% of attacks after Modi government came to power', *Hindustan Times*, 16 July 2017.

[14]Chaitanya Mallapur, 'Communal violence rose by 28% from 2014 to 2017, but 2008 remains year of highest instances of religious violence', *Firstpost*, 9 February 2019.

audience claps even as their fellow citizens die painfully for no reasonable cause, except assertion of power; or perhaps just sport.

Such crimes are punishable by law. But we rarely see punishment meted out to the perpetrators of aggression and murder. In fact, the opposite is true. On 8 July 2018, the then union minister of state for aviation, Jayant Sinha, honoured and garlanded eight men who had been accused of murdering a Muslim coal merchant, Alimuddin Ansari, in June 2017. A fast-track court had sentenced eleven men and these eight men were out on bail.[15]

In other cases, social media posts instigated mobs to kill. The ban on beef and attacks on meat-eaters was satirized by the humorous poet Saghar Khayyami thus; 'Nafraton ki jung mein dekho to kya-kya hogaya/Sabziyan Hindu huin/ bakra musalman ho gaya'. (Just see what has happened in this war of hate, vegetables have become Hindu and the goat has become a Muslim.)[16] The foremost task of a democratically elected government is to protect its people, particularly vulnerable sections against violence. Khayyami's lines are a sad comment on the inability of the people in power to do so.

According to a report by the civil liberties group *Human Rights Watch* titled 'Violent Cow Protection in India', made public in February 2019, killings in the name of cow protection have become an integral part of the political agenda of the ruling party. The details of the report are harrowing. On 18 March 2016, a group of men murdered two Muslim cattle herders who were on their way to sell bulls at the annual cattle fair in Jharkhand. The attackers, who were associated with a cow protection group, accosted thirty-two-year-old Mohammed Mazlum Ansari and eleven-year-old Imteyaz Khan, accused them of selling cattle for slaughter, whipped them to death, and strung their bodies from a tree. This was the first killing by lynching in Jharkhand. The eight men involved were sentenced in 2018.

Attackers who call themselves cow protectors, or gau rakshaks, are associated with extreme right-wing groups. The victims are invariably Muslims, Dalits, and Adivasis. In all almost all cases, the police stalled investigations and ignored procedures. Policemen, it is alleged by human

---

[15]'Union Minister Jayant Sinha garlands 8 lynching convicts, faces opposition flak', *Times of India,* 8 July 2018.

[16]Mahmood, 'The secular agenda of humorist Urdu poetry'.

rights activists, are complicit in the killings and cover-up of crimes. In July 2018, the Supreme Court issued a series of directives to the government to adopt preventive, remedial, and punitive measures that address lynching.[17]

In Uttar Pradesh, the state government's crackdown on slaughterhouses and the meat trade has had an unexpected fallout. Previously, farmers sold cattle that had passed the age of productivity to butchers. Now, selling of cattle to butchers is a crime punishable by law. Consequently, aged cows are let loose. Desperately searching for food, cattle that are no longer of any use to farmers and to dairy producers create havoc in fields of grain and destroy crops.

For a long while, there was no pushback from civil society, mainly because the government had come down heavily on human rights organizations and civil liberty activists. Funds of non-governmental organizations have been frozen, their premises raided, and prominent human rights activists arrested and jailed even though cases against them are yet to be proven in court.[18] Civil society is expected to keep a watch on the government and its acts of omission and commission. The government, which came back to power with an impressive number of elected members in May 2019, was determined to curtail activism and suppress voices that challenge its policies. The silence, however, proved transitory.

On 9 December 2019, the government introduced the Citizenship (Amendment) Bill in the lower house of Parliament. At the heart of the bill lies the dangerous idea that citizenship is dependent on the religion people belong to. Cleared by the cabinet in the previous week, the bill, which was passed by Parliament on 11 December 2019, provides for citizenship for non-Muslim refugees who seek to escape religious persecution in Pakistan, Bangladesh, and Afghanistan—three countries in which Islam is the official religion.

It has been pointed out by numerous commentators that the idea of citizenship based on religion violates the Constitution of India, that it is

---

[17]'Violent Cow Protection in India: Vigilante Groups Attack Minorities', *Human Rights Watch*, 18 February 2019, available at <https://www.hrw.org/report/2019/02/18/violent-cow-protection-india/vigilante-groups-attack-minorities>.
[18]'Civil Society Groups Attack Modi Govt for Cancellation of 9,000 NGO licenses', *Huffpost*, 29 April 2015.

inherently discriminatory, anti-Muslim and that the grant of citizenship rights to non-Muslims will adversely affect the demographic balance in states in the northeast of India. The implications of the bill for the region are spelled out in the chapter on the Northeast. What is troubling is the clear anti-Muslim slant. If India wants to provide a home to refugees fleeing religious persecution in neighbouring countries, two of which border India, then why should not Ahmadiyyas—who are non-citizens in Pakistan—and Hazaras—who face religious discrimination in Afghanistan—be given refuge? The bill, it was argued by many, was anti-democratic and anti-secular. Violations of secularism, which is based on Article 14 of the Indian Constitution that guarantees equality and freedom from discrimination, infringe the basic presumption of constitutional democracy, equality, or at least its weaker form of non-discrimination. If religion was introduced into the concept of citizenship, the National Population Register (NPR) and the National Register of Citizens (NRC) would be based on religious criterion. The perceived danger that the bill posed was that minorities would be proclaimed non-citizens and banished into detention centres being built across the country.

The Citizenship (Amendment) Bill was passed by both houses of Parliament by relying on the 'brute majority' of the BJP. On 15 December 2019, students belonging to Jamia Millia Islamia, a central university in New Delhi, came out in large numbers to protest against the Citizenship (Amendment) Act (CAA).[19] The procession marched through the streets of an upper middle-class colony in South Delhi, with students carrying banners that rejected the CAA. They demanded withdrawal of the legislation that connected citizenship rights with religion. The police attacked the procession of students, entered the varsity, vandalized the library, and beat up young people in the reading room and in toilets. Students were injured, the library was ransacked, and the campus was damaged.[20] The violence inflicted on the student body set off a chain of protests by university students and citizens in the rest of the country. Thousands of citizens, particularly university students, marched and demonstrated against the inhuman treatment

---

[19]'At the stroke of midnight, how universities across India united for Jamia students', *India Today*, 16 December 2019.

[20]'Students Across the Country Protest Police Violence in Jamia Millia', *The Wire*, 16 December 2019.

meted out to students of Jamia Millia Islamia and Aligarh Muslim University (whose students had come out in protest against the attack on Jamia Millia) by the police and the administration.[21] The objective of major demonstrations that took everyone, particularly the government, by surprise was to uphold the Constitution and to challenge the division of the country on religious grounds. Public readings of the Preamble to the Constitution transformed the Constitution from a legal document into a supremely democratic one.

Student protests have been remarkably creative and imaginative. Singing revolutionary songs, young people carried posters expressing their determination not to allow the proposed NRC to be implemented in the country. Women demonstrated in many parts of India, and the sit-in by women in Shaheen Bagh for over ninety days became a symbol of protest against possible violations of the Constitution. Little children painted the national flag on their cheeks and performances were staged against the backdrop of portraits of Gandhi, Ambedkar, and Bhagat Singh. Photographs and visuals in the newspapers and on television channels indicated the democratic nature of the protest—a young woman holding up an admonishing finger to the police, students offering roses to flummoxed police personnel, novel art forms depicting the plurality of India and confirming the determination to protect it, and chants of solidarity with Muslim fellow citizens. This was India's civil society moment. Thousands of citizens had peacefully assembled on the streets and in public places to demand that the government observe constitutional morality.

Matters came to a head in late February 2020 in the northeast of Delhi. Pro-CAA groups led by right-wing leaders chanting provocative slogans clashed with anti-CAA protestors on 24 February at the Jaffrabad-Maujpur road sit-in. Over the next two-and-a-half days, Delhi witnessed the worst form of Hindu-Muslim violence since Partition. Rampaging mobs wreaking violence over a 5-kilometre radius left fifty-three persons dead, many more injured, and thousands deprived of their livelihood as shops, workplaces, and houses were burnt down. Muslim places of worship were particularly targeted.[22] The irony is that leaders of the

---

[21]'At the stroke of midnight, how universities across India united for Jamia students', *India Today*.

[22]'Explainer: What do we know about the communal violence that left 53 dead in Delhi in February 2020', *Scroll.in*, 6 March 2020.

constitutional and peaceful anti-CAA protests have been named by the Delhi police as responsible for the communal violence.[23] It is ironic because in a democracy, civil society has the right to monitor acts of omission and commission of the government. In today's India, peaceful protest is labelled as treason. The power of civil society to speak back to power has been relentlessly cut back.

The message is clear. Major riots involving large number of deaths, arson, displacement, and destruction may not have taken place in India after 2013. But, as suggested earlier, we cannot abstract big riots from the incivility and the brutality of everyday life and see them as isolated incidents. These are the high points of cycles of violence that have bedevilled India and its citizens at crucial junctures in our history. Large-scale riots are one indication of violence, but as long as discrimination and violence against minorities is produced and reproduced in society, India will never be free of the spectre of violence.

Everyday targeting of minorities is one side of the story of communal violence and discrimination in India. There are other sides to the sordid story of violence between groups on the basis of religious mobilization irrespective of who is in power. India has to acknowledge a troubled and a troubling fact: In most, if not all incidents of violence, the Muslim community is at risk. In a democratic society, care is taken to protect minorities that are vulnerable to the power of 'brute majorities'. The majority principle is merely workable. There is nothing that is inherently of value in the naïve belief that democracy means majority rule. Democracy is about equal protection of the rights of every individual, irrespective of arbitrary factors such as birth into a religious or a caste community. That is why liberal democrats take care to defend the rights of vulnerable minorities against the onslaught of pure numbers. That is why liberals privilege unelected bodies like the Supreme Court over popularly elected legislative chambers. The judiciary is expected to check the power of elected majorities. Where majorities are allowed to rule, discrimination becomes institutionalized, violence becomes the new normal, and loss of livelihoods and lives becomes a commonplace occurrence. The mob takes over and subsumes the body politic into its own crowd mentality. Democracy is replaced by mobocracy. Chaos

---

[23]Mohana Basu, 'Over 1,100 activists condemn Delhi Police action against anti-CAA protestors amidst lockdown', *The Print*, 30 May 2020.

reigns. Life becomes so much more frightening, so much more insecure, and so much more anxious if the institutions of justice kneel before political power. This is the fate of societies that are held hostage to the politics of communal violence.

## COMMUNAL VIOLENCE: POLITICS OF THE PROCESSION

On 28 March 2018, an extremist Hindu right-wing group took out a procession on the occasion of Ram Navami in Bihar Sharif in the state of Bihar. Even as the number of participants in the procession swelled, even as they began to brandish weapons ranging from sticks to the trident and even as they began to shout obscenities against minorities, leaders heading the procession diverted its route. The procession entered Muslim mohallas. The consequence could have been foretold.

On the same day, four persons died in clashes between Hindus and Muslims in the Raniganj-Asansol belt in the Paschim Bardhaman district in West Bengal. The casualties would have been higher except for the wisdom of the imam of a mosque in Asansol. He had lost his young son in the clashes. Still, he warned that if anyone from his community retaliated in kind, he would leave town. This voice of sanity and humanity amidst the madness sparked off by the religious procession calmed inflamed passions and averted further disasters. We doff our metaphorical hat to the imam.

In Rajasthan, on the same occasion, a religious procession included a float glorifying Shambhu Lal Regar, who is currently in prison for hacking an innocent Muslim to death and cynically videotaping his death to the tune of his own anti-Muslim slogans. After the festival, communal tension spread to more districts of the state. Across swathes of North India, according to a report in *The Hindu*, daily interactions between the majority and the minority communities have been rendered fraught with the probability of violence. Processions such as these are drawing new fault lines in society.[24]

The religious procession is not new to Indian history. Taking out processions on religious occasions has been, since the late nineteenth century, deployed as a strategy to cement identities and flex muscles. Historians tell us that till the end of the nineteenth century, Muslims

---

[24]'Exposing fault lines: the violence over Ram Navami processions', *The Hindu*, 31 March 2018.

and Hindus lived in some degree of harmony, and very often took part in each other's religious processions in the Bombay Presidency. Bitter communal riots in the aftermath of the 1892 reforms introduced by the colonial government that resulted in deaths and suffering changed this.

The 1892 reforms expanded the number of non-official members in legislative bodies. The reforms did not involve direct elections, but even the idea of representation set off competitive mobilization on the basis of religion. It is perhaps one of the political ironies of modern times that the institutionalization of the competitive market, and representation based on competitive elections or nominations to legislative assemblies, have catalysed and reproduced intense rivalries and hardened boundaries that separate communities. The market and representative democracy uphold the principle of freedom, but they also spark off competitiveness and bolster conflict. These processes, if not checked by the rule of law, acquire virulent forms. In Maharashtra, the 1892 reforms accomplished precisely this: they sparked off a chain of competitive politicization. This resulted in *bloody* riots.

The riots, writes Ram Gopal, the biographer of the nationalist leader Bal Gangadhar Tilak, upset the communal equilibrium of Pune. Hindus flocked to Tilak and implored him to intervene. The riot prompted Tilak to think of regenerating, what he considered to be, the lost pride of Hindus. One way in which this could be accomplished was by the revival of festivals that had died out after the end of the Peshwa regime in Maharashtra. Among these festivals were public meetings centred around Ganapati and the Maratha warrior Chhatrapati Shivaji who had fearlessly fought the Mughal empire as well as neighbouring sultans to expand his domain.

The transformation of a festival from a personal to a collective celebration led, over time, to the consolidation of identity around representations of Hindu gods and icons, the production of competitive nationalism, and passionate denunciations of colonialism. Five Ganapati statues were set up in Pune and funds collected for celebrations. The ten-day festival was marked by elaborate performance of rituals and delivery of fiery lectures to the tune of patriotic music. Tilak wrote in his newspaper, the *Kesari*, that the Ganapati festival was comparable to the Olympian and Pythian festivals of the Greeks. According to Gopal, the thousands of people who participated in the event cultivated a sense of solidarity under the aegis and protection of god Ganesh.[25] Pageants staged during the festival comprised choirs of young men dressed in the uniform of Shivaji's soldiers. The following year, hundreds of bands were singing songs accompanied by musical instruments. 'The caustic dramatic dialogues in between the songs...had a subtle mixture of current politics.[26] In 1894, a procession to commemorate the festival defied the orders of the District Magistrate that it should not pass by a mosque, and triggered off a communal riot.

By the opening years of the twentieth century, the festival had spread to different parts of western India. A hitherto private ritual for the worship of Ganesha was converted into a public spectacle, a site for the singing of revolutionary songs and the dissemination of nationalist literature. Fiery anti-colonial speeches were greeted with rousing acclaim. The coalescing of a political community around a Hindu god was created and recreated through the staging of plays, stories of liberation from demons, and revolutionary music. Memories of historical and political figures like Shivaji were celebrated with the same fervour as the festival of the God of good fortune, Ganapati. In eastern parts of India, the worship of the Goddess in Bengal and the practice of Kurbani, or animal sacrifice, in Islam were turned into public displays. These festivals constructed political constituencies that lined up behind their leaders.

History tells us that public displays of religious passions slide into eruptions of communal violence in a shockingly short period of time. It is almost as if violence against the other community, and offering of human sacrifice to the gods, is an extension of religious celebrations. Processions that wend their way to the place of worship do not always take the shortest possible route, they intentionally enter the residential, or even the work spaces of the other community. These incursions provide opportunities to entrepreneurs and organizers of violence to mobilize crowds, wreak havoc on the other community, burn, maim, and kill.

The psychiatrist Sudhir Kakar in his book *The Colors of Violence* writes that among the various incidents that precipitate communal riots, two occur with such regularity that they may fairly be called archetypes. One of them has to do with rumours of killings of cows and the other relates to disputes over religious processions. The former cause is specific

---

[25]Ram Gopal, *Lokmanya Tilak*, Mumbai: Asia Publishing House, 1965, pp. 82–88.
[26]Ibid., p. 89.

to India. In 1886, writes Kakar, a riot occurred in various cities of Punjab. In Ambala, the precipitating incident was a change insisted upon by Muslims in the route of the Hindu festive procession. In Ludhiana, the riot began with a report that a cow had been sacrificed in a Muslim's house. In the same year in Delhi, a riot began with a clash between Hindu and Muslim processions whose routes crossed each other. In 1969, a riot was precipitated in Ahmedabad when a Muslim vegetable seller inadvertently hit a cow. In India, cow-related grievances can lead to or transform a procession into a mob. The same phenomenon was evident in the inter-war years in Europe when extreme ideologues of the Left and the Right were creating mass movements imbued with messianic fervour.[27]

A procession, argues Kakar, is necessary for the creation of a physical group, or a group which is represented in the bodies of its members rather than in their minds. This shift from individual minds to a collective body is essential for the group to become an instrument of actual violence.

The sensory experience of belonging to a relatively abstract entity, for example fellow Hindus, touches a very different chord of the self. The self-experience of the individual is determined more by concrete bodily communication and physical sensations. He gets wrapped up in the crowd. He is continuously and sensually pounded through all the avenues his body offers. As we have seen in the opening paragraphs of this chapter, Elias Canetti has made the same argument about the French Revolution. The experience of being part of a crowd transgresses generally established and universally valid distances and boundaries.

It follows that the crowd acts as a unified entity. The individual as a physical being is carried along by a collective project or even the lack of a project. She forswears her sense of individuality or judgement of right and wrong. She has no problem in touching or being touched by strangers when she is part of a crowd. In line with this interpretation, Kakar insists that the religious procession produces the most physical of all groups. Mere presence in a crowd that has produced and responded to hysteria over imagined or real slights, or provocative statements, dissolves the boundaries between our self and other corporeal selves during that period of time.[28]

[27]Sudhir Kakar, *The Colors of Violence*, New Delhi: Viking, 1995, pp. 55–56.
[28]Ibid., pp. 56–57.

Kakar draws out psychological processes that overwhelm individuals in a procession. The individual is carried along a path that she has not spontaneously chosen. She becomes part of a crowd that is quickly transformed into a mob. In a short span of time, the mob is converted into a body of people who hack, set fire to, maim, and kill human beings. Some of them do so intentionally, others are carried along on a wave of irrational impulses.

There is more to the story of the procession. When the procession takes a route that has been disallowed to them by public authorities, and enters a neighbourhood dominated by the other community, we can practically foresee the death and annihilation that loom menacingly over the horizon. The diversion of the procession is seldom haphazard, in most cases it has been cleverly planned by strategists. The intention is to obliterate boundaries between spaces inhabited by different communities and take over neighbouring spaces. The procession marks out and appropriates the space as its own. The violence that is embodied in the procession, whose participants carry sharp weapons and shout slogans of hate, is followed by the looting of shops, sacking of places of worship, burning of sacred books, and desecration of everything held holy by the other community. Often, reprisals follow. Angry responses to provocative slogans lead to more murders and mayhem.

Investigations of communal riots show us that a tangible link can be established between slogan-mongering, affirmations of the collective self, accusations against other communities, and the outbreak of violence. The trigger that translates communal sentiments into violence is provided by political entrepreneurs who provide deadly weapons and inflammatory slogans to crowds, design deviations in routes, and often mark shops, factories, or households run or inhabited by the other community as targets for annihilation. A religious festival quickly turns into a political rally and then into a spectacle of violence, providing multiple opportunities for leaders to produce and reproduce an aggressive 'nationalist' constituency.

It follows that processions can turn into riots only if the administration and the police do little to prevent violence. It has by now been established that communal riots happen only when the government allows them to happen. People who engage in violence know that the political party, or at least powerful individuals within the party that is in power, will grant them immunity. Even if the leadership of the party in power does not support violence between communities, it may do little to stop these incidents.

## THE COMMUNAL RIOT AS CROWD VIOLENCE

Once colonialism and some sections of extreme nationalism hammered the fact that religious identity can be effectively harnessed to the objective of securing power, the project of living together has never been free of violence in the country. As if it were almost an extension of Partition violence, communal riots between Hindus and Muslims have rocked India periodically. Incidents of communal violence began in the 1960s, cementing distrust between communities. According to Home Ministry reports, serious communal riots occurred in 1968 and 1969. The report counted 865 incidents of communal violence mainly in Bihar, Gujarat, and Uttar Pradesh.[29]

Interestingly, the end of the 1960s witnessed a decline in the hegemony of the Indian National Congress. The Congress was formed as a coalition of regional and local leaders who controlled villages, castes, religions, and classes. They were held together in what has been called the 'Congress system' by charismatic national figures such as Jawaharlal Nehru. In the 1967 elections, the Indian National Congress lost power in eight state assemblies. Indian politics fragmented without an overarching ideology to hold together disparate streams of beliefs. Though the lower ranks of the Congress, it has been alleged, overlapped with the religious right in the pre-Independence period, the leadership of the party had ensured that the party did not institutionally or ideologically commit to communalism. But in the decades that followed, the party leadership was accused of turning a blind eye towards, and even of masterminding, major riots.

This became clear in one of the most serious of these riots which occurred in 1984. The Sikh community was subjected to an appalling pogrom after the assassination of Prime Minister Indira Gandhi. In June 1984, the Indian Army was ordered to launch an assault on the holiest of Sikh shrines, the Golden Temple. Called Operation Bluestar, it was launched in an effort to flush out Khalistani terrorists led by the

---

[29]N. C. Saxena, 'Nature and Origins of Communal Riots in India', in A. A. Engineer (ed.), *Communal Riots in Post-Independence India,* New Delhi: Sangam Books, 1984, pp. 51–68.

leader, Bhindranwale. The exercise generated rage and animosity among the Sikh community. It saw the military assault as a defilement of the premier shrine of the community.

In November 1984, Indira Gandhi was assassinated by her two Sikh security guards in retaliation for Operation Bluestar. The assassination sparked off a massive pogrom against the Sikh community in Delhi and elsewhere by goons, reportedly under the direction of Congress leaders, between 1 and 3 November 1984. Gurudwaras were set on fire, Sikhs were beaten with iron rods, men were killed by forcing burning tyres over their throats, entire families were ruthlessly butchered, houses were burnt, neighbourhoods went up in flames, rude huts covered with asbestos sheets were shattered, shops were razed to the ground, and lower-middle-class and middle-class colonies bore the brunt of the politics of reprisals. Over two days, Delhi witnessed nothing but blood and mayhem that evoked chilling memories of Partition. Innocent Sikhs who had no role in the assassination of Indira Gandhi were butchered in appalling acts of retribution. Reportedly, 3,000 people died and thousands of families were displaced. Horrific cases of brutality inflicted on men, women, and children continue to haunt memories.[30]

What was worrying was that many Hindus seemed to tacitly approve of the merciless killing of innocent members of a community with which they were closely bound by ties of marriage and kinship. The seeds of alienation were sown in the 1970s and 1980s, when militancy erupted in Punjab and demands were made for a separate Sikh state. The assassination of Indira Gandhi completed this vicious phase of alienation. Chakravarty and Haksar write that beginning with Bluestar and culminating with the carnage, the Sikhs had begun to feel like a marked community. 'Never before had these ten million citizens felt like a minority…. The carnage dealt a shattering blow to the already battered emotions of the Sikhs.'[31]

A majority of Hindus began to speak of victimization and of feeling like a minority in a country in which they formed 80 per cent of the population. The sentiment would be laughable if it had not bred terrible consequences. Over the years, it would go on to wreak havoc.

---

[30]Uma Chakravarty and Nandita Haksar, 'Introduction', *The Delhi Riots: Three Days in the Life of a Nation,* New Delhi: Lancer International, 1987, pp. 13–32.
[31]Ibid., pp. 22–23.

## THE CASE OF AHMEDABAD: 2002

Erik H. Erikson in his study *Gandhi's Truth* asks: why did Gandhi choose to stay in Ahmedabad (from 1915 to 1930, first at Kochrab in the city and then at the Sabarmati Ashram) in the first place? Why did he choose the 'Manchester of India'?[32] Ahmedabad, Erikson suggests, is a true city. It breathed, if one may say so, the logic of mercantile life. Its industry had grown from native crafts to small enterprises and then to a large industry by an uninterrupted process so consistent that the city could truly be said to have a corporate identity. This gave it a character both solid and limited, both strong and ingrown, both alive and isolated, which it had been able to harness through the centuries into remarkable energy.[33] Gandhi chose Ahmedabad, wrote Erikson, because he spoke Gujarati, which was the official language in the city. The language had always been spoken, studied, and cultivated in the city. Gandhi chose Ahmedabad because it was an ancient centre of handloom weaving, because it had become the seat of the most modern mechanism of spinning and weaving, and because the weaving tradition was deeply embedded in a system which made guilds, caste, and religion intimately interdependent. The city provided an appropriate context for Gandhi, who called for a rapid modernization of awareness and aspirations. At the same time, Gandhi acknowledged those aspects of the ancient social structure which alone could provide irreplaceable elements of a traditional identity. Gandhi could do no better than to settle in a modern place that had preserved some ancient structure, so that from there he could travel and study.[34]

Though the Sabarmati Ashram continues to bear testimony to some of the remarkable experiments that Gandhi conducted on non-violence, the city has led the country in the scale and the number of communal riots between Hindu and Muslim communities till 2002. The first riot in the city occurred in 1946 on the eve of India's independence. In the first major communal riot of 1969, 1,500 people died. Ninety per cent of the people killed belonged to the Muslim community.[35] The

---

[32]Erik H. Erikson, *Gandhi's Truth: On the Origins of Militant Nonviolence,* New York: W.W. Norton and Company, 1969, p. 258.

[33]Ibid.

[34]Ibid., pp. 260–61.

[35]Ghanshyam Shah, 'Communal riots in Gujarat: reports of a preliminary investigation', *Economic and Political Weekly,* Vol. 5, Nos. 3–5, 1970, pp. 187–200.

next major riot took place in 1985 but minor riots occurred in 1971, 1972, 1973, 1977, 1980, 1981, and 1982. After the 1985 riots, minor riots erupted in 1986, 1987, 1989, 1990, and 1992. In 1993, another major riot occurred followed by minor riots in 1994 and 1996. In 1999, a major riot was followed by minor riots in 2000 and 2001. The 2002 case was different.

We can see at least three ways in which this case was different. One, the employment of violence was completely one-sided. Rather than wait for the rule of law to take its course after the Godhra incident when Muslim mobs stormed a train compartment returning from Ayodhya and murdered Hindu passengers, mobs proceeded to administer brutal vigilante justice. Two, although government ministers and bureaucrats have been cleared by various special investigation agencies and courts of complicity in the riots, it is also painfully evident that the government could not prevent attacks on vulnerable people by vigilante groups. Three, whereas earlier riots had more or less taken place in old Ahmedabad, particularly the walled city and the industrial areas, this time the entire city was affected. According to the official version, the number of deaths in Gujarat stand at around 900. The figure is contested by civil society organizations that estimate the number of people who died reached 2,000 and that a large number of deaths in rural areas went unrecorded. One lakh people were displaced.[36] Ahmedabad accounted for some of the most horrific cases of deaths.

The irony is that Ahmedabad was the site of Gandhi's experiments in truth and non-violence. But these lessons, it appears, were only half-heartedly internalized in the collective psyche. In 1919, reports of Gandhi's detention by the colonial government swept the city, and mobs set fire to the jail, the telegraph office, and the Collector's office. But Gandhians walked the streets to counsel patience and reassure workers. Regrettably, no Gandhian walked the streets during the frightening communal riots that had become a recurrent feature of the city after 2002. More disturbingly, for the most, civil society organizations in Ahmedabad either kept silent or participated in the violence. Breman suggests that but for 'a few exceptions, the institutions that represent civil

---

[36]T. K. Oomen, *Reconciliation in Post-Godhra Gujarat: The Role of Civil Society,* New Delhi: Pearson Longman, 2008, p. 47.

society took no action at all when this horrific violence broke out'.[37]

T. K. Oommen, writing on reconciliation attempts in the aftermath of the 2002 violence in Gujarat, arrives at the same conclusion. What is more troublesome, writes Oomen, is that a section of civil society organizations, mainly the militant Hindu outfits, actively participated in the violence against the Muslims.[38] Though some civil society organizations began to mobilize legal, psychological, and material aid to the victims in the relief camp, overall, civil society did not protest against the violence or against the failure of the government to protect its own citizens. Today, Ahmedabad is a divided city with Hindus and Muslims living in different neighbourhoods, with Muslim neighbourhoods labelled 'Pakistan', and the unofficial boundary between the two neighbourhoods actually called 'the border'.

## THE AYODHYA CASE

Among other philosophical questions asked by medieval scholars was the following: How many angels can dance on the head of a pin? The question can be considered to be irrelevant. Logically speaking, angels are insubstantial and cannot possibly dance, let alone on the head of a pin. The question, however, is not a piece of sophistry nor does it form part of the vanities of philosophic debates. It metaphorically highlights the profound difference between the notion of time and that of space. Space is always contested because more than one event cannot happen at the same point in space at the same time. If a second angel or at least her corporeal form was to try to dance at exactly the same point in space as the first one, she will have to push the first dancer off that point. On the other hand, time is plural, because millions of incidents can happen at the same point of time. Many of them will contradict each other, many will overlap with each other and others will wend their own distinct paths towards different directions. Time accommodates them all.

We see the clear difference between space and time in the history of the Ayodhya movement. The Babri Masjid in the town became an issue of power politics the moment the Hindu community staked claim to the exact point in the inner space of the mosque where the Muslims offered

---

[37]Jan Breman, *The Making and Unmaking of an Industrial Working Class: Sliding Down the Labour Hierarchy in Ahmedabad,* New Delhi: Oxford University Press, 2004, p. 292.

[38]Oommen, *Reconciliation in Post-Godhra Gujarat,* pp. 74–75.

their prayers. In 1885, Mahant Raghubir Das approached the district court in Faizabad and asked for permission to build a canopy over the mosque. It was argued that Lord Ram was born at that precise point in space. To avoid any possibility of violence, the colonial government constructed a fence which separated the inner dome where the Muslims prayed from the outer courtyard where Hindus were allowed to worship. In 1949, an idol of the infant Ram was placed in the inner dome. In a bid to avoid catastrophe, the government locked the gates of the mosque. Henceforth, no one was allowed to worship there.

In February 1986, the locks were opened by the Congress government led by Prime Minister Rajiv Gandhi, so that the Hindu community could have a darshan of the spot where Lord Ram was born. No rituals were permitted. Since the late nineteenth century, the judicial battle between the two parties revolved around the exclusive legal title to the contested space. This is the nature of space. Both sets of claims could not be accommodated; one claim had to be consigned to the wayside. The contestation catalysed a chain of events that bore serious consequences.

As discussed earlier, the BJP incorporated the rebuilding of the Ram temple into its 1990 election manifesto. Subsequently the party proceeded to mobilize people around this project. As processions in support of the temple made their way through the country, provocative sloganeering and hate speech reduced India's terrain of plurality and multi-religiosity to an arid wasteland. A trail of destruction, violent riots, arson, and carnage followed these processions. The campaigns culminated in the amazing spectacle of one of the leaders of the BJP riding a chariot and leading a procession, that was called a pilgrimage, from the restored temple of Somnath to the site of the Babri Masjid.

By 1992, the BJP had acquired considerable presence in politics and was ruling four states, including Uttar Pradesh. The Supreme Court had rejected a petition that Hindus be allowed to demolish the mosque. On 6 December 1992 about 70,000 people assembled in the Ram Katha Kunj for a public meeting with 500 sadhus and sants to perform puja. Several persons broke through the cordon on the terrace and started pelting police personnel with stones. Around 12.30 p.m. 80 people had climbed on the structure and damaged it. Buy 2.30 p.m. the crowd swelled to 75,000. Many climbed onto the tomb and then 'began a frenzied demolition with shovels, iron rods, and pick axes'. By 4.30 p.m. the entire structure was demolished.[39]

Mark Tully, BBC's India correspondent, wrote about the destruction of the mosque then and much later. He reported that a crowd of 150,000 that had assembled at the site suddenly surged forward, broke through the police cordons defending the mosque, swarmed over the building, and started tearing it down. 'As I watched,' he wrote, 'the last cordon collapsed and the police walked away with their wicker shields held high above their heads to protect themselves against the stones raining down on them. I realized I was witnessing a historic event, the most significant triumph for Hindu nationalism since independence and the gravest threat to secularism.'[40]

The Babri Masjid was demolished. In 2019, a five-judge bench of the Supreme Court gave its verdict on the case. The case was about legal title to the disputed site. In a unanimous verdict, the Bench ruled that the entire land under dispute should be handed over to a trust. The government was entrusted with the task of setting up the trust that would be responsible for building a temple. The Sunni Waqf Board, which was party to the legal dispute, was to be given five acres of land elsewhere in Ayodhya or near the site for building a mosque. The Bench of the then Chief Justice of India, Ranjan Gogoi, Justices S. A. Bobde, D. Y. Chandrachud, Ashok Bhushan, and S. A. Nazeer overrode the December 2010 judgement of the Allahabad High Court. The court had divided the disputed area of 2.77 acres among three parties: the Nirmohi Akhara, the deity Ram Lalla who was seen as a juridical person with rights, and the Uttar Pradesh Sunni Waqf Board.

The Supreme Court ruled that the earlier judgement was legally untenable. After considering the cases made by all parties, the court further ruled that the preponderance of possibilities ensured that the Hindus had been continuously worshipping at the site, the Muslims had not, and therefore the land was granted to the former community. Though the court held that the demolition of the mosque in 1992 was an illegal act, it may be argued that the Supreme Court seems to

---

[39]P. V. Narasimha Rao, *Ayodhya 6 December 1992*, New Delhi: Penguin/Viking, 2006, pp. 153–154. The book was published posthumously after Rao's death in accordance with his wishes. He had assembled all the documents in the book.

[40]Mark Tully, 'How the Babri mosque destruction shaped India', *BBC News*, 6 December 2017.

have rewarded those who had committed an illegality.

What is evident is that contestation over that point in space was not a spontaneous move. The court ruled that only the Hindus have the right to that precise point in space on which the mosque stood. The philosophical question of how many angels can dance on the head of a pin had been answered—only one angel can, the other will be pushed off. Time, on the other hand, is plural. History will narrate a sorry tale of how numerous campaigns to strip us of our shared history and common heritage by the destruction of a mosque were built up. A special court exonerated thirty-two individuals who had been accused of complicity in the destruction of the mosque on 30 September 2020.

Numerous tales will be told of the mosque that once stood where a massive Ram Temple will now be built. Sheela Rohekar has foregrounded the tragedy of modern India in her novel *Taviz*, set against the background of the destruction of the Babri Masjid. Annu is the son of a Hindu mother, Reva, and a Muslim father, Anwar. Anwar is killed in a communal riot in Ahmedabad, and Reva marries again, this time a Hindu man. Her new mother-in-law and her second husband heap humiliation on Annu because he is the son of a Muslim. He is not allowed to come close to, let alone touch, utensils used for prayers, he is told repeatedly that he is a half-blood and therefore illegitimate, and he is estranged from his stepfather.

Annu is disoriented, he neither belongs with his mother nor to his murdered father. He keeps asking himself the question—Main kaun hoon? Who am I? Buffeted by the desire to belong, he denies his Muslim parentage, joins a Hindutva organization, and takes part in the campaign to build a temple in Ayodhya as a kar sevak. During a demonstration in front of the Babri Masjid in 1990, Annu is killed by a police bullet. When his friends begin to bathe his body and prepare him for cremation, they find that he was circumcised, that he was a Muslim. They begin to maul and desecrate the dead body on the suspicion that he had infiltrated the ranks of the kar sevaks to discredit their campaign. Annu is finally cremated but the leader decrees that his ashes should be thrown into the dust.[41] This is the story of how a space was cleared to build a temple. Many people lost their lives in the process, others lost

---

[41]Heinz Werner Wessler, 'Who am I?: On the narrativity of identity and violence in Sheila Rohekar's novel *Taviz*', *Orientalia Suecana*', Vol. 60, 2011, pp. 49–59.

their dignity, and yet others were deprived of their right to worship. Further tragedies followed the destruction of the Babri Masjid.

## THE BOMBAY RIOTS

In the week that followed 6 December 1992 and the destruction of the Babri mosque, riots broke out in Bombay. According to the Srikrishna Commission report, set up by the central government to investigate the violence, the riots left close to 900 dead and as many as 2,036 people injured. The Commission identified two phases of the riots. The first phase was inaugurated by Muslim leaders to express anger at the destruction of the mosque. The Commission reported that the first phase of rioting by Muslims was a spontaneous reaction of leaderless and incensed mobs.

The second phase was inaugurated in January 1993 by Hindu mobs. The violence was a response to the killing of Hindu workers, reportedly by a Muslim group. The Srikrishna Commission report held that the second phase was brought to fever pitch by inciting propaganda unleashed by Hindu communal organizations.[42]

As the city erupted in a frenzy of murders, arson, and retaliation, Mumbai was destroyed. The deaths became the reason for every kind of mayhem in the city. The loss to property is incalculable. Informal settlements were destroyed; shops, workshops, godowns were set on fire; entire families were subjected to torture and killed; and gangs roamed and controlled the streets of the city. The administration could not enter major parts of the city because entrances to roads had been taken over by gangs. The violence affected not only shanty towns and slums, but also the middle and the upper class of city dwellers. The city, writes Meena Menon, was held to ransom by rampaging mobs bent on vengeance.[43]

During repeated cycles of violence, people suffered untold losses of life, property, livelihood, and families. The worst hit was the largest slum in Asia, Dharavi, where a high proportion of Muslims live and work. Their businesses and houses were burnt down. The landscape of Dharavi, home to almost 6 lakh people and possibly more, is defined by

---

[42]'Bombay riots 1992: Scars remain, victims still plead for justice', *Indian Express*, 8 December 2011.

[43]Meena Menon, *Riots and After in Mumbai: Chronicles of Truth and Reconciliation*, New Delhi: Sage Publications, 2011, pp. 21–23.

precarious multistorey shacks topped by tin sheds. The shanty town has
also been seen as the site of creativity. 'The heart of the capital city', says
the protagonist in Graham Greene's novel *The Heart of the Matter* (1948),
'is the shanty town'. Dharavi, home to the informal economy, is no
exception. The problem is that rudely-constructed dwellings and factories
are precarious and highly inflammable. They were easily destroyed.

Bombay burned. Small businesses and traders suffered. Caught
viciously in this violence were daily wage workers. Their workshops
were set on fire. The riots furthered the process of the ghettoization of
the Muslim community, which moved from the central spaces of the city
to arid areas on the outskirts to live among their own. After the riots,
Mumbai was ripped apart by a series of bomb blasts, which reportedly
took the lives of 257 people.[44] The government set up the Srikrishna
Commission to enquire into the riots. The commission was disbanded by
the Maharashtra government in January 1996 but reconstituted in May
of the same year due to pressure of civil society groups. The Commission
submitted its report in February 1998 after recording the evidence of
502 people and took on record 2,903 documents as evidence.[45]

## THE GHETTO

The greatest impact of communal violence, whether in Mumbai or
Ahmedabad, has been on residential patterns in cities. Take the instance
of Ahmedabad. The virulence and the scale of the 1969 riot earmarked
the onset of ghettoization. This was the time when Juhapura came to
be a refuge for the victims of violence. Juhapura is one of the largest
settlements of the Muslim community with about 3 lakh people. It
contains about 46 per cent of the total Muslim community in the
urban agglomeration. Located on the highway that leads to the capital
city, Gandhinagar, Juhapura borders the Vejalpur area, which is Hindu
dominated. The road between the two areas is considered the border
and the settlement is perversely stereotyped as Pakistan.[46] Originally,
Juhapura consisted of poor Muslim households, but after the 2002

---

[44]'Timeline: 1993 Mumbai blasts and after', *The Hindu*, 21 March 2013.

[45]Zeeshan Shaikh, 'Mumbai riots 1992: 'Srikrishna Commission report and action taken, *Indian Express*, 6 December 2017.

[46]Neera Chandhoke, Silky Tyagi, Neha Khanna, and Praveen Priyadarshi, 'The Displaced of Ahmedabad', *Economic and Political Weekly*, 27 October, Vol XLII, no 43, 2007, pp. 10-14.

pogrom, affluent Muslim families have moved into the area.

Juhapura falls outside the boundaries of the Municipal Corporation and most of the land is agricultural land. Therefore, the ghetto lacks infrastructure and services—health facilities, schools, power supply, roads, drainage, street lighting, and transport. Whatever infrastructure has been created in the area, such as micro credit networks, schools, shops, eating places, and mosques, have been built with private funds. Juhapura is not connected to the city by public transport since it is located on the highway.[47] The location of the ghetto has, therefore, deprived people of employment, access to good schools, and health facilities.

Though the ghettoization process began in 1969, Hindus and Muslims still resided in mixed neighbourhoods. Within these neighbourhoods, the two communities lived in housing clusters that were separated by a fence or a street. By the 1980s, the ghettoization process intensified and by the 1990s only a few mixed neighbourhoods remained. It was these mixed neighbourhoods that were systematically and brutally targeted in the violence of 2002. The worst affected areas were on both sides of the railway track in Ahmedabad.

The victims of violence were herded into poorly funded and grossly inadequate relief camps, mainly set up by Muslim religious organizations and some civil society organizations. In a short time, these camps were rapidly wound up, and the inhabitants, after being given pathetically inadequate funds as 'compensation'—sometimes as low as ₹1,200[48]— were now on their own, at the mercy of a society that had proved complicit in the carnage, either actively or through studied silence. The state government, recognizing neither the plight nor the needs of the victims of communal violence, simply refused to take any action to help these people to rebuild their shattered lives.[49] At this point a few civil society organizations, particularly Islamic organizations such as the Tablighi Jamaat, the Jamaat-e-Islami, and the Jamiat Ulama-i-Hind, and specifically the Islamic Relief Committee, which is the relief wing of the Jamaat-e-Islami, stepped in to help people relocate and resettle. Some land was acquired on the outskirts of the city, and the victims were resettled in four pockets—Juhapura, Ramol, Vatva, and Dani Limda.

---

[47]Ibid.
[48]Ibid.
[49]Ibid.

In these bare, stark, inhospitable areas, civil society organizations helped potential inhabitants to construct rickety one-room tenements, without water supply, electricity, access to internal roads because there were none, and sanitation and sewerage. And it is here, in these barren spaces, that the victims of the communal carnage in Ahmedabad have been settled and expected to begin their life anew, amidst even more deprivation than they had faced in their original habitats.

The word 'ghetto' codes many messages, none of which carry positive connotations. It evokes resonances of a community clustering together in a constricted and circumscribed spatial location. It arouses memories of how inhabitants are stigmatized by other inhabitants of the city. Throughout history, ghettos enclose not the favoured but the disfavoured section of the population. The origin of the ghetto lies not in the free choice to live among one's own community, but in forced circumstances that are not within the control of the residents, notably fear. Vulnerable groups prefer to live among their own, even if where they must live is not to their liking. Above all, ghettos are easy to target in times of crisis; therefore, the inhabitants live amidst the perpetual production and reproduction of terror and anxiety.

It follows that the inhabitants of a ghetto are deprived of four sets of basic rights that are the due of every citizen in a democracy: (a) the freedom to move freely and reside wherever one may choose, (b) the right not to be physically harmed or deprived of property without legitimate reasons, (c) the right not to be deprived of liberty without due cause, and (d) the right to social and economic goods which are the fundamental preconditions of living a life of dignity. In sum, they are denied the right not to be discriminated against and to be treated with equal concern.

Ghettos narrow the cultural and thereby the political horizons of the inhabitants, close off options, and prohibit creative mingling of perspectives. In the process, the idea that cultural communities as living mutable entities created and transformed through intermingling with other communities is negated. A culturally plural context provides a vibrant background for assessing and reflecting on one's norms, beliefs, and cultures. Interaction with other persons who are like us, or not like us, provides us with a valuable basis of understanding and knowledge, and gives to us the capacity to evaluate and rework our own options. When such an opportunity is closed off, this leads to narrowing of perspectives, constriction of personalities, and intolerance. This is applicable both to Hindus and Muslims.

## CONCLUSION

Riots inscribe in blood the core question: who will control society and the state, who will hegemonize symbolic representations of society, and who will command the material benefits this society has to offer? The shameful objective of purveyors of violence, who engineer and direct mass killings, is to redraw the normative map drafted by Indian democracy and the Constitution—that of equality of political status irrespective of religion, caste, ethnicity, gender, and class. A poem written by Jigar Moradabadi in 1960 is a powerful indictment of what politicians do. 'Unka jo kaam hai, woh ahl-e-siyaasat jaanein/mera paigam mohabbat hai, jahaan tak pahunche.' (Let the politicians bother about what they do, my message is of love, it should reach the entire world.)[50]

It is time we paid heed to the sentiments expressed in this stanza. It is time that we realize that involvement in violence diminishes us sadly.

Communal violence is not the only kind of violence seen in India. But it is painful because it is clearly a continuation of the violence that culminated in the Partition of India. At the time of Partition, Muslims had a choice: to emigrate to Pakistan or stay on in India. A substantial number of Muslims preferred to stay on and become a part of the new democratic and secular order the Constituent Assembly constructed for the country. They are legitimate citizens of India, endowed with the same rights as other citizens. Numerically speaking, they form a minority, and it is the responsibility of the majority to ensure that no harm comes to the minority.

When Indians adopted the Constitution on 26 December 1950, they symbolically signed two social contracts. One contract was with the present and future governments that were elected to power. A democratically elected government had to work within the framework established by the Constitution; the power of the rulers was curtailed by an elaborate system of checks and balances and by the fundamental rights of citizens. Institutions were established to secure the citizen from

[50]Jigar Moradabadi, 'Un ka jo tarz hai', www.Rekhta.org, accessed on 14 March 2021. Translation provided by the author.

untrammelled powers exercised by governments. The second contract Indians signed was with each other. The Constitution created a political community bound to each other by allegiance to itself and by the fact that we share a set of political practices embodied in institutions, the legislature, rule of law, the judiciary, civil society, and above all our fundamental rights.

Violation of a right harms the body politic, it harms democracy and justice, and it harms you and me. If a basic right of our fellow citizens is violated, we should be agitated about this violation. For the incorporation of this obligation to our fellow citizens into political thinking, into our values, and into vocabularies that are ritually employed in and through an activity the ancient Greeks termed politics requires a great deal of hard work. We have to foreground our obligations to each other by constructing a political consensus on the need to be responsible for our fellow citizens.

The construction and the consolidation of this political consensus is, of course, a project that requires the harnessing of creative imagination and courage on the one hand, and careful reasoning, persuasion, and dialogue on the other. The task also demands the investment of rather high degrees of energy and time. But this is essential because a political consensus on what constitutes, or should constitute, the basic rules of society is central to our collective lives. The political is not a given, it has to be constructed through determined and sustained political intervention.

In India, the creation of this political consensus is a difficult task simply because Indian society is marked by discrimination based on religion. It is not easy to tackle social discrimination but we have to do so through reasoning, persuasion, and dialogue. We need to do this in order to safeguard our existence as a civilized democracy. Unless a society learns to value and respect different ways of life and different religions, members of vulnerable communities will always be subjected to hate speech and acts that maim and diminish dignity. The right of a group to respect, and its right to exist with dignity and with the assurance that its practices and its beliefs are protected from aggression, is an essential aspect of democracy. Can a civilization as great as India afford to be silent in the face of discrimination on the grounds of religion?

Finally, we need to appreciate that the language and culture of different religious communities expand and enrich our grasp of the complexities and the dilemmas of the human condition. A monocultural society, or a society that allows only one system of belief to flourish is, by definition, soulless and bare. Stripped of the excitement of learning new languages, acquaintance with new values, familiarity with new cuisines, literature, music, art, sculpture, and ways of conceiving the world, monochromatic societies are dull, predictable, and tedious.

Life in a plural society, on the other hand, promises adventure and novel ways of understanding ourselves and our worlds. Where after all would Bollywood films, that fuel romantic imaginations of the young and old, be without love poetry written in Urdu by Gulzar or Javed Akhtar? Awareness of difference expands our horizons, deepens sensibilities, cultivates empathy, and enhances solidarity. Living in a plural society allows us to launch on a new journey and a new adventure every day. For this, we need to leave religious discrimination and violence by the wayside and proceed as a political community towards the path of a democratic political community.

## Chapter 3

# CASTE-BASED VIOLENCE

*I do not ask/for the sun and moon from your sky/your farm, your land, your high houses or your mansions/I do not ask for gods or rituals, castes or sects/Or even for your mother, sisters, daughters. I ask for my rights as a man.*

—Sharankumar Limbale, 'The White Paper'[1]

## INTRODUCTION: HISTORICAL INJUSTICE

'Once that boy from my hometown/threw the bread I had touched on the ground/and ran home crying/My touch polluted his bread,' wrote the Marathi Dalit poet Prahlad Chendvankar in a poem titled 'Majha Gaowala' (My Fellow Villagers) in 1988, 'Nowadays that same fellow doesn't leave a crumb in my lunch box/Once the tea shop owner made me stand outside, gave me tea in the cup he kept outside, made me drink the tea outside—and I had paid good money/Nowadays the same tea shop owner calls again and again/"Come on in, sir, come in"/Once the police patil/always spoke to my father, servant of the village, with a dirty curse/Now he never sees me without snapping to attention with a salaam/So, my friends! I agree my home town folks are changing but I also know that even if the rope is burnt the twist is still there because like a fly snared in snot when the time comes to marry daughters/he is stuck in horoscope, caste, family, line, kin/He can never get free.'[2]

---

[1]Sharankumar Limbale, 'The White Paper', translated by Priya Adarkar, in Arjun Dangle (ed.), *Poisoned Bread*, Hyderabad: Orient Longman, 2009, pp. 74–75.
[2]Prahlad Chendvankar, 'Asmitadarsh', translated by Jayant Karve, Veena Deo, and Eleanor Zelliot, in Veena Deo and Eleanor Zelliot, 'Dalit Literature—Twenty-five Years of Protest? Of Progress?' *Journal of South Indian Literature*, 1994, Vol. 123, pp. 41–46.

The rope has burnt away; the twist remains. This popular saying in probably all Indian languages speaks of troublesome and painful knots in personalities, obdurate social relations, and the bulges in collective psychologies. These knots do not untie easily, even if the rope burns or loosens. One of the most difficult knots which has strenuously resisted every attempt to untie it completely is caste-based discrimination against Dalits. It might have slackened a little, but many, often intangible and often tangible knots in the rope continue to chafe lakhs of people. The rope ties the so-called lower castes to the power of the so-called upper castes. This is an ugly but constitutive aspect of social relations in India.

The caste system is a mega category that defines relationships between the four main castes, as well as the inner structure, logic, and function of each caste. Caste is an indication of who we are, how we are defined in terms of duties and rights or the lack thereof, what our relationship with people who are like us is, and what our relationships with people who are not like us should be. Caste defines status or the shortfall in status.

A community that was, since the hoary past, placed outside the system was called 'untouchable'. The pejorative term was rejected by the members of the community once they became aware of their political and civil rights as citizens of a democratic India. In the twentieth century, the community also rejected the term 'Harijan', or 'children of God', given to them by M. K. Gandhi. The nomenclature was interpreted as offensive and patronizing by activists who had been struggling to free themselves from the shackles of an unjust system. They fought and continue to fight obnoxious perceptions, attitudes, insults, abuses, denial of opportunities, banishment to the margins of society, and rampant violence. The community calls itself Dalit. According to Dalit scholars the term signifies those who struggle.

The battle against the many injustices that the upper-caste Hindus have heaped upon their own people has been long, bitter, and at times has bred terrible repercussions and backlashes. Some sections of the community have benefited from the project of remedial justice instituted by affirmative action policies, others continue to suffer quotidian violence. Despite the intense struggle of the Dalit movement, violence by the upper, and increasingly, as Anand Teltumbde suggests, the backward castes, continues to loom menacingly over the lives of the Dalit community.

The affirmative action project instituted by the Indian government after Independence has failed to deliver justice to the Dalit community. It has failed to remedy historical injustice.

The concept of historical injustice takes note of a variety of historical wrongs such as wartime brutalities, appropriation of land and extermination of indigenous people, slavery, genocide, colonialism and imperialism, mass rapes, and mutilations during territorial partitions, apartheid, and extraction of wealth through imperialism and the system of bonded labour, among others. Some injustices are inflicted on vulnerable groups in times of exception such as annexation and partition, war, riots, and civil strife. Other injustices like slavery and untouchability fall into a different category altogether. They are an integral part of the way a system organizes economic, social, and political relations. These practices serve to order and legitimize an exploitative division of labour between social groups.

## THE MAKING OF A CASTE ORDER

In India as well as in other countries of South Asia—Bangladesh, Pakistan, Sri Lanka, and Nepal—a rigid, hierarchical, and exclusionary caste system has, for many centuries, subjected Dalits to three-fold injustice: extreme economic deprivation, institutionalized humiliation through disrespect, and lack of voice or participation. These three aspects of injustice flow from a principle that is completely arbitrary and thus indefensible: birth into a caste that has been marked as lowly and as outside the caste system.

Though there is no consensus on how and why or indeed when the caste system developed, it is generally agreed that Hindu society is divided into four castes—Brahmins, Kshatriyas, Vaishyas, and Shudras. These castes are ranked according to the functions each performs. Then, as noted above, there are those who were placed outside the system and classified as the 'untouchables': those whose touch defiles the highly placed Brahmin and other castes as well. Ironically, these practices of pollution and purity have influenced egalitarian religions such as Indian Islam, Sikhism, and Christianity as well.

Discriminatory practices were consolidated over time, even though protest stalked the practice of untouchability, much as the vengeful Goddess Nemesis single-mindedly pursues hubris. In the sixth century, philosophers belonging to the Charvaka School of materialist philosophy that is critical and materialist, as well as Buddhism, rejected untouchability among other precepts of Brahmanical Hinduism. From the sixth to the sixteenth century, the Bhakti movement of devotional mystics launched a powerful and concerted attack on the dreadful practices of pollution and purity. Till today, the poetry of the sixteenth-century weaver, Kabir, who exposed the hollowness and the hypocrisy of organized religion and its gatekeepers is remembered, recited, and sung. 'O Pandit... Tell me, whence did defilement spring? How came you to discern defilement?.../Defilement you eat, defilement you drink, defilement created the world/Kabir says, they are free from defilement, who keep no company with Maya.'[3]

Till the turn of the twentieth century, a number of social reform leaders and groups, driven by the quest for a moral order and by the belief that untouchability was a later appendage to a highly metaphysical Hindu order, tried to retrieve the ethical spirit of the religion by tackling this inhuman practice. Others threw up their metaphorical hands in despair, broke away and established new religions such as Buddhism and Sikhism. A 'divinely ordained' social hierarchy and practices of exclusion became the object of struggle, the target of social reform movements, and often the butt of satirical comments. The social practice, however, endured. Interestingly, caste became a significant political category in Indian politics. Over time, the import of caste increased exponentially in Indian politics.

Historians argue that caste was foregrounded as a central category of politics through a series of colonial interventions, especially the census. Various census reports reflected the belief held by Oriental scholars and British administrators that Indians were governed by religion and by caste. Caste was given as much centrality as religion was, as suggested in the first chapter. The belief was based on the identification of, translation, and interpretation of selected scriptures.

The colonial bias in favour of abstract and intensely metaphysical texts becomes clear when we take a look at the selection, translation, and privileging of texts considered representative of Hinduism by Orientalists.

[3]Translation by the Rev. Ahmad Shah. Cited in Srinivasa Ramanujam, *Renunciation and Untouchability in India: The Notional and the Empirical in the Caste Order,* New Delhi: Routledge India, 2019, p. 13.

Translations of the Vedas, Upanishads, Manusmriti, Bhagavad Gita, Mahabharata, Brahma Sutras, and the works of Kalidasa into European languages were regarded as an interpretive exercise, and as providing a window into Hindu society. The problem is that these texts were abstracted from their social context, as well as from internal debates and discussions, and privileged as the defining features of Hinduism. They were seen as embodying eternal truths irrespective of the fact that these truths had been contested and challenged throughout the history of ideas, and by biographies of social movements.

Surprisingly, Indian intellectuals and leaders of the freedom struggle joined the Orientalist acclaim of a rich and sophisticated Vedic tradition without acknowledging its adverse impact upon society—the consolidation of Brahmanical superiority and the caste system. Nor did they take into account debates around the consolidation of the sacred texts. If the textual tradition provided an anchor for the recovery of the collective self, the self was deeply fractured along lines of caste contestation. The philosopher J. N. Mohanty tells us that the Vedas that were composed possibly around two thousand years before the Common Era (BCE) cover an entire range of subjects, but above all one finds in them an exemplary spirit of enquiry into the 'one being', or 'ekam sat', that underlies the diversity of empirical phenomenon, and into the origin of all things.[4]

The Vedas had laid out the philosophical thesis that in the beginning of things there must have been a being and not non-being, for nothing can emerge out of nothing. This being was identified as the spirit within us. Therefore, the highest wisdom lay in realizing the identity of the subject and the object (tat tvam asi). But if the real that we find behind the empirical nature is the universal spirit within, then what is the nature of the empirical world? This, suggests Mohanty, became the leading question of dispute among commentators on the Upanishads and various schools of Vedantic philosophy.

What is important is that the lessons in wisdom given by the Vedas were challenged both by supporters and opponents of the philosophy. Towards the end of the Upanishadic period was born Gautama, the founder of Buddhism (560 BCE). His teachings, after he attained

---

[4] J. N. Mohanty, *Classical Indian Philosophy,* New Delhi: Oxford University Press, 2000, p. 1.

Enlightenment, were devoted to the central question of how to escape suffering. Though he renounced the notion of the soul because he believed that all phenomenon material or non-material are impermanent, he continued to believe in karma, in rebirth, and in eventual deliverance, or moksha.[5]

The emergence of Buddhism was politically significant because it represented a generalized discontent with Brahmanical power and the monarchical state. The philosophy mounted a strong challenge to the superiority of the Brahmanical class, to ritualism, and to the caste system that had banished its own people to the margins of society. The challenge to hierarchy was neutralized when Indian intellectuals began to appropriate Buddhism. Towards the ends of the nineteenth century Swami Vivekananda, in his famous address at the Parliament of Religions in Chicago, suggested that Buddhism had completed the highly metaphysical task of the Vedanta. In a short period of time, the Buddha came to be seen as the eighth avatar of Hinduism. The critical edge of the philosophy had been blunted, somewhat alarmingly.

The main lines of division were drawn between philosophical schools that believed in the Vedas and those that did not, or the Sramanic tradition. But within the tradition, according to Mohanty, we see considerable sceptical self-criticism. Both Gautama and Mahavira, the founder of Jainism (599–527 BCE) were influenced by intellectual dissenters within the Vedic tradition. These dissidents rejected sacrificial rituals as well as Upanishadic monism. For example, an influential philosophy that belonged originally to the Vedic tradition had a strong strain of atheism and naturalism. This was Samkhya philosophy, associated with the legendary figure of Kapila. The philosophy eschews notions of the Brahman and subscribes to theories of the five elements. Other sceptics refused to accept the claim that the Vedas code absolute knowledge, questioned the doctrine of omniscience, and believed that the conclusions of these texts were contradictory, as well as controversial.[6]

Also excluded from dominant and metaphysical conceptualization of Hinduism was the heretical materialist school of Lokayata or Carvaka philosophy. This philosophy was originally one of the branches of Vedic

---

[5]Ibid., pp. 2–3.
[6]Ibid., p. 4.

learning, but over time it developed an anti-Vedic materialism.[7] The origin of Carvaka philosophy is the thesis that the self is the body not the soul. This school of philosophy was left out of the dominant constructions of Hinduism, both by the colonialists and the nationalists. It just did not fit into the model of theism, and of the ultimate objective of the merger of soul with the divine.

Pradeep Gokhale argues that though the Carvaka school of philosophy is comparatively neglected and disrespected, it represents the true philosophical spirit of the eternal quest for truth. All other schools accept certain authentic texts as their own, and hesitate to question the goals of life, or the maxim of life after death, justified as these are in in trans-empirical terms. But if the true philosophical spirit lies in questioning and examining dogmas and religious beliefs, this spirit is embodied in Carvaka philosophy.[8]

The marginalization of critical and rational philosophical schools both by the Indologists and the nationalists, discussed in the previous chapter, gives us cause for considerable thought. If a rational, materialistic, empiricist, and sceptical philosophical school such as Carvaka had been given prominence in the forging of a Hindu tradition, perhaps India would have escaped being slotted into the spiritual versus materialist dichotomy that seems to have tied down the collective imagination. The consequences have not been too favourable. This stereotyping of Indian society as exotic and other-wordly has not helped us forge an equitable future. India, with all its material inequities, symbolic oppressions, and casteism which erupts into conflict over resistance at the veritable drop of a hat, has been slotted into a spiritual pigeonhole.

Till today, Indian society fails to accept the enormity of caste inequities, fascinated as it is with the metaphysical spirit. In short, the privileging of a highly metaphysical tradition as the public philosophy of India leads us away from social oppressions and power. It cannot help us to pinpoint power equations or remedy inequities.

Colonialism, as we see, has had a tremendous impact on the structuring of social relations within the community. This is evident not only in the privileging of the Vedanta as synonymous with Hinduism

---

[7]Ibid., pp. 3-4.
[8]Pradeep Gokhale, *Lokaya/Carvaka: A Philosophical Enquiry,* New Delhi: Oxford University Press, 2015, pp. 1–48.

and the marginalization of a critical, rational, and materialist tradition. The impact can also be seen in the way colonial officials thought of India, as predominantly Hindu, and in the way they could not deal with practices and institutions that deviated from a metaphysical tradition. Therefore, whereas the colonialists were comfortable with the philosophical tradition of Vedantic Hinduism since it cohered to their beliefs of what religion should look like, they were simply flummoxed when it came to a community that had been perversely typed as the untouchable and that did not form part of the caste system. Colonial administrators simply did not know what to do with this group.

Oliver Mendelsohn and Marika Vicziany write that British census officials were confused about whether the untouchable community could be classified as Hindus. These officials found a way out—by categorizing in the 1872 Census the Chamars, the largest untouchable caste of India in the province of Bengal, as part of what was awkwardly called 'Semi-Hinduised Aborigines'. In other parts of India, the Mahars and the Pariahs were placed along with Buddhists and Jains into a category called the 'Outcastes or Not Recognizing Castes'. The anxieties of British census officials were infinitely complicated by the insistence of their Hindu assistants that 'such low persons' could not be classified as part of the Hindu religion. The same kind of comments were made by the census commissioners during the 1891 and the 1901 census operations.[9]

Perspectives on whether the former untouchables could be classified as Hindus changed dramatically by the 1911 census. The need to mobilize more and more people in the freedom struggle, expanded representation of Indians in the legislative councils, and separate electorates introduced by the 1909 Indian Councils Act, or the Morley-Minto Reforms, introduced a new set of dynamics into the political scene. Leaders of the freedom struggle became concerned with the demographic strength of their constituency relative to other religious communities. After all, competitive elections rest on the politics of numbers. For Hindus, their demographic strength could only be augmented if the untouchables were included within the Hindu community.

The Muslim League objected to what it saw as the artificial inflation of the Hindu community. In 1911, the census commissioner, Edward

---

[9]Oliver Mendelsohn and Marika Vicziany, *The Untouchables: Subordination, Poverty and the State in Modern India,* Cambridge: Cambridge University Press, 1998, pp. 26–29.

Albert Gait, issued a preparatory circular to the provincial commissioners on the matter. Communities could be regarded as Hindu if appropriate answers to six questions could be found. Among these questions were the following: Do the members of the caste or tribe worship Hindu gods? Are they allowed to enter Hindu temples or make offerings to the deity? Will 'good' Brahmins consent to act as their priests? Will clean castes take water from them? And, finally, do they cause pollution by their touch or proximity?

The 1910 circular was unearthed and published by the print media. This caused an uproar in the Hindu community, which felt that the circular had been motivated by the leaders of the Muslim community. As part of his defence against mounting criticism, the census commissioner reiterated that statistically the Hindu community included what was now termed 'Depressed Classes'. In the 1931 Census, the term used for the former untouchable community was 'Exterior Classes'.[10]

## THE MAKING OF CASTE AS RESISTANCE

Political processes often breed unanticipated consequences. Attempts by the census commissioners to identify and locate a neglected and oppressed community resulted in the creation of a political category called the Depressed Classes. This gave to members a collective identity, enabled identification with other members, and fostered political consciousness. A community that had been disadvantaged by reasons of birth was now offered a chance to struggle for its rightful place in an independent India. It awaited a leader to guide the political struggle. This leader was Dr Bhimrao Ambedkar.

Ambedkar was a gifted and a remarkable scholar who had the learning, the intellectual resources, and the skills to challenge the way the interests of his community were consistently overlooked by leaders of the freedom struggle. The nationalist movement was compelled to recognize that it was simply not enough to fight for the freedom of Indians from colonial rule; Indians had to be liberated from the shackles that bound them to an indefensible caste system. The Dalit community was not going to wait for upper-caste Hindus to reform the community. Dalits, under the leadership of Dr Ambedkar, demanded equal political

---

[10]Ibid., pp. 28–29.

status, recognition of historical injustice, remedial justice, affirmative action, and separate electorates.

Dr Ambedkar, in effect, gave to the concept of freedom a new twist. Freedom from colonialism had to be accompanied by freedom from social fetters that had truncated the ability of vulnerable sections of society to come into their own. Delivering his address at the opening plenary session of the First Round Table Conference on 20 November 1930 as the representative of the Depressed Classes, Dr Ambedkar expressed this point of view.

> We know that political power is passing from the British into the hands of those who wield such tremendous economic, social and religious sway over our existence.... But we will consent to that on one condition and that is that the settlement of our problems is not left to time. I am afraid the Depressed Classes have waited too long for time to work its miracle. At every successive step taken by the British Government to widen the scope of representative government, the Depressed Classes have been systematically left out. No thought has been given to their claim for political power...we will not stand this any longer. The settlement of our problem must be a part of the general political settlement and must not be left over to the shifting sands of the sympathy and goodwill of the rulers of the future.[11]

The message had important implications for the concept and the practices of justice. Freedom for the Dalit community could only be achieved when the upper castes recognized their own complicity in the perpetuation of injustice on their own people. And substantive concepts of freedom, equality, rights, and justice could only be achieved when Indians realized that they must compensate for historical injustice through affirmative action policies. Caste was no longer a matter for social reform in order to realize the basic tenets of Hinduism, as reformers had thought. Caste was a political relation of super-ordination and subordination that compromised the ideology of the freedom struggle in India. The question had to be asked: whose freedom? Can India really be free if its own people remained in social bondage? The

---

[11]Narendra Jadhav, *Ambedkar: Awakening India's Social Conscience,* New Delhi: Konark, Publishers, 2014, pp. 131–32.

freedom struggle had to transit from formal to substantive freedom, a process that even Gandhi's concept of swaraj could never capture in its metaphysical image. Caste oppression was a matter for politics, for political struggle, for the realization of the democratic spirit that permeated the spirit of the freedom struggle. Dr Ambedkar and the anti-caste movement contributed substantially to the widening out and the deepening of the struggle for independence. Political freedom had to be accompanied by freedom from social bonds.

Notably, the Dalits did not ask for a separate state as the leaders of the Muslim League did from the 1940s onwards. They demanded an overturning of the social and economic order, and therefore of the political order. Partition and secession are qualitatively different from struggles to overthrow social oppressions. Leaders who want a state of their own turn their backs on the oppressions of the society they live in. They simply say—just keep your society rotten, corrupt, and hierarchical, we are leaving you. Because they do not interrogate social discrimination and oppression, they carry these oppressions of the society they leave, with them, into the new state. Getting a state of one's own is difficult, and I do not wish to undermine the struggle for independence. But political freedom is incomplete without social and economic freedom. It is precisely this multi-dimensional freedom that Dr Ambedkar struggled for. And it is this that represents politics in the best sense of the term. Those who struggle for a new order, those who are fired by the desire for emancipation, wish to transform society so that everyone can get her and his just due. This is Dr Ambedkar's contribution to Indian politics.

The politics of substantive freedom acquired a sharp political edge because the question of how equal political status for all in an independent India could be achieved was catapulted to the forefront of the agenda. How would a democratic India go about acknowledging and remedying historical injustice? What were the roads society had to follow to deliver social justice for the most disadvantaged? These questions were tackled through affirmative action policies. However, caste-based discrimination proved resistant to multiple interventions in many ways and violence continues to dodge the lives of a community that has been subjected to three-fold historical injustice.

## POST-INDEPENDENCE INDIA AND THE DALIT QUESTION

The continuation and reproduction of violence in postcolonial India can be typed as one of history's major ironies because in few newly independent countries were equality and redistributive justice given such centrality in the political imagination. No leader of the freedom struggle could ignore the contribution of Dr Ambedkar to transformative politics. Nor could the Constituent Assembly do so. Independent India adopted an ambitious programme of affirmative action, which sought to turn existing inequities and hierarchies on their head. To accomplish this task, the project took cognizance of background inequalities and set out to compensate for historical injustice.

Basically, affirmative action ensured the physical presence of Dalits in state-maintained educational institutions, in public employment, and in elected assemblies. The Constitution and laws criminalized the practice of untouchability. In the interests of affirmative action, exceptions were made to Article 14 of the Fundamental Rights chapter of the Constitution that guarantees the right to equality.

Undeniably, affirmative action policies that centre on acknowledgement of harm done and the politics of presence have contributed to the repair of historical wrongs to some extent. Given the gap between policy and their administration that marks the implementation of public policy in India, the project of affirmative action has not done too badly. The advantages of the project are, however, unevenly distributed. The constituency of affirmative action has benefited from these policies, but in bits and pieces. We see the making of an educated and professionally qualified Dalit middle class. Magazines run cover page stories on the rise of Dalit millionaires and on the establishment of a Dalit Chamber of Commerce and Industry. Significantly, the Dalit movement has succeeded in prising open worlds that, for a long while, had been closed to the community. Activists have seized the right to voice through collective action, defined social justice, and they influence and shape public debates on redistributive justice.

Equally spectacular has been the phenomenon of cultural and literary assertion by the leaders of the community. Today, Dalits write their own histories and biographies. A vibrant literary movement denounces the ostracism of an entire community from mainstream society and chronicles the nerve-wracking experience of being treated as outcaste. Challenging prevailing literary conventions, rewriting the script of literary and poetic production, inserting the community into critical narratives of the Indian nation, and intent on representing their own community, Dalit writers have profoundly dented the way we think of others and of ourselves.[12]

This genre of literature has gained considerable acclaim and English translations of Dalit literary works, for example Narendra Jadhav's *Untouchables* (2007), Omprakash Valmiki's *Jhoothan* (2008), and Baby Kamble's *The Prisons We Broke* (2009) have expanded the canon of postcolonial literature and aesthetics in Indian and Western universities. Above all, democratic politics, election strategies, commitment to affirmative action, and the space afforded by civil society for mobilization have enabled a suppressed community to recover agency and speak back to institutionalized power. Finally, the Dalit movement has generated a politically correct vocabulary in the public domain.

## THE PARADOX OF AFFIRMATIVE ACTION

In many respects, caste-based practices have changed for the better, at least in urban India. Yet, practices of discrimination and violence, often palpable, sometimes masked, sometimes unintended, continue to blot the lives of many members of the community.

For instance, education levels among Dalits have improved in the post-primary and higher educational levels. They have benefited as much as non-Dalits. Still, children from lower castes are disadvantaged compared to upper castes. Several reports tell us that Dalit children are subjected to discriminatory and unequal treatment ritually dished out by teachers and by peers. It is not surprising that these experiences injure the self-esteem and self-worth of the student and have serious implications for their interest in schooling and higher education. Consequently, children fail or perform poorly, and tend to discontinue studies once they leave school. Clearly the reason for school dropouts is systematized social prejudice and hateful practices more than anything else.

The product of systemized discrimination is violence, often in blatant and more often in veiled forms. More significantly, violence is not a one-time affair. The impact of violence ranges from permanent psychosomatic damage to irreversible bodily harm. Anand Teltumbde,

---

[12]Martand Kaushik, 'Dalit literature goes global', *Times of India,* 5 April 2015.

who has recorded the collective biography of Dalits in India, writes that massive atrocities on Dalits have taken place over the years. On an average, more than two Dalits are murdered every day. More than five Dalit women are raped every day.[13] The National Crimes Record Bureau data shows that the number of rape cases against SC women went up from 1,346 in 2009 to 2,536 in 2016, an increase of 88.4 per cent nationally. The increase in Haryana was 167 per cent.[14]

Uttar Pradesh, Bihar, and Rajasthan head the list of states that have seen substantial numbers of crimes against the community. A 2015 report by the Media Institute for National Development in Tamil Nadu found that 30 per cent of cases under the Scheduled Caste and Scheduled Tribe (Prevention of Atrocities) Act (POA) were closed because of mistakes in the process of fact collecting. The law, held the report, has not been used to its full potential. It is not unusual to find investigative agencies, such as the police, belong to the same caste as the perpetrators of violence. The odds are heavily weighted against those who have been subjected to these crimes. In some parts of the country, attempts by Dalits to assert the right to equality have led to terrible backlashes and to caste riots.

Violence can range from the unthinkable and the terrible to the trivial. On 12 May 2015, a Dalit bridegroom was forced to wear a helmet over his traditional bridal headgear. Pelted with stones by upper-caste Hindus because he had dared to mount a horse and lead his marriage procession, our determined bridegroom reached the venue of the wedding under police protection.[15] Matters have not improved since then. In February 2020, a Dalit bridegroom was dragged from his horse and beaten in Rajkot.[16]

Violence takes on shocking proportions in other contexts. In July 2016, four Dalit youths were stripped and brutally thrashed in Una, Gujarat, by cow vigilantes. Jignesh Mevani, a young Dalit leader, emerged as the face of protests in the region. He led a massive demonstration against the lynching of men whose occupation involves skinning of the carcasses of cows. This is considered the lowliest and most degrading occupation in the sub-caste hierarchy among Dalits. The long march

[13] Anand Teltumbde, *Republic of Caste,* New Delhi: Navyana, 2018, p. 26.

[14] Ibid., p. 167.

[15] 'Dalit groom attacked for riding a horse', *The Hindu,* 13 May 2015.

[16] 'Rajkot: Dalit groom on horse dragged down, beaten', *Times of India,* 17 February 2020.

resolved that Dalits would not remove the carcasses of dead animals, and that they would scatter truckloads of bones in public places. Mevani's campaign was funded by crowds of people belonging to his community. On balance, the campaign, which had an eclectic mass base, won against some formidable opponents in the December 2016 elections to the Gujarat legislative assembly. Mevani shifted the Dalit discourse from identity politics to political economy. Political economy is enormously significant. Yet, identity issues have not gone away, and they continue to dictate the most inhuman atrocities against Dalits simply on the basis of their identity.

In June 2018, three young men were attacked and killed in cold blood even as the residents of the Dalit village Kachanatham in Sivaganga district in Tamil Nadu were watching a popular television serial. Their power supply was cut off and a mob armed with swords swarmed into their homes. One of the victims, Shanmuganathan, was an MBA graduate who had given up his job to cultivate his family's land. He had dug a borewell to ensure water supply to his fields and to others as well. It was clear that the violence was instigated by people who resented educated Dalit youths taking up government jobs and emerging as leaders in the village.[17] Dalits have been killed for sporting a moustache, for riding a motorcycle, for marrying outside his or her caste, for riding a horse to his wedding, and for watching television at home.

Consider the enormity of injustice wreaked on the heads of Dalits for trivial reasons. The consequences are, however, not trivial. On 26 April 2019, a twenty-one-year-old Dalit man, Jitendra Das, was thrashed to death by upper-caste men, merely because he sat on a chair in front of them at a wedding in Shrikot area of Tehri Garhwal. These men assaulted him again when he was on his way home. A badly injured Jitendra collapsed and was taken to the hospital. He died of his injuries. This young man was a carpenter and the sole breadwinner of his family.[18] People are humiliated and killed in a modern and democratic India just because they belong to the lower castes. This is the irony of our history as an independent, democratic nation.

---

[17]Vignesh V., 'The great divide', *New Indian Express*, 3 June 2018.
[18]Kalyan Das, 'Dalit youth thrashed for sitting on a chair, eating at wedding, dead', *Hindustan Times*, 5 May 2019.

## THE URBAN CONDITION

To escape labelling, targeting, and consequent discrimination, Dalits have increasingly migrated to urban areas. In the anonymity of urban spaces, it might be possible for people who have been subjected to perverse stereotyping, humiliation, and overt violence in their villages to drop their last names, not out of choice but out of necessity, and to hide their identity. They might wish to move into a decent neighbourhood occupied by the upper castes or apply for jobs that command dignity and respect. The urban experience might offer opportunities and the freedom that comes with anonymity.

In Narendra Jadhav's *Outcaste*, the author recounts the story of his father who was not impressed with Bombay, 'I was disappointed and longed for the clean air and rolling fields back home in Osar.'[19] But he also accepted that in the village he could not have entered a tea shop without being identified as a Mahar. He would have been driven out instantly. By contrast, Bombay appears to be a city of freedom.

But Mumbai can also replicate the oppressions of rural India in different but equally repressive forms. Mohandas Naimishray observed in *Apne Apne Pinjre* that though Bombay had huge poverty and unemployment, there were no walls that separated men from men. He was not asked about his caste. But caste creeps silently but surely into his life, it finds a way to shape Naimishray's experiences of the urban space. He notes that the temple does not allow Dalits to enter. The stigma of untouchability remains, even if the oppression is not as brutal or as blatant as in rural environments. The city promotes facelessness compared to the village. Still, Dalits have to hide their caste to get things done. For instance, they are forced to opt for namelessness if they wish to live in an upper-caste colony. If they are, perchance, found out, they will be asked to leave.[20]

Caste dodges the heels of its bearer in different ways. Surveys have shown that Dalits are underrepresented in industry because of the persistence of strong prejudices against the lower castes. The economist Ashwani Deshpande reports that firms do not bother to respond to applications for jobs by Dalits. In order to test the persistence or lack of

---

[19]Narendra Jadhav, *The Outcaste: A Dalit's Life*, translated from the Hindi by Arun Prabha Mukherjee, Kolkata: Samya, 2003, p. 82.

[20]Mohandas Naimisharay, *Apne Apne Pinjre* (Hindi), New Delhi: Vani Prakashan, 2013.

such discrimination, her research team submitted multiple applications for near-entry-level jobs in the private sector. Each application was under a fictitious name. One application carried an upper-caste Hindu name, the second carried a Muslim, and the third carried a Dalit name. In each set of applications, the upper-caste applicant had a lower degree than the lower caste applicant. In total, 4,808 applications were submitted in response to 548 advertisements over a period of 66 weeks. The team discovered that upper-caste candidates with lower qualifications had a better chance of getting a job than Dalits who had higher qualifications.[21]

The belief that employment in the job market is based on merit has been blown open by a number of studies. Jobs are heavily skewed in favour of upper-caste Hindu men and against Dalits, Muslims, and women. Dalits have moved to towns and cities to access the world of opportunities, but many of them remain caught in jobs that had traditionally been allocated to the lower castes. Notoriously, these jobs fall in the category of cleaning and sanitation activities. The National Human Development Report (India) 2016 reported that 99 per cent of people who do manual scavenging, a job that requires direct contact with excreta and is considered the worst surviving symbol of caste discrimination, are Dalits. Women constitute 5 per cent of this number. Manual scavenging is officially banned in the country; yet, the latest census data confirmed the existence of this form of employment in which cleaners die of suffocation. According to the data, 180,657 households are still engaged in this degrading work. Maharashtra with 63,713 households involved in the work tops the list; Madhya Pradesh, Uttar Pradesh, Tripura, and Karnataka follow.[22]

Large numbers of cleaners die every day in the heart of the capital city because they are compelled to descend into sewer manholes and septic tanks without protective gear. They are consequently asphyxiated. Whether it is Delhi or Mumbai, scores of people engaged in manual scavenging die before their time because they have no option except to take jobs that are slotted for their caste. A substantive part of the

---

[21] Ashwini Deshpande, *The Grammar of Caste: Economic Discrimination in Contemporary India,* New Delhi: Oxford University Press, 2011, pp. 187–88.

[22] Subhash Gatade, 'Waiting for Swach Bharat: A Close Look at the Question of Caste, Sanitation, and Policy Approaches in India', in Kalpana Kannabiran and Asha Hans (ed.), *India Social Development Report 2016: Disability Rights Perspectives,* New Delhi: Council for Social Development and Oxford University Press, 2016, pp. 252–61.

community continues to suffer economic deprivation in urban slums and shanty towns.

It is impossible to separate issues of material deprivation and humiliation that Dalits suffer in their daily lives. Humiliation is a covert form of violence. Omprakash Valmiki in *Jhoothan* recounts his shock and disbelief when he witnesses the persistence of untouchability in metropolitan Bombay. An upper-caste family that he had come to know, the Kulkarnis, treated him as if he was their son, with love and respect. 'One day', he writes, 'a common friend, Professor Kamble, had come to meet the family. 'Kulkarni and Kamble,' the author continues, 'were deep in conversation about Marathi plays and Patil and I were listening to them quietly. I noticed that Kamble's cup was different from the rest of us. I asked Sudama Patil on our way out why Kamble had been served tea in a different cup. Finally, he said, "Maharashtrian Brahmins, that too from Poona, they don't allow Mahars to touch their dishes." As I listened to him my ears started to boil as though someone had poured mercury into them.... When I saw well-educated people in a metropolitan city like Bombay indulging in such behavior, I felt a fountain of hot lava erupting within me.'[23]

His challenge of the tradition of separate plates and glasses for the Dalits and his open declaration that he belongs to the Chuhra community of Uttar Pradesh results in the break-up of a potentially romantic relationship with Savita, the daughter of the family. 'I said as plainly as I could that I was born in a Chuhra family of U. P. Savita appeared grave. Her eyes were filled with tears.... Suddenly the distance between us had increased. The hatred of thousands of years had entered our hearts. What a lie culture and civilization are.'[24]

What are the lessons we learn from these autobiographies and these reflections on the urban condition, one that is supposedly marked by steady progression towards a more tolerant and open society? Perhaps these lessons can only lead to anguished questions. Once people embrace the anonymity of the city, are they liberated from irrational discrimination and inhuman prejudices? What does the perpetuation of prejudice tell us about the project of affirmative action?

---

[23] *Jhoothan: A Dalit's Life,* translated from the Hindi by Arun Prabha Mukherjee, Kolkata: Samya, 2003, p. 95.

[24] Ibid., p. 98.

## THE PARADOX OF AFFIRMATIVE ACTION

Undoubtedly, as remarked above, affirmative action policies have bred some positive results. Some redistribution has taken place, the community has secured the right to voice, but equality which encourages and fosters respect between fellow citizens continues to elude most Dalits. This is no small matter; it cannot be brushed under the carpet on the assumption that what matters is that people should have enough to live on. How does it matter if they are not treated as equals or with respect? Yet, matters are not so simple. The notion of recognition which challenges the belief that individuals are self-contained has always been a powerful theme in political philosophy. It acquired new relevance in the days that followed the collapse of the Berlin Wall in 1989. Ironically, the collapse of existing socialist societies was to inaugurate an era of hyper-ethnonationalist movements, especially in the region of the Balkans and the Caucasus. The consequences of the upsurge were somewhat serious. Countries dissolved, federal systems melted away, and several new states emerged out of the debris of old ones often through processes of armed struggle, ethnic cleansing, and genocide. The scale as well as the pace at which existing states broke, and new states were created, was quite unprecedented in history. Theorists rediscovered the concept of recognition to argue that the self-esteem of human beings depends not only on access to material preconditions of a dignified life, such as an income, food, health, education, and a healthy environment, but also respect that comes from recognition.

When others recognize us as worthy of respect, not only because we are accomplished in any way, not only because we are skilled cricketers like Virat Kohli, or creative writers like Amitav Ghosh, classical singers like Rashid Khan, or imaginative artists like M. F. Hussain, but simply because we are human, we develop self-esteem and self-respect. Individuals are not the source of their own self-respect; they are dependent on others for this feeling that leads to confidence and to assurance.

When people disrespect us for an arbitrary reason, such as birth into a community that has been labelled in derogatory ways, our souls shrivel and our bodies arch in pain as if someone has landed a powerful punch to our solar plexus. Discrimination and disrespect harm the recipients often beyond repair. The damage done by lack of respect is as serious as damage by physical harm. It results in diminished human beings.

We have to come to terms with a subtler form of violence, violence as disrespect and humiliation that scars minds. *Antaspot*, an autobiography by Kumud Pawde, chronicles the extreme mortification of a lower-caste woman. The story begins with an intriguing statement made by the author. She states that she does not like listening to praise. 'I might seem ill-mannered',[25] she says, 'to others'. They do not realize that beneath the praise there is resentment that a woman from a low caste has not only done her doctorate in Sanskrit, but also teaches the language of the scriptures. Upper-caste people look askance at me, "Well isn't that amazing? So you're teaching Sanskrit at the government college are you?'[26] The statement carries a wealth of meaning and is derogatory to Dalits, implying that now the upper castes have to learn a sacred language from a Dalit, a member of a community that was forbidden to speak the language.

Caste, she remarks sadly, cannot be eradicated. Struggling to find a job in the university, she confronts obstacle after obstacle. Finally, Kumud Pawde gets married and also gets a teaching job in her own college. At the end of the story, she admits that she got the job because she had married an upper-caste man. She is no longer Kumud Somkuwar, she is Kumud Pawde. Marriage to a man from a higher caste opened the gates of opportunity. The caste of her maiden status, however, the author remarks sadly, remains deprived.[27]

Humiliation is a form of violence. The denigration of a person merely because she belongs to caste X and dismissal of her ambitions and her accomplishments lead to a violent break in her relationship to herself, her self-esteem, and her sense of worth. Violence as disrespect and insult, howsoever subtle it may appear, breeds fearful consequences. Underlying these painful narratives of untold damage done to people's minds and bodies is incomprehension and perplexity. Why would the accomplishments of individuals be belittled only because of a factor outside their control: birth into a community that has been typed in vicious ways? This is what they ask themselves.

Sharankumar Limbale in the stanza with which this chapter opens, asks in the 'White Paper' with despair—why am I targeted? Poets note

---

[25]Kumud Pawde, 'The Story of My "Sanskrit"', translated by Priya Adarkar, in Arjun Dangle (ed.) *Poisoned Bread*, New Delhi: Orient BlackSwan, 2009, pp. 110–22.

[26]Ibid., p. 111.

[27]Ibid., p. 122.

with desolation that their voice remains unheard. Baburao Jagtap writes: 'Brother, our screams are only an attempt/to write the chronicles of this country/—this naked country/with its heartless religion/The people here rejoice in their black laws/and deny that we were ever born.'[28] When people who have been handed down humiliation and disrespect as their patrimony rebel in verse, in song, in literature, in rhetoric and in struggle, we see the birth of a political miracle. Yet we must also note sadly that protest and resistance, rebellion and anger, have bred a backlash the enormity of which stuns our senses, or at least should paralyse the common conscience of India.

## VIOLENCE AS RETALIATION

It is difficult to sort out the complex of causes that have led to an escalation of violence against Dalits, either as disrespect which leads to psychological harm or as strong-arming which leads to physical injury. They overlap in particularly ugly ways, resulting in caste-based violence. But if we were to make a rough map, one major factor that feeds into violence is collective memory of the practice of untouchability that has shaped inter-caste relations over centuries. The practice has been challenged and derided. The sanctity of human rights jurisprudence and constitutional morality has been reinforced repeatedly, yet ignoble caste-based violence persists. A second factor that has fed into violence is resentment. Upper castes and the landed backward castes are bitter about affirmative action policies that grant the Dalit community access to education, employment, and representation. Resentment is fed by the empowerment of the Dalit community, a vigilant anti-caste movement, assertions of new rights to cultural space, celebration of Dalit heroes and mythology, the right to dress the way people want to, the right to celebrate festivals the way they want to, the right to own or rent a house in a locality of one's choice, the right to freedom of literary expression, and the right to speak back to the upper castes in an idiom of their own. The third factor is the resistance of young educated Dalits to live and work according to existing caste distinctions. Assertions of basic human rights have carved out new domains for resistance and rejection of existing hierarchies. The consequences can be dreadful but

---

[28]Baburao Jagtap, 'This Country is Broken,' translated by Vikas Sarang, in Arjun Dangle (ed.) *Poisoned Bread.*

they do not deter further and sustained resistance to discrimination and violence.

Basing his insights on fieldwork in Rajasthan in 1993, Oliver Mendelsohn concluded that caste hierarchies and exclusions had changed. The Dalits were no longer dependent on the upper castes for access to material and symbolic resources.[29] A number of sociologists conclude on the basis of their work in different regions that the traditional link between caste, land, and occupation had weakened. Dalits are reluctant in rural Punjab, concluded Surinder Jodhka and Prakash Louis, to work on farms owned by Jat farmers. They emphasize equal rights, particularly their right to a legitimate share of the common resources of the village. But this has resulted in frequent caste-based conflict and violence in rural Punjab.[30]

The cases cited below illustrate the shameful depths to which people overpowered by anger and envy can descend. These cases also illustrate the determination of the Dalit community to speak back to a history not of its making, to fight for fellow citizens even if the intervention comes too late, to claim space and reclaim rights. The importance of resistance cannot be emphasized enough but outcomes can be bitter. The interplay between discrimination/humiliation and resistance has resulted in violence.

Anand Teltumbde has chronicled the sordid atrocities wreaked on an educated Dalit family of Bhaiyalal Bhotmange in September 2006. The family owned a piece of land in Khairlanji in Maharashtra. This provided enough cause for resentment among the landed middle castes. The family was routinely subjected to insults by the middle castes.[31] Though their land was irrigated, members of the family had to draw water at night or at daybreak to avoid conflicts with the rest of the villagers. When the family tried to build a pucca house in place of a thatched hut at the edge of the village, the panchayat, dominated as it was by the backward castes, prevented it from doing do. The hut had

---

[29] Oliver Mendelsohn, 'The Transformation of Authority in Rural India', *Modern Asian Studies*, Vol. 15, No. 4, 1993, pp. 805–42.

[30] Surinder S. Jodhka, 'Caste and Untouchability in Rural Punjab', *Economic and Political Weekly*, Vol. 38, No. 19, 2002, pp. 1,813–23; Surinder S. Jodhka and Prakash Louis, 'Caste Tension in Punjab: Talhan and Beyond', *Economic and Political Weekly*, Vol. 38, No. 28, 2002, pp. 2,923–26.

[31] Anand Teltumbde, *Khairlanji: A Strange and Bitter Crop*, New Delhi: Navayana, 2008.

no electricity connection. The Bhotmanges were also denied easy access to drinking water.

The main cause of resentment among the upper castes was that Surekha, the mother of the Bhotmange family, was educated, hardworking, courageous, outspoken, and intolerant of discrimination. The children went to college and possessed mobile phones and bicycles. There came a time when Surekha stood up to the upper castes who tried to carve a path out of the land owned by the Bhotmanges. She and some of her relatives filed a police complaint against the use of abusive language and casteist slurs by the villagers. The family was threatened with dire consequences. On 29 September 2006, some villagers, who had been accused of attacking a relative of the Bhotmanges, were arrested but later released on bail.

The middle castes decided that it was time the family was taught a lesson for nothing else other than the defence of their right to live with dignity. Two tractors carrying men who were out on bail, accompanied by a mob of sixty to seventy men and women, proceeded to surround the house. The mob, intent on violence most foul, was armed with sticks, cycle chains, and other improvised weapons. Various people who made up the murderous mob attacked the family for having dared to file a police report against the landed castes. The father, Bhaiyalal, had been working in his field and was on his way back home. He was forced to witness the appalling and merciless brutality inflicted upon his family. He rushed to report the incident to his extended family. A complaint was filed in the police station, but the police hesitated to act against people who belonged to the dominant community.

For the family, the nightmare had just begun. Surekha, the sons Roshan and Sudhir, and daughter, Priyanka, were subjected to cycles of unspeakable violence. The children were twenty-one, nineteen, and seventeen years of age respectively. A group of women dragged Surekha and her daughter to the centre of the village and stripped them. They were paraded, battered, raped several times, and finally killed. Bhotmange's two sons were beaten up. When they refused to rape their mother and sister on demand, their genitals were crushed and mutilated, and they were murdered.

The story does not end here. The desecrated and broken bodies of the four members of the family lay on the ground, but the mob, intoxicated by the sight and the smell of blood, did not spare the dead. Reportedly, the bodies of the two dead women were raped in mind-numbing acts of necrophilia. The torture of corpses went on for two hours. Subsequently, the bodies were dumped into the Pench canal that had irrigated the fields of the Bhotmanges. The bodies were recovered from the canal by the police, but post-mortems were carried out in a perfunctory manner. Twenty-eight people from the village were arrested.

Reports of the torture and the massacre became public, and Dalits in the Vidarbha region of Maharashtra erupted in protest. On 1 November, Dalit women organized a long march in the district town of Bhandara shouting slogans and asking for police action. These protests catalysed larger protests by other organizations. Young people joined in and the whole of Maharashtra was up in arms. Police repression followed, Dalit bastis were attacked, and young men, women, and children were abused and thrashed. Young boys in schools and colleges were tortured while they were in custody. After mass protests, hundreds of Dalit lawyers, doctors, businessmen, and professionals were beaten up and arrested. But the protests were too widespread and could not be ignored. The state government was forced to request the Central Bureau of Investigation (CBI) to probe the crime. It also designated the Sessions Court in Bhandara as a fast-track court with the responsibility of applying the provisions of the Prevention of Atrocities Act (POA).

Within two years, Judge S. S. Das of the District and Sessions Court of Bhandara pronounced death sentences on six persons and life terms for two. The motive of the case was shifted from caste to revenge. The POA was not invoked. Nor were the provisions of the Indian Penal Code that provide for punishment for outraging a woman's modesty invoked. The High Court confirmed the decision, though it converted the death sentence of two accused into life imprisonment. The Khairlanji case was treated as just another criminal case. Teltumbde draws an important lesson from the case. Every village in India is a potential Khairlanji, he writes. The case codes the quintessence of caste: everyone must keep his place in the hierarchy, or the consequences will be terrible.[32]

The ancient Greek lawgiver Solon had suggested that Athenians were clever as foxes when they looked after their own interests, but

---

[32] Teltumbde, *Khairlanji*, p. 14.

as soon as they came together, they lost their wits. Individuals might hold grudges against others for irrational reasons, but this does not mean that they wreak horrifying violence on others. Things change when people come together in a mob and when violence is triggered off by a catalyst that might appear to most people as minor. People lose control over their actions, develop a collective will to destroy, and are ready to be led into insane directions by rabble rousers. The anger of a few persons breeds rage in the crowd. It proceeds to imprint the bodies of the victim with the scars of terrible violence.

The number of incidents that involve rage and resentment at what are seen as unjustifiable rewards cannot be counted. On 7 January 2013, S. Anandhi and M. Vijayabaskar wrote a piece titled 'Where buying a motorcycle can spark a riot' in *The Hindu*. They recounted an ugly incident that took place in Dharmapuri in Tamil Nadu when 300 Dalit houses and property were destroyed by a mob of Vanniyars. The mob was angered by reports of the marriage of a Vanniyar woman to a Dalit youth and the subsequent suicide of the girl's father. Other reasons that contributed to the violence were simmering discontent against the upward mobility of the Dalit—education, some degree of well-being, and the reclamation of the right to voice. Eleven districts in the state had already witnessed caste violence and destruction of property. In this riot, fifty two-wheelers were destroyed.

Resentment that a community that had been deprived throughout history had managed to gain education and some degree of wealth has taken on terrifying forms. During the attacks on Dalits in Dharmapuri, assailants kept chanting that they were punishing the Dalits because they had acquired wealth and cattle, because their houses have tiled roofs, because their children are educated, and because their women wear gold ornaments.[33] This was considered enough justification for violence and arson.

This resentment has a gendered aspect, like many such cases often do. On 23 March 2014, in the village of Bhagana in Hisar district of Haryana, four young girls—the youngest was thirteen and the oldest was eighteen years old—belonging to the Dhanuk community of Dalits, were abducted drugged, raped in the fields, and set upon by five men

---

[33]S. Anandhi and M. Vijayabaskar, 'Where buying a motorcycle can spark a riot', *The Hindu*, 7 January 2013.

of the Jat community. Their bruised bodies were dumped in the bushes outside the railway station in Bhatinda, Punjab. Two years later, the thirteen-year-old survivor could only remember the weight of male bodies that forced themselves on a child. An FIR was filed against the five men under the POA. The sarpanch who was related to one of the accused had tried to prevent the filing of the FIR and it was filed only when 200 people surrounded the police station in Hisar. The medical reports confirmed rape. The men were arrested.

Dalit families protested against the incident. Certain the land-owning dominant caste would take revenge on them, they refused to go back to their villages. Most of the Dalits were either farm labourers or domestic help, a class that is helpless before the powerful castes. 'The system belongs to the Jats', said one protestor to *The Hindu*, '...they've given money to the police. They can confess without fear of anything happening to them.'[34] It was also reported that in retaliation the Jats had socially boycotted the Dalit community, forcibly grabbed 208 acres of common land, and prevented the implementation of any social welfare schemes. Many Dalit families left the village and others who stayed on were threatened and coerced. The village witnessed the planned exodus of Dalit families and appropriation of common land. The government evicted families from the site of protest that they had made their home. On 8 August 2015, the Bhagana Kand Sangharsh Samiti called a meeting at Jantar Mantar and the attendees embraced Islam. Buddhism, protestors felt, could no longer protect them.[35]

Festering resentment that a community has been able to surmount overwhelming obstacles and live with some degree of dignity has had other political consequences. For some time now, India has been in the throes of an agrarian crisis; agriculture has been rendered unprofitable, and prices for commodities, as well as wages, have dramatically deteriorated. Agrarian economists document that children of the farming community prefer to leave the village and search for professional jobs. Given the scarcity of jobs in urban areas and the difficulties of getting admission into reputable educational institutions, many of the younger generation are both under-educated and unemployed. It is precisely here that rage

---

[34]Aradhna Wal, 'Reliving a nightmare', *The Hindu*, 12 May 2014.

[35]Deepender Deswal, 'Bhagana Dalits convert to Islam for "dignified life"', *The Tribune*, 9 August 2015.

against the Dalit community, which has been granted benefits under affirmative action programmes, reveals itself in violence. An interesting outcome of this has been the demand for extension of affirmative action policies to other castes.

In Maharashtra, the generally well-off Maratha community has resorted to protest and even violence since 1992, when it began to demand reservations. In August 2018, a major protest movement was launched. A correspondent from the *Times of India*, Sugandha Indulkar, interviewed Virendra Shashikant Pawar, one of the leaders of the Maratha Kranti Morcha. The latter admitted that among other things the movement was asking for, such as amendments to protective legislation for the Dalit community, were reservations in educational institutions and government employment. He also admitted that children of the otherwise affluent community do not get admission into their preferred colleges and higher education institutions. But children who belong to the non-Maratha community have managed to secure both education and employment. The problem is aggravated in the case of marginalized farmers. Frustrations have mounted and this has led to the demand for reservations for economically backward castes. Either include us in the Other Backward Caste category or abolish all reservations, Pawar demanded during the interview.[36]

The demand is ironical because reservations have been designed for groups who are doubly disadvantaged insofar as they suffer from both social and economic discrimination. There is a distinctive difference between projects of distributive justice that try to reorganize ownership of economic resources equitably and remedial justice that ensures benefits to a historically disadvantaged community to compensate for that historical injustice. Redistributive justice recognizes that resources are unjustly monopolized by a small group of elites and sets out to institutionalize equitable redistribution through a variety of means; for example, progressive taxation. In India, the project of distributive justice has failed to ensure a degree of equality and levels of inequality remain frighteningly high. In January 2020, the human rights group Oxfam released a study in Davos ahead of the fiftieth annual meeting of the World Economic Forum. The study reported that the richest 1 per cent

---

[36]'Maratha youth denied right to preferred education, while their friends who have reservations move ahead in life', *Times of India*, 10 August 2018.

of the population in India owns more than four times the wealth held by 953 million people who make up the bottom 70 per cent of the population. The gap between the rich and the poor cannot be resolved without deliberate inequality-busting policies, and too few governments are committed to these, said Amitabh Behar, CEO of Oxfam India.[37] Groups, therefore, increasingly opt for the same measures that were initially formulated for the doubly disadvantaged by historical injustice. And this brings them into confrontation with Dalit groups. Now all manners of groups claim the right to affirmative action. However, if affirmative action policies are designed in abstraction from programmes of redistributive justice that benefit all citizens irrespective of caste, affirmative action comes to stand in for redistributive justice.

## THE RIGHT TO CULTURE

The assertion of another right which has occasioned resentment and violence is the right to an alternative culture and the right to celebrate spaces and icons. One of the main achievements of the Dalit community has been the reclamation of political history and cultural symbols. In mainstream narratives of culture, these achievements have been marginalized. Dalit efforts to recover a history that is peripheral to dominant history, mythology, festivals, rituals of commemoration, and memory have been little short of Herculean. They have had to suffer for their endeavours to overturn dominant memories.

Consider one such case. On 1 January 2018, an estimated 3 lakh Dalits gathered in the village of Bhima Koregaon in Maharashtra. The meeting celebrated the outcome of a battle fought 200 years ago in 1818, between the British Army's Mahar Regiment and Peshwa Baji Rao's Maratha army. In the battle, the upper-caste Peshwa's army, which outnumbered the Mahar Regiment, was defeated. Twenty-two Mahar soldiers were killed. The battle heralded the end of the Maratha empire and inaugurated the domination of British colonial power over western India. The colonial administration raised an obelisk at the site of its victory. The obelisk carries the names of forty-nine soldiers, including the twenty-two Mahar soldiers who had died in the battle. On 1 January 1927, on the 109th anniversary of the battle, Ambedkar visited the war memorial to

[37]'Wealth of India's richest 1% more than 4-times of total for 70% poorest: Oxfam', *Mint*, 20 January 2020.

pay obeisance. Ever since, Dalits assemble at the war memorial in Bhima Koregaon on the same day every year. It is celebrated as Shaurya Diwas, or as the victory of the oppressed over the oppressor.

Dalit organizations had planned festivities on a grand scale in the space around the obelisk on 1 January 2018. Several lakh Dalits had gathered around the victory pillar when, allegedly, some right-wing groups carrying saffron flags pelted them with stones. Prakash Ambedkar called for a Maharahtra Bandh on 2 January in protest.[38]

Schools, colleges, and shops were closed as an outraged Dalit community protested against premeditated attacks on a peaceful gathering memorializing its own history. Hundreds of Dalit activists marched through the streets of Mumbai shouting the slogan 'Jai Bhim'. According to reports, on the third day of the bandh, the police tried to put down the revolt using lathis. More than hundred people were arrested and detained.

The print and visual media reported the clash as a caste-war between Dalits and Marathas. Hindu right-wingers alleged that the Dalit community was anti-national because it celebrated the defeat of Brahmanical forces. They celebrate, in other words, the victory of the lower castes against the upper castes.

Matters were not settled. In June 2018, the government arrested nine prominent human rights activists and intellectuals. It was alleged that the activists were connected with the violence at Bhima Koregaon.[39] The list of activists and intellectuals who were imprisoned was expanded subsequently and now include Anand Teltumbde, Gautam Navlakha, and Stan Swamy. The celebrations on 1 January 2018 at Bhima Koregaon was preceded by a meeting on 31 December 2017. Human rights activists, social workers, leaders of Dalit organizations and their supporters, and former justices had assembled at the Elgaar Parishad rally at Shaniwarwada in Pune. Jignesh Mevani was one of the key speakers at the meeting. According to the police, the Elgaar meeting that saw hundreds of Dalits congregate in the city was subversive. The police held that the meeting was funded by Naxalites, and that it planned the violence that erupted on 1 January 2018 at the victory obelisk. The activists who

---

[38]'Bhima Koregaon violence: What happened on 1 January and the events that followed', *FirstPost*, 4 October 2018.
[39]'Elgar Parishad Case: Pune police file charges against 19', *Indian Express*, 19 December 2019.

were present at the Elgaar rally were further charged with conspiracy to kill Prime Minister Narendra Modi. They were arrested under the Unlawful Activities (Prevention) Act, 1967 which does not allow for anticipatory bail.[40] More than two years later, some activists are still in jail for a crime they did not commit.

The Bhima Koregaon incident is politically significant because as suggested above, Dalit activists and academics have tried to resurrect a history that has been consigned to the wayside by the upper castes and celebrate icons that have been demonized by the upper castes. For instance, every October, Hindus celebrate the killing of the demon Mahishasur by Goddess Durga during Navratri, Durga Puja, and Dussehra. Legend has it that Mahishasur, half-man, half-buffalo, could not be killed by any human being. The gods of the Hindu pantheon—Brahma, Vishnu, and Mahesh—created Goddess Durga for this purpose. She descended to earth and proceeded to kill the 'demon'. In Devi temples, a fair Durga (who is seen as upper caste) is depicted stabbing a dark and demonic Mahishasur.

Dalit communities across the country have revitalized the story of the 'demon' as that of a real-life Dalit hero who suffered caste-based injustice and became a martyr. The resurrection of the hero, unjustly represented as a demon, is tied to reinterpretations of the history of the Dalits, whose gods have been demonized in mythology. Dalit intellectuals have argued that in ancient India, a group of Indo-Aryans conquered the subcontinent and tortured and enslaved the indigenous inhabitants. The Dalits and Adivasis are seen as the descendants of the indigenous people of the country who had escaped cruelty at the hands of the Aryans. For them, Mahishasur is a king of the indigenous tribes who was unfairly killed by the invaders. The upper castes are accused of reducing Dalit heroes to less than human simply because they resisted Brahmanical oppression. The upper castes in turn rally against this subversive trend in history. In sum, attempts to reclaim Dalit heroes from the margins of mythology and claim cultural spaces where a history of the subalterns can be written and celebrated and where this history can provide an anchor for identity formation have been savagely attacked by upper-caste organizations as anti-Hindu.

---

[40]Ibid.

## EVALUATING AFFIRMATIVE ACTION AS REMEDIAL JUSTICE

What are the lessons that we learn from even a partial rendering of stories of caste-based discrimination? Though the Indian government after Independence moved fairly quickly to dissolve the spectre of untouchability through affirmative action policies and through the banning of untouchability, violence against the Dalit community continues to bedevil the community in some form or the other. It is perhaps time to ask what affirmative action policies have done for the community.

In 1969, the sociologist I. P. Desai presented the findings of his research on the practice of untouchability in rural Gujarat. In public arenas that were governed by law, such as schools and post offices, he told us, untouchability was least practiced. Only one school in fifty-nine villages had separate seating arrangements for Dalit children, and only 4 per cent of the post offices practiced discrimination in their transactions with Dalits. When it came to the private sphere of social transactions, however, matters were different.[41] In 90 per cent of the villages that he surveyed, Desai found that Dalits were not allowed to enter the houses of caste Hindus. Dalits were prohibited from entering temples frequented by caste Hindus. In 10 per cent of the villages that were surveyed, Dalits were not allowed direct access to common water sources. They were consequently dependent on caste Hindus for access to water.[42] Other villages had created separate wells from where the Dalits could draw water.

Though discrimination could be found in seating arrangements in the public arena of panchayats,[43] it was really in the private sphere that untouchability continued to be practiced seriously. Desai concluded that Dalits had benefited because 'they do not have to suffer humiliation every day at the hands of the upper castes'[44]. But though the attitude of caste Hindus had changed at least in public transactions, their beliefs about untouchability had not altered. The world of the Dalits had advanced in the sphere of public transactions that are governed by law, but not in the sphere of private relationships—friendship, intimacy,

---

[41] I. P. Desai, *Untouchability in Rural Gujarat*, Mumbai: Popular Prakashan, 1976.
[42] Ibid., pp. 62–63.
[43] Ibid., p. 258.
[44] Ibid., p. 114.

dining together, visiting each other—which lie outside the ambit of the law. More recent research tells us that the attitude of caste Hindus has not changed. In 2006, a research project conducted by scholars and social activists in 565 villages in 11 states of India revealed systematic evidence of untouchability and infliction of atrocities on the lower castes despite a powerful Dalit movement, and in defiance of laws that render untouchability an offence.[45]

Have the Dalits finally come into their own as equal citizens of India? Perhaps yes, and this despite all odds. A more troubling question follows: have the Dalits finally come into their own as citizens who are treated with respect or as equals by the government and by fellow citizens? The answer is mixed and on the whole troubling. It is even more troubling to recognize that the upper castes relentlessly focus on dismantling laws that protect the Dalit community.

On 2 April 2018, Dalit groups across the country called a Bharat Bandh in protest against a Supreme Court ruling of 20 March of the same year. The highest court in the land had struck down clauses in the POA on the ground that the legislature had not intended the Act to be used as an instrument to wreak vengeance or blackmail. The Act, ruled the court, should not result in perpetuating the spread of casteism which adversely impacts social integration and constitutional values. 'We have seen the working of POA in the last three decades and its abuse has been judicially acknowledged.'[46] The court laid down safeguards to protect any alleged offender of the PO, such as provisions for anticipatory bail and the institutionalization of a preliminary enquiry before registering a case.

The Rajiv Gandhi government had enacted the Scheduled Castes and Scheduled Tribes (Prevention of Atrocities Act) in 1989 to buttress constitutional provisions of abolition of untouchability and grant of equality. The Statement of Objects of the bill explicitly stated that despite various measures to improve the social and the economic status of the SCs and STs, they remain vulnerable, are denied civil rights, and

---

[45]Ghanshyam Shah, Harsh Mander, Sukhadeo Thorat, Satish Deshpande, and Amita Baviskar, *Untouchability In Rural India,* New Delhi: Sage Publications, 2006, pp. 165–66.

[46]Faizan Mustafa, 'SC/ST Act: Court ruling will have chilling effect on reporting crimes against Dalits' *The Wire,* 20 March 2018.

subjected to various offences, indignities, humiliations, and harassment.[47]

It is this weakening of protection against atrocities that aroused Dalit groups to action. Dalit activists demanded that protections, which had been removed by the Supreme Court, should be restored, and this should be accompanied by a broadening of the category of caste crimes and untouchability. Mass protests alarmed the government and on 9 August 2018, the Parliament passed a bill to overturn court's decision to water down the provisions of the POA. After a slew of petitions in the Supreme Court asking for a review of the earlier decision, on 1 October 2019, the court restored the provisions of the Act. 'This,' ruled Justice Arun Mishra, 'is a nation where we have not been able to provide the modern methods of scavenging to Harijans due to lack of resources and proper planning and apathy. The court condemned its own judgement given on 20 March 2018 stating that it was against basic human dignity to treat all members of the SC/ST community as liars or crooks.'[48]

Legislation to protect a community that is doubly disadvantaged by reasons of class and caste has proved inadequate. Parliament had enacted the Untouchability Offences Act in 1955. This failed to be effective. On 25 December 1968, in Kilvenmani, Tamil Nadu, twenty-three children, sixteen women, and five men all belonging to the Dalit community were burnt alive. They were locked in a hut which was then set on fire. The cause for this mass murder was practically inconsequential. Dalit labourers had been agitating for higher wages. A landlord secured his own interest by bringing in labour from outside. This was met by resistance by the agitators who had organized themselves under a communist flag. The landlords retaliated brutally. They arrived in police lorries, surrounded the Dalit basti, beat up the inmates, and set fire to their huts. Forty-four charred bodies were found in the morning. The Dalits were punished for demanding more wages, a right that arguably vests in the working people. They were beaten and burnt because they defied and resisted upper-caste landlords. All the laws of the land failed when it came to protecting citizens of the country.[49]

---

[47]Ibid.

[48]Krishna Rajagopal, 'SC recalls verdict diluting SC/ST anti-atrocities law', *The Hindu*, 1 October 2019.

[49]'The Hindu Explains/Keezhvenmani: The first chronicle of violence against Dalits in independent India', *The Hindu*, 25 December 2018.

The Untouchability (Offences) Amendment Act was amended and recast in 1976 as the Protection of Civil Rights Act. The Act made untouchability an offence. However, it suffered from so many loopholes that atrocities continued to mar the lives of the SCs. In 1977, fourteen Dalits were burnt alive in Belchi, and many more were killed in Pipra in Bihar in 1980.[50] Constitutional and legal provisions were found inadequate and the POA enacted in 1989 aimed to provide comprehensive protection for the Dalit community. The POA defines several aspects of caste practices as atrocities against the Dalits. The definition of atrocity ranges from the violence of everyday life to exceptional cases of mass violence, from routinized violence to extraordinarily dramatic enactments of brutality, and from residential segregation to ritualized humiliation.

The number of incidents against the Dalit community, however, continued to increase because the implementation of the POA has been as inadequate as the administration of earlier laws. It is generally believed that power wielded by the upper castes, the presence of a reluctant police force, and an even more indifferent prosecution accounts for the carelessness with which caste atrocities are received and dealt with by public authorities. In a large number of cases, the accused were acquitted because of their higher caste, technical lapses in the prosecution's case, negligent police investigations, and/or outright denial that the person who had brought the case to court had been insulted because of his or her caste. This flaw in the judicial system, which is meant to dispense justice to all without fear and favour, has promoted atrocities against Dalits. When human lives are lost, when people have been brutalized, when the upper castes flourish their physical power to put caste enemies in their place, the judiciary is obliged to restore human rights and penalize violators. We see the opposite happening in the case of caste violence in India.

More than seventy years after the adoption of the Constitution, a series of laws criminalizing the practice of untouchability, and prescribed affirmative action policies, we are still stuck with caste-based discrimination. Till today, what caste we belong to continues to influence social relations, codify inequalities, govern access to opportunities and

---

[50]Santosh Singh, 'A lasting signature on Bihar's most violent years', *Indian Express*, 4 June 2012.

privileges, and dictate how we will be treated.

The continuation of caste-based prejudices and consequent disrespect compromises democracy and violates justice. Respect is vital for human beings; it determines how they think of themselves and how they relate to others. The great German philosopher Georg Wilhelm Friedrich Hegel has told us that a good life is dependent on being held in regard by others. Human self-consciousness, he argued, depends on being recognized by others as someone who possesses worth. In recent years, political theorists have recovered the concept of recognition to argue precisely the same case.

The concept of recognition is located in the interface between the individual and the community. We achieve consciousness of ourselves as people who matter when others show us through their actions and their behaviour that we matter. Conversely, the potential for moral injury arises from disrespect. We realize that human beings are not autonomous of society; on the contrary, they are vulnerable because their self-respect is dependent on the approval or the disapproval of others.[51]

Theories of recognition help us understand that it may not be enough to grant individuals access to material resources through redistribution, it is equally important to respect them. For when an individual is subjected to disrespect in her daily dealings in the public or in the private sphere, or when she is subjected to humiliation, the consequences can be serious—the spectre of demoralized, diminished, and degraded beings on the one hand, and the eruption of struggles for respect through recognition on the other. One more right has been added to the list of rights that are essential for living a life that we recognize as human—the right to recognition that ensures respect and, therefore, dignity.

## CONCLUSION

We are forced to conclude that the link between affirmative action and respect has proved rather tenuous in India. Of course, the forging of such a link is not an easy matter. Politics can negotiate the distribution of resources. The matter requires vision, courage, and commitment and, as history has shown, it can be done. How does politics negotiate recognition? How does it lay down parameters of what human beings

---

[51] Axel Honneth, *The Struggle for Recognition: The Moral Grammar of Social Conflicts,* Joel Anderson (trans.), Cambridge: Polity, 1995, p. 131.

owe each other simply because each of us is human? Far too many troubling factors cast their dark shadow on this issue, factors that relate to the stereotyping of others as the polluting, the untouchable, the inferior, or indeed the 'enemy at the gates'. These stereotypes are not easily amenable to political negotiation or intervention. And for precisely this reason, recognition manages to dodge the project of affirmative action.

We recognize with troubled hearts and anxious minds that millions of Indian citizens who have been, for centuries, denied a basic opportunity to live a life of dignity because of circumstances outside their control continue to be subjected to prejudice, discrimination, indignities, and physical violence in democratic India even if they are granted the right to education, to representation, and to employment. This is a lack that has to be addressed and negotiated through meaningful action that concentrates on what we owe our fellow citizens. Laws are not enough; they can be implemented in a society which instils respect for fellow citizens. How this can be achieved is a different and a full debate. Here, it may be enough to realize that, among other things, what the state owes citizens, and what we owe our fellow citizens, is recognition.

Finally, how do we explain the persistence of caste-based violence in India? It has been argued that adherence to an unholy and reprehensible tradition that regards a community in perverse ways contributes majorly to discrimination. The government has institutionalized affirmative action and this has contributed immensely to resentment that a caste that had been marginalized in popular understanding has been able to acquire education, professional competence, and employment. Resentment has resulted in major violence. This resentment is clear in the Khairlanji massacre, in the Dharmapuri attack on Dalits, at attempts to water down protection for Dalits, and in the spectre of violent resistance to celebrations of alternative histories.

It is true that a number of ignoble motives underpin caste riots just like they underpin communal riots: attempts to grab remunerative land, the settling of personal scores etc. Running like a strong skein through these incidents is a dangerous story: that of struggle for power. Incidents of violence are not random or abstracted from deeper struggles over power in society by groups that feel that they have a divine right to rule. These incidents are signifiers of these struggles. The aim of caste riots is to redraw the normative map drafted by democracy and the Constitution—that of equality of political status irrespective of religion, caste, ethnicity, gender, and class. Caste violence seeks to restore a hoary older social order based on hierarchy and exclusion, domination and subordination, and dispense with the new democratic order that upholds as an organizing principle of the political community, the principles of non-discrimination and equality. Caste and communal violence throw onto the political horizon the one question that is crucial to democracy: what should the relative standing of persons in society irrespective of their religious beliefs or their caste be?

Looked at from another perspective, the constitutionalizing of political equality in India has actually succeeded in a perverse way. It has bred uncertainty and fear among social groups who believe that they and they alone have the right to dominate others by reasons of birth into a particular caste. Struggles in the arena of caste politics are struggles over which group should occupy what status in society. Violence in this case erupts over claims to universal rights to equality, freedom, and justice. Caste violence inscribes in fine and painful detail the way groups resist the institutionalization of a new and equitable political order. Today, groups that have been subjected to humiliation fight against this order. This is what democratic politics is about. Resistance needs to be furthered and consolidated but we must not devalue the political significance of acts that question shameful acts of governments and people. The history of Dalit oppression, subjection to violence, and consequent resistance is best summed by the Dalit poet Siddalingaiah, a professor of Kannada in Bangalore University, Karnataka. There was a time, he writes, that my people were those:

> Who die of starvation, who are kicked till they faint,
> Who cringe before others, reaching out to hands and feet
> Who keep their hands folded, devotees of those above them,
> These, these are my people.
> …
> Who, treated to fiery speeches, are scorched and burnt to ashes…

But now, he writes in the poem 'Thousands of Rivers', has come a time when his people came like a mountain:

They arrived in hordes
my men, yesterday!
Black faces bearded with silver
burning eyes red with rage
burst through the blankets of sleep
breaking the barriers of day
breaching the bounds of night...

...

They rose, my men in mountains
shouting the red song
Down, down inequality
Down Caste Hierarchy...

...

my people, have seized the throats of those cut-throats.[52]

Dr Ambedkar had insightfully remarked in 1946 that the problem of Dalits is not social in nature, it is completely unlike the problem of dowry, widow remarriage, and age of consent. The problem is that of securing to the community liberty and equality of opportunity at the 'hands of a hostile majority which believes in the denial of liberty and equal opportunity to the minority and conspires to enforce its policy on the minority. Viewed in this way the problem of the Untouchables is fundamentally a political problem.'[53] Violence, we may add, is equally a political problem.

---

[52]Siddalingaiah, 'My People' translated into English by K. Narasimha Murthy and 'Thousands of Rivers' translated by P. Rama Murthy in H. S. Sivaprakash and K. S. Radhakrishnan (eds.), *A String of Pearls*, Bangalore: Karnataka Sahitya Academy, 1990, reproduced in 'Two Poems of Siddalingaiah', available at <https://bavivekrai.wordpress.com>.

[53]B. R. Ambedkar, *What Congress and Gandhi have Done to the Untouchables*, Bombay: Thacker, 1946, p. 190.

## Chapter 4

# INDIA'S MANY INSURGENCIES: KASHMIR

*'Abruptly mounting her ramshackle wheel,/Fortune had pedalled furiously away;/The sobbing mess/is on our hands today.'*

—W. H. Auden[1]

## INTRODUCTION: KASHMIR, A DANGEROUS PLACE

The Valley of Kashmir that forms part of the erstwhile state of Jammu and Kashmir (J&K) is one of the most beautiful places in the world. It has also been called one of the most dangerous places in the world. Here, the armies of two neighbours, both nuclear powers, confront each other on highly inhospitable terrains and in daunting weather conditions. On the other side of the conflict, we see a formidable collection of Kashmiris who have taken up the gun against the Indian state in pursuit of self-determination, mercenaries who rush to conflict regions because it is here that they can garner a great deal of monetary profit, and agents of armament firms who sell destructive arms and munition to various militants. The Kashmir issue falls within the predictable category of low-intensity war. This form of war is not less ruinous than conventional war. Conventional wars come to an end after a time, political wars that involve (a) state as well as non-state actors and (b) pursuit of objectives that are not sanctioned by the constitution, such as secession, are unending.

They cease, perhaps, when those in power show some imagination, a great deal of courage, and, above all, generosity. They end when rulers exhibit a willingness to listen to and respect grievances, restore justice, and re-establish constitutional protection for the citizens of the region. In

---

[1] W. H. Auden, *The Collected Poetry of W. H. Auden,* New York: Random House, 1945, p. 3.

turn, this can only be done when draconian laws are lifted and the local elite show some determination that it will respect the fundamental rights of the people of the region once again. We will see in this chapter and the next one that unjust laws have contributed to the reproduction of militancy. We will see how the fundamental rights of citizens who have not picked up the gun are repeatedly, insistently, and brazenly violated both by the militants and the security forces. And we will see how governments also resort to violence to quell violence. Does violence from any quarter resolve the problem of political discontent? The jury is still out on the issue. On balance, however, violence only breeds violence, it can never resolve problems; it may even exacerbate them.

What has violence accomplished in the Valley of Kashmir? The Valley has been rocked by discontent ever since 1989. It has witnessed waves of protest that have ebbed, risen, and swamped society. And it has been under the control of armed forces since the time the state acceded to the Indian Union in 1947. At the precise point when we, who are condemned to be spectators of history, think the Kashmir issue has simmered down, another burst of anger and resentment sweeps the Valley and affects the rest of the country. Moreover, as India and Pakistan confront each other as potential opponents in a destructive war, anxiety rises. War clouds, time and again, dangerously hover over the region.

This became painfully apparent when on 14 February 2019, a convoy of the Central Reserve Paramilitary Forces (CRPF) was attacked by a lone vehicle in Pulwama in Kashmir. The driver, identified as a member of the dreaded Jaish-e-Mohammed—Adil Ahmed Dar—rammed his explosives-laden SUV into a bus. Forty CRPF personnel died in the attack.[2] On 26 February 2019, the Indian Air Force conducted an aerial strike at a site reportedly used for training terrorists in Balakot, which lies in Pakistan's Khyber Pakhtunkhwa province. The Pakistani air force, taken by surprise, carried out a counter-attack. In the aerial dogfight an Indian pilot was shot down. Tensions escalated. His safe return to India contributed much to the calming down of political anger.[3]

On 5 August 2019, the central government, in a series of rapid moves, imposed a complete lockdown on the former state of J&K, suspended civil liberties, closed down the internet and other means of

---

[2]'Pulwama Attack 2019', *The Hindu*.

[3]Prabash K. Dutta, 'What Balakot air strike achieved in one year', *India Today*, 26 February 2020.

communication, and put prominent political leaders and activists under house arrest. Thousands of troops occupied the state. After three months, detention of the entire political leadership that had fought elections and come to power—that had resisted separatism, that was considered as part of the mainstream of Indian politics, and that considered the Kashmir Valley to be an integral part of India—was extended indefinitely under the draconian Public Safety Act.[4] The BJP government at the centre altered the political status of J&K. Legislation was rushed through both houses of Parliament to approve the dilution of Article 370 that had granted special status to the state and secured regional autonomy, and rendered Article 35A, which prohibited 'outsiders' from acquiring land in the state, ineffective. More seriously, the state of J&K was abolished. The state was divided into two union territories, that of Ladakh and J&K. The people of J&K were not only deprived of their civil liberties, their state was obliterated. This was completely unprecedented in the history of J&K or indeed in the history of India. The consequences of this undemocratic and unconstitutional act are yet to be seen. But the future does not augur well. Since March 2020, prominent Kashmiri leaders have been released. The demand for the restoration of statehood for J&K and that of special status for the state is on the anvil. Where this demand will lead to is an open question, but nonetheless anxiety-ridden.

What has violence produced in the state? Perhaps violence reproduces nothing but violence, it can never lead to anything creative; it cannot even secure political compliance, let alone loyalty of the people. History shows us that political wars can only end through political negotiations, innovative thinking, and an ability to look into the near future; not by the imposition of intensely coercive laws and by expanding the reach and the immunities of security forces. In this chapter, we look at J&K, or simply the Kashmir Valley, to see how through a combustible mix of bad politics and policies, violence erupted in the Kashmir Valley and some parts of Jammu. All governments at the centre, irrespective of the political party they belong to, have contributed to the problem. In the process, fortune has pedalled speedily away.

In order to understand the various dimensions of the conflict and the tremendous violence it has unleashed, we need to understand the

---

[4]Rebecca Ratcliffe, 'Kashmir leaders placed under arrest amid security crackdown', *The Guardian*, 5 August 2019.

troubled history of Kashmir after 1947. We also need to understand, in all its complexity, the principle of self-determination which forms the anchor of much of political discontent. The principle has had a difficult history in international law. We need to study it because the impact of international principles upon domestic law and oppositional politics cannot be overestimated; it creates the framework within which the state acts to protect its territorial sovereignty. International principles such as self-determination and human rights also form the legitimizing plank of dissent and insurgency. Therefore, we begin with a short and concise history of the principle of national self-determination and move on to discuss the utter ruin of a region that was, and will hopefully continue to be, the most beautiful place on this earth.

## SEPARATISM AND THE PRINCIPLE OF SELF-DETERMINATION: A SHORT HISTORY

In 1945, members of the United Nations committed themselves to the sanctity of territorial borders. This makes sense when we remember that colonial powers had arbitrarily drawn administrative boundaries of colonies in Sub-Saharan Africa on a map of the subcontinent hanging on a wall in Berlin in 1885. In keeping with colonial ambitions, colonial boundaries were drawn instrumentally, with complete disregard for the fact that ethnic communities were divided by frontiers or that two ethnic communities that had been hostile to each other now came to coexist in the same state. The origins of much of the civil war that besets the continent of Sub-Saharan Africa go back to 1885 and the Berlin Conference.

Nevertheless, the UN, rather than open up the border issue to civil war adopted the principle of 'uti possidetis juris'—you shall possess as you possess. This was considered necessary because decolonization loomed large over the world. The principle was first conceived of by the newly independent countries of South America. Sub-Saharan Africa was one region where the break-up of states could have threatened not just the stability but the very existence of newly independent countries. Members of the Organization of African Unity, fearing this kind of eventuality, agreed at the Cairo meeting of the organization held in July 1964 that borders were binding.

These states thereby sanctioned the principle of 'uti possidetis juris'. Once a country acquired independence from the colonial power, territorial borders were not to be touched. The exception to the international consensus was of course India, which was split into two countries in 1947. But this was seen as the product of a political pact masterminded by the colonial power, Britain, and accepted by the two parties to the settlement. The formation of an independent state of Pakistan through the partition of territory and people fell outside the ambit of self-determination of colonial countries and people.

The second interesting turn in international politics after World War II followed logically the principle of 'uti possidetis juris'. The United Nations abandoned the principle of national self-determination. The principle was catapulted to the forefront of international attention by the defeat of gigantic multinational empires—the Ottoman, the Austro-Hungarian, and the Russian. In the wake of the collapse of these mammoth empires, the specific question that the international community was confronted with was the following: on what basis, or on what principle, could the future of the constituent units of the empire be decided? The principle that the American president Woodrow Wilson put forth, during the deliberations of the League of Nations, as a resolution to the problem was that of national self-determination. Simply put, wherever nations had been a part of a larger collective such as an empire, these entities had the right to independent statehood. The link between nations and self-determination, or specifically the right of a nation to a state of its own, appeared particularly strong at this phase of international history.

The principle was not a new one; it had emerged as a corollary of democratic revolutions in the late seventeenth and eighteenth centuries in Europe and in the United States. Self-determination was conceptualized, in these cases, as the right of the people living within a state to determine the form of their political community. By the middle of the nineteenth century, the principle took on another avatar. Ethno-national groups, or groups whose members were tied together by the principle of what Michael Ignatieff has called 'blood and belonging'[5] and who had been caught up in the political and the territorial grip of multinational empires, had begun to agitate for their own state. For instance, the Poles

---

[5]Michael Ignatieff, *Blood and Belonging: Journeys into the New Nationalism*, London: Vintage, 1994.

in the Russian and the Magyars in the Austro-Hungarian Empire had advanced claims to self-determination.

But even as ethnic nations in the Balkans began to fight for either independence or national aggrandizement, Russia crushed the Polish Rebellion in 1863, the Austro-Hungarian Ausgleich of 1867 was settled on dynastic grounds, and the British repressed the Irish Rebellion of 1916. Europeans had in any case colonized Africa in the nineteenth century even though the principle of national self-determination was doing the rounds in multinational empires. There was simply no consensus on whether nations had the right to determine their own form of state given the continuation of colonial rule. Nor was there any consensus on which nation had the right to self-determination, and why 'this' nation and not 'that' one had this right.

After the end of World War I, the principle of national self-determination provided to the victorious powers a convenient means for the redivision of Europe. However, the application of the principle proved arbitrary, contradictory, and self-serving. Whereas defeated territories in Eastern Europe, Balkans, and the Middle East were split up to create numerous new states, which national group was entitled to its own state, and which was not, was contingent on the political calculations of the great powers. Ironically, states that were created through the application of the principle of national self-determination did not possess homogenous nations. Yugoslavia and Czechoslovakia were multinational states, and Romania included a considerable number of minorities within its territory.

It is one of the supreme ironies of history that colonies, where freedom struggles had begun to construct nations out of a host of disparate people, were denied this right. This really meant that not all nations possessed the right of self-determination, only some did. Conversely, only those groups that were granted this right were considered to be nations, or so it was inferred. Other groups were denied both the status and the right. In the hands of the international community, the principle of self-determination proved amorphous, and it continues to be so till date. Ultimately, the ambiguous and troubled principle of national self-determination was not incorporated into the Covenant of the League of Nations.

This was in retrospect a politically sagacious move because, by the beginning of the twentieth century, the concept of the nation was split between what came to be known later as civic and as ethnonationalism. Wilson, who enthusiastically supported the principle, was simply not aware of these complexities in the concept of the nation, or of the knots in the filament that tied nations to self-determination, or properly states of their own. For Wilson, the concept of a self-determining people, as professor of politics Allen Lynch has noted, was rooted in the Anglo-American tradition of civic nationalism, or the right of communities to democratic self-government.[6] The idea that the right could also emanate from traditions of collective or ethnic nationalism or the belief that nations are collective agents that possess a distinct identity and shape the identities of their individual members was quite alien to Wilson. British writer Derek Heater argues that historical doctrines of democracy, sovereignty, and nationalism were in their own way replete with possibilities of diverse interpretations. But Wilson, by blending them together, announced 'like some frontier-town quack' that he had concocted a panacea for Europe's, if not the world's, ills.[7]

In short, Wilson's understanding of the concept of the nation, upon which the right of self-determination supervened, was partial and, therefore, flawed. It is not surprising that the moment he began to confront difficulties in implementing the principle that a nation should determine its own political community and state in Eastern and Central Europe, Wilson began to voice reservations about the concept. Ironically, he also began to question the legitimacy of the hyphen that connected the concept of the nation with that of self-determination.

Expectedly, the American president was, in a relatively short period of time, forced to acknowledge that 'in point of logic, of pure logic, this principle which was good in itself would lead to the complete independence of various small nationalities now forming part of various Empires. Pushed to its extreme, the principle would mean the disruption of existing governments, to an undefinable extent.'[8] He also did not seem to be cognizant of the problem of 'dispersed minorities', for example,

---

[6]'Woodrow Wilson and the Principle of National Self-determination; As Applied to Habsburg Europe', in Henry Huttenbach and Francesco Privitera (eds.), *Self-determination from Versailles to Dayton, Its Historical Legacy*, University of Bologna: Angelo Longo Editore, 1999, pp. 15–30.
[7]Derek Benjamin Heater, *Citizenship: The Civic Ideal in World History, Politics, and Education*, Manchester: Manchester University Press, 2004, p. 95.
[8]Lynch, *Self-determination*, p. 19.

that a large number of Germans lived in Bohemia. Later, he admitted as much. Heater chronicles Wilson's melancholy confession of his own ignorance about this issue, as well as of his discomfort that huge numbers of nationalities were coming to him, each demanding a state of their own.[9] In sum, Wilson's lack of knowledge of the kind of ethnonationalism and ethnic nations that had been consolidated in East Europe during the nineteenth century rendered his own support for the principle of national self-determination questionable.

At about the same time, Vladimir Lenin of the Soviet Union had begun to declare that the principle of national self-determination was both suitable and desirable for multinational states. But though the principle was included in the Soviet Constitution, Lenin's view of self-determination was as flawed as Wilson's understanding. He distinguished between secession as an instrument of class struggle against oppression and separation that leads to fragmentation instrumentally.[10] Nevertheless, the Soviet commitment to national self-determination sent shivers of disquiet along the liberal spine. If rival ideologies come to acclaim the same principle as politically significant, and if these ideologies manage to occupy quite the same political and conceptual space, something somewhere must have gone wrong. For these, as well as other reasons, the principle did not garner much support from the rest of the international community.

The victorious powers, however, employed this principle to split up numerous defeated territories in Eastern Europe, the Balkans, and the Middle East and create new states. Notably, who got their state and who did not was contingent on the political calculations of the great powers.[11] More significantly, though the right of self-determination was seen as a property of nations, the people who belonged to a nation were not consulted when the map of Europe was refashioned at the Paris Peace

---

[9]Heater, *Citizenship*, p. 96.

[10]This position is clearly spelt out by Lenin: 'the right of nations to self-determination implies exclusively the right to independence in the political sense, the right to free political separation from the oppressor nation... This demand, therefore, is not the equivalent of a demand for separation, fragmentation and the formation of small states.' Vladimir N. Lenin, *Questions of National Policy and Proletarian Internationalism,* Moscow: Foreign Languages Publishing House, undated, pp. 138–39.

[11]For instance, under the 1919 Treaty of Saint-Germain-en-Laye, Italy annexed German speaking South Tyrol, in clear breach of the principle of self-determination.

Conference. Except in a few frontier regions, neither a plebiscite nor a referendum was held to ascertain the wishes of the people. Simultaneously, the vast lands, possessions, and inhabitants of the German Empire were distributed among seven developed nations—Australia, Belgium, Britain, France, Japan, New Zealand, and South Africa. The birth of the principle of national self-determination as a precept of international law was, in other words, rooted in ambivalences and immersed in contradictions from day one. There was no clear interpretation of the principle to guide practice. This confusion continues to mark international practices related to self-determination in Kashmir till date.

However, by the time the moment of decolonization came around, the principle of *national* self-determination had been practically banished from the domain of international law. The end of World War II saw the emergence and constitution of a new global order oriented around the establishment of the United Nations. This period also witnessed large-scale decolonization of the colonized world. However, though the right of colonized people to independence via the principle of self-determination was recognized as the cornerstone of the new order, the identity of the unit upon which the right devolved was radically transformed. Now, the political unit that possessed the right of self-determination was an entity called the 'people', rather than the nation.

The main reason for dropping the hyphen between the nation and the right of self-determination was the rise of Nazism in Germany and the genocide of the Jewish community by Hitler's government. Considering that this crime against humanity had been carried out in pursuit of a pure Aryan nation and that of a monocultural state, the concept of nationalism, that of the nation and the right of the nation to a state of its own, created a great deal of disquiet in the international community. The principle of self-determination was, consequently, set aside. The Soviet Union, however, insisted on the inclusion of the right of self-determination at the 1945 San Francisco Conference, which met to decide the institutional configuration of the United Nations. Subsequently, the principle was incorporated into the Charter of the United Nations. But now, it was not the *nation* that had the right of self-determination; a political unit called the *people* had this right.

Article 1(2) of the Charter of the United Nations lists the 'self-determination of peoples' as a defining goal of the organization. Article

55 of the Charter further states that the UN shall promote goals such as higher standards of living, full employment, and human rights '[w]ith a view to the creation of conditions of stability and well-being which are necessary for peaceful and friendly relations among nations based on respect for the principle of equal rights and self-determination of peoples'. That is, whereas the UN accepted the right of self-determination as one of the objectives that member states were expected to aspire towards, the right now supervened upon the people who lived in a colonized territory. The territory was more important than the people who lived in it.

The distinguished jurist Sir Ivor Jennings had famously declared that the principle of self-determination that states 'let the people decide' was ridiculous. 'The people,' he remarked, 'cannot decide until somebody decides who are the people.'[12] In 1945, the UN firmly decided who the people who had the right to their own state were. The 'people' were all those persons who inhabited a territory that sought independence from a colonial power. It was this particular entity that had the right of self-determination. It followed that once a colony had acquired independence, no territorial unit within the country could demand a state of its own. The principle of self-determination was only permissible in the context of colonialism *provided* the colonized territory was separated from the metropole by a body of water.

The United Nations, in effect, committed that territorial borders were sacrosanct. The idea that 'people' rather than the 'nation' possessed the right of self-determination carried two major implications. One, the United Nations clearly privileged the liberal democratic notion of the 'people' as the locus of popular sovereignty and as the bearers of citizenship rights over ethnic nations and ethnonationalism. Two, since the 'people' were all those persons that inhabited the territory seeking independence from the colonial power, subnational groups *within* the territory did not have the right to their own state. In short, the United Nations proclaimed its intention of discouraging subnationalism. Once a country had attained freedom from colonial domination by virtue of the principle of self-determination, secession was not to be tolerated.

The only case of secession that was recognized by the United Nations

---

[12]Ivor Jennings, *The Approach to Self-Government,* Cambridge: Cambridge University Press, 1956, p. 56.

after 1945 was that of Bangladesh. But Bangladesh was not placed in the category of national self-determination within the colonial context. The new country was recognized by the United Nations three years after the country had seceded from Pakistan, and after Pakistan had recognized the new state. The independence of Bangladesh was considered a fait accompli. Earlier, the UN had refused to accord recognition to secessionist conflicts in two states in Sub-Saharan Africa: Katanga in the (Belgian) Congo and Biafra in Nigeria. The world body clearly stated that the attempt to violate the territorial integrity of Congo, which was a member state of the UN, was unacceptable.

The Security Council Resolution 169 of 24 November 1961 condemned the secessionist movement in Katanga. The same course of action was adopted in the case of Biafra. U. Thant, a former Secretary General of the UN, made the position of the world body clear when he stated on one occasion that '[s]o far as the question of secession of a... member state is concerned, the United Nations' attitude is unequivocal. As an international organization, the UN has never accepted and does not accept, *and I do not think it will ever accept the principle of secession* of a part of its member state.'[13]

## SELF-DETERMINATION, SEPARATISM, AND KASHMIR

This principle of self-determination took a rather hard knock in the period that followed the end of the Cold War that followed the collapse of the Berlin Wall in 1989. The breakdown of existing socialist societies inaugurated an era of hyper ethnonationalist and secessionist movements, especially in the region of the Balkans and the Caucasus. The consequences of the upsurge were somewhat serious. Countries dissolved, federal systems melted away, and several new states emerged out of the debris of old ones, often through processes of armed struggle, ethnic cleansing, and genocide. The scale as well as the pace at which existing states broke and new states were created was quite unprecedented in history. Scholars estimate that the membership of the United Nations was enlarged in the first phase from the late 1940s to the 1960s because of decolonization. After 1989, membership

---

[13]Cited in James M. Cooper, 'Therapeutic Jurisprudence and the Rights of Self-determination', in Burton M. Leiser and Tom D. Campbell (eds.) *Human Rights in Philosophy and Practice,* Dartmouth: Ashgate, 2001, p. 489. Italics in the original.

of the international body increased because of secession. Despite all reservations of the international community towards the principle of self-determination, it came to be attached to ethnic nationalism which upholds genocide.

Even as state-breaking and state-making exerted a profound domino effect across the world, a new lease of life was infused into hitherto dormant separatist movements. Among some examples are the insurrectionary movements of the Nagas and Bodos in India, the Chechens in Russia, separatist movements in Azerbaijan (Nagorno-Karabakh) and Moldova (Trans-Dniester), Balochistan in Pakistan, West Papua in Indonesia, the Oromos and the Somalis in Ethiopia, the Kurds in Turkey, Sudan, and till May 2009 the Tamils in Sri Lanka, and South Ossetia and Abkhazia in Georgia. Regional elites in Canada, the United Kingdom, and Europe, such as Quebec, Scotland, Catalonia, the Basque country, and Corsica, continue to demand independence, admittedly off and on. And the Kashmir Valley erupted in flames in 1989.

Before 1947, the year when India gained independence, the princely state of J&K was not part of British India. The political status of the state was, however, ambiguous, just like the other 565 princely states that accounted for about 45.3 per cent of the total land area of the country. Whereas these states were technically not part of British India, they were not entirely independent of British sovereignty either. Via the Doctrine of Paramountcy, the British Sovereign exercised suzerainty over the princes through a variety of treaties and political arrangements. The suzerainty of the British monarch over these princely states lapsed with the passing of the Indian Independence Act in July 1947, as did all treaties and agreements in force. Though in principle the rulers, some of whom controlled kingdoms barely larger than a substantial landholding, had the right to decide their own futures, the subtext was that they could not remain independent or retain their status as autonomous principalities *within* the territory of either India or the newly constituted state of Pakistan. The last British viceroy in India made it clear that the princely states did not have many options. They were left with one of two choices: join either India or Pakistan, logically the one that their state bordered geographically.

The territory of J&K, which borders India as well as Pakistan, is crucial for both countries. The former state of J&K, located in the northwest of India, borders Pakistan on the west, China on the north and east, and Indian Punjab and Himachal Pradesh in the south. The region consists of three geographical regions—the Kashmir Valley, Jammu, and Ladakh. The Valley is inhabited predominantly by Sunni Muslims, Jammu is dominated by Hindus, Kargil in Ladakh has a population of Shia Muslims, and Buddhists inhabit the subregion of Ladakh. The hub of conflict is the Vale of Kashmir and before August 2019, the geographical terminology indicating J&K was referred to simply as Kashmir. The case of Jammu and Kashmir, or more precisely the Kashmir Valley, has been discussed extensively by many authors; therefore, instead of repeating the long history of the origins of the conflict, let us sum it up as follows.

The region is strategically important for both countries because of its geopolitical location. Moreover, it contains invaluable resources, particularly river water. Above all, because it is a Muslim-majority region, the former J&K provided the touchstone for the two rival ideologies of the subcontinent in 1947. These ideologies were the Indian doctrine of secularism and accommodation of all religious groups, and the Pakistani claim that their country provided a homeland for the Muslims of the subcontinent. However, the monarch, Hari Singh, dreaming of perpetual sovereignty, refused to accede to either India or Pakistan in August 1947 despite all advice to the contrary. He signed a standstill agreement with Pakistan which guaranteed the non-interruption of trade, travel, and communication through Pakistani territory. The independence of the princely state was short-lived, however. It lasted precisely seventy-three days.

Pakistan was given the opportunity to intervene in the region on the proverbial platter when, in August 1947, parts of the erstwhile J&K, particularly the district of Poonch, rebelled under the leadership of demobilized soldiers against the misrule of the maharaja, oppressive taxation policies, and because of reports of massacres of Muslims in Hindu-dominated eastern Jammu districts during Partition. By 3 October, the rebels, who had acquired control over much of Poonch, along with the pro-Pakistani chieftains of Muzaffarabad and Mirpur in western Jammu district, proclaimed the formation of 'Azad Kashmir' in Pakistan. Shortly afterwards, Gilgit and neighbouring states, including Hunza and Nagar, signed Instruments of Accession with Pakistan on 18 November 1947. Matters worsened when, in October 1947, the Government of

Pakistan backed an armed incursion into the state by some several thousand Pashtun tribals from the North West Frontier Province. After taking the town of Muzaffarabad, the raiders headed for Baramulla and moved on towards Srinagar, inflicting terrible atrocities on the population and killing almost 3,000 of the 14,000 population of Baramulla.[14]

According to all reports, the attack, which was meticulously planned and executed, could not have taken place without the backing of the Government of Pakistan. Hari Singh requested the Indian government for military aid. The Government of India promised military aid on the condition that the state of J&K accede to India *before* troops were sent there. The monarch signed the Instrument of Accession on 26 October 1947. The instrument was accorded legality when it was accepted by Lord Mountbatten, the Governor General of India. Indian troops were airlifted to the besieged territory.

But precisely at this point of the narrative occurs a twist in the tale, a twist that haunts politics in Kashmir till today. In the letter that accompanied the acceptance of the Instrument of Accession, Lord Mountbatten stipulated that *after* the invader was expelled from the territory, and *after* law and order had been restored, the question of the state's accession should be settled by reference to the people, or through a plebiscite. This was consistent, stated Mountbatten, with the policy adopted in the rest of the princely states.

However, the right moment for the promised plebiscite never came for a number of reasons, notably the internationalization of the issue. The Security Council of the United Nations resolved (Resolution 47) that a plebiscite would be held after Pakistani and Indian troops withdrew. The withdrawal never happened; therefore, the plebiscite could not be held. And it cannot be held today because not only has the Valley been

---

[14]Though Pakistan claimed that the government had no role to play in the invasion, substantial evidence proves otherwise. For example, according to Alan Campbell-Johnson, press attaché of Mountbatten, Jinnah (at a meeting of the Joint Defence Council in November 1947 in Lahore) told Mountbatten that the accession of J&K to India was not bona fide because it rested on fraud and violence. Johnson reports that Mountbatten agreed that the accession had indeed been brought about by violence. But, the violence, added Mountbatten, came from the tribes for whom Pakistan, and not India, was responsible. Jinnah proposed that both sides should withdraw at once and simultaneously. 'When Mountbatten asked him to explain how the tribesmen could be induced to remove themselves, his reply was "if you do this, I will call the whole thing off".' Alan Campbell-Johnson, *Mission with Mountbatten,* London: Robert Hale Ltd., 1952, p. 229.

militarized to an alarming extent, third parties have stepped in to garner benefits from the simmering conflict and war.

On 1 January 1949, the first Indo-Pak war ended and the two countries signed a ceasefire agreement. Subsequently, the very framework of the J&K problem was radically transformed because the July 1949 Karachi Agreement formalized the de facto division of the former state of J&K between India and Pakistan. The ceasefire line stopped at the Siachen Glacier (at map coordinate Point NJ9842), and both troops withdrew behind the ceasefire line. India retained less than half of undivided J&K—that is, a major part of Jammu, Ladakh, and the Kashmir Valley. One-third of the region which consists of a sliver of territory extending from the north to the south of western Jammu district, comprising the Punjabi-speaking districts of Poonch, Mirpur and Muzaffarabad, Hunza, Chilas, Gilgit, and Baltistan is under the control of Pakistan. Pakistan also controls Skardu in Ladakh. The division legitimized the ground position of troops of both the countries. Aksai Chin, occupying 16.9 per cent of the area of the state and with almost no population, came under the control of China during the 1950s. In 1963, Pakistan ceded to China another 2.33 per cent of the land claimed by India. The former state of J&K was therefore divided between three countries.[15]

The government of J&K was not only granted complete jurisdiction over other areas of policymaking, but also given the right to have its own flag, elect its own constituent assembly, and adopt its own constitution. Further, the provisions of the Indian Constitution could be applied to the state only with the concurrence of the state government. In 1952, the relationship between the central government and the government of J&K was finalized. The talks resulted in an unwritten understanding known as the Delhi Agreement that maintained the status quo on J&K's constitutional position. It was this special provision that granted the state regional autonomy that was eroded by the central government in August 2019.

A violent movement in pursuit of the cause of self-determination arose in the Valley and in two districts of the Jammu region, some forty-three years *after* the default of this particular obligation by the Indian state. The original uprising in the Valley in 1990 was, within a space of

---

[15]Since we are speaking of the period before the state of Jammu and Kashmir was divided into two union territories in August 2019, the term J&K is used.

about three years, practically hijacked by mercenaries coming into the Valley from outside, particularly from Pakistan and Afghanistan. These mercenaries proceeded to fight for a cause that, arguably, had little to do with the original grievances of the Kashmiri people. By the early years of the 1990s, the Kashmiri-led movement had been hijacked by an extremist group—the Jammu and Kashmir Hizbul Mujahideen (HM)—that had been assiduously built up by the Government of Pakistan. In contrast to the objectives of the Jammu and Kashmir Liberation Front (JKLF) that led the original movement in 1989 of uniting the two parts of J&K and establishing a sovereign state, the HM was a fundamentalist organization that wanted to integrate the region into Pakistan.[16]

By the end of the 1990s the HM was sidelined by even more extremist groups—the Lashkar-e-Taiba and Jaish-e-Mohammed. As Islamist organizations in the Valley harnessed extremist political passions to their own objectives of establishing an Islamic state, extreme violence was inflicted not only on government organizations but also on the innocent people living in the region. From the objective of securing justice for the people through restoration of civil liberties and lifting of coercive laws, militant groups moved to an intolerant ideology based on violence towards all. It is difficult to figure out what a majority of the people of the Valley want: do they want fuller democracy? Is theocracy an option? How is the opinion of the people of Kashmir different from those who purport to speak for them? The cause that armed militants espousing a hard-line Islam fight for has little to do with the waylaying of democracy and the return to the constitutional promises the Indian state made to the people of the region.

## THE ROAD TO VIOLENCE

Discontent has escalated over the years because all political parties who have ruled India from the centre have contributed to the whittling away of the constitutional status of the region. All governments, irrespective of the political party they belong to, have diluted the special status of the former state. Article 370 remained on paper; in practice, it has been subjected to constant modification. The Supreme Court in 1984 ruled in *Khazan Chand and Others vs the State of Jammu and Kashmir* that J&K

---

[16]Sumantra Bose, *Contested Homelands: Israel-Palestine, Kashmir, Bosnia, Cyprus and Sri Lanka*, New Delhi: HarperCollins and India Today Group, 2007, pp. 175–81.

occupied a special position in the constitutional set-up of the country and that Article 370 forms the basis for a constitutional relationship between the Indian union and the state. In July 1952, Nehru signed an agreement with Sheikh Abdullah, the prime minister of the state. The union flag, it was decided, would occupy a prominent place in the state, along with the flag of the state. The fundamental rights of the Indian Constitution were made applicable to the state and the jurisdiction of the Supreme Court now extended to fundamental rights, as well as to disputes between the centre and the state.[17]

In the period that followed, the power of the central government over the state was expanded beyond the limits defined in the Delhi Agreement. The infringement of the Constitution and of the political pact was rapidly compounded by infringements of the federal pact. 'The developments of 1954', writes Bose, 'were the beginning of the end for Article 370, which has effectively been dead in letter and in spirit since that time. Strangely, the autonomy clause formally remains in India's constitution.'[18]

In the 1980s, the regional party, the National Conference, partnered with the national party, the Indian National Congress, in a series of compromises. In the 1987 elections, the voter turnout was as high as 75 per cent, but the elections themselves were marked by coercion, electoral malpractices of a high order, and massive rigging.[19] To compound the problem, the political space was practically closed off to new political agents, or to political agents that did not belong to either the ruling regional party or to the central party, which in tandem had succeeded in monopolizing political power. The election proved to be *the* major catalyst for the eruption of discontent. By the turn of the 1990s, resentment at the manipulation of electoral democracy and erosion of the special status of the region broke out in a series of violent demonstrations.

Between 1989 and 1993, the Valley of Kashmir witnessed a series of violent protests that brought normal life to a standstill. The scale and the intensity of protests involving bomb explosions in the capital city of the

---

[17]For an account of these negotiations in the period and thereafter see Sumit Ganguly, *Conflict Unending: India-Pakistan Tensions since 1947,* New York: Columbia University Press, 2001, pp. 23–28.

[18]Sumantra Bose, *Kashmir: Roots of Conflict, Paths to Peace,* New Delhi:Vistaar, 2005, p. 69.

[19]Ibid., p. 49.

Kashmir valley, Srinagar—closures, strikes, arson, attacks on government offices, bridges, and buses, and murders of government officers—took everyone by surprise. It seemed to have even astonished the political organization—the JKLF—which had initiated and spurred the popular unrest in the Valley. On 21 February 1990, half a million Kashmiris marched from Srinagar and other parts of the Valley to the holy shrine of Charar-e-Sharief.[20] 'They travelled in carts, wagons, and motorcycles and even on foot, through sleet and freezing rain, chanting slogans and poems calling for freedom.'[21] On 1 March 1990, a crowd of more than one million from every part of the Valley, many wrapped in shrouds, gathered at the headquarters of the UN Military Observers Group in Srinagar. 'Impassioned speeches were made; memoranda addressed to the UN Secretary-general demanded that he urge India to concede to Kashmiri's their inherent right of self-determination.'[22]

## A SHORT HISTORY OF VIOLENCE

The consequences could have been foretold. Since 1989, an entire generation has grown up in the shadow of the gun wielded by both sides of the conflict in Kashmir, state coercion, draconian laws, encounter deaths and forced disappearances, militancy, and terrorism as well as the rhetoric of religious war.[23] Though the citizens of J&K had been given the assurance that they would be able to determine their own future, it is only in the Muslim-dominated Valley that the demand for the right of self-determination arose in violent forms at the turn of the 1990s, in 2000, 2010, and 2016. J&K has a plural society, and *no* group apart from the Muslim separatists in the Valley has articulated a desire to separate from India.[24] On the contrary, Buddhist organizations in Ladakh and

---

[20]The shrine of Charar-e-Sharief, which is located in the south of Kashmir, is dedicated to the fourteenth-century Sufi saint Sheikh Nooruddin Wali, known to Hindus as Nand Rishi. The shrine represents the finest confluence of two traditions in the valley, the Hindu Saivite tradition and Islam, that had merged into Sufism.

[21]Wajahat Habibullah, *My Kashmir: Conflict and the Prospects of Enduring Peace*, Washington, D.C.: United States Institute of Peace, 2008, p. 74.

[22]Ibid.

[23]Inpreet Kaur, 'Warring Over Peace in Kashmir', in Waheguru Pal Singh Sidhu, Bushra Asif, and Cyrus Samii (eds.), *Kashmir: New Voices, New Approaches*, Boulder: Lynne Reinner, 2006, pp. 13–32.

[24]Victoria Schofield, *Kashmir in Conflict: India, Pakistan and the Unending War*, New Delhi: Viva, 2004, p. xiii.

Hindu organizations in Jammu have demanded fuller integration into India. Some of these organizations have also demanded that the special status of J&K should be abolished. Jammu has, not unexpectedly, become the centre of hardcore politics of the religious right.

In the democracy that they are a part of, the people of J&K have, except for a decade when militancy was at its height, exercised the right to vote in local, state, and central elections. And they have done so even when the state has been subjected to a lockdown. But just because people vote, it does not mean that the problem has been solved. Violence on the streets can go hand in hand with electoral politics. The people of the Kashmir Valley have been buffeted by violence from all sides;. The experience of living in a region amidst violence has been movingly narrated by Basharat Peer in his *Curfewed Night* and Mirza Waheed in his *The Collaborator*. A powerful literary culture, mainly in English, has been nurtured by memories of loss, as in Sudha Koul's *The Tiger Ladies*.[25]

In a land where people have been dispossessed in many ways by the loss of their common inheritance, shared memories, and social interaction, poets and writers express their angst and horror at what violence has done to their homeland and their people in song and verse. Agha Shahid Ali, the voice of the Kashmir Valley, powerfully wrote of 'Summer 1992—when for two years Death had turned everyday in Kashmir into some family's Karbala.'[26] Most families were to experience little but death and destruction from 1990 onwards.

The creativity of poets and authors is not limited by facts or interpretations of facts. Creative artists articulate sentiments of nostalgia, of liberation and freedom, longing and loss, fear and resistance, dread that they will be penalized for resisting, and aspirations and dreams of happier times that may be around the corner. There is in conflict regions a big question mark that hangs darkly over the future. The poet articulates despair, she speaks of grief, she verbalizes terror, she puts into words deep longing for freedom, and her poetry embodies

---

[25]Bahsharat Peer, *Curfewed Nights*, New Delhi: Random House, 2010; Mirza Waheed, *The Collaborators*, New Delhi: Penguin Books India; and Sudha Koul, *The Tiger Ladies*, Boston: Beacon Press, 2002.

[26]Basharat Shameem, 'English Writing in Kashmir: A Literary Culture's Rise from Conflict', *NewsClick*, 27 March 2019.

reveries. Her dreams are a response to empirical developments, but she does not reduce violence to empirical evidence. For her, violence is not a statistic: so many people died, so many people survived at great cost. To the poet, violence is trauma, memories of which resist banishment. These agonized memories continue to inhabit the shadowy realm of the mind, dominate and submerge consciousness of the present, and evoke fear of what is to come.

But violence also evokes protest. Much of the poetry that comes to us from conflict zones is protest poetry. This enriches our understanding of what violence is. But it still does not allow us to grasp the full extent of what the Kashmir problem is and what it means for the people of the Valley. As for the rest of India, the inordinate emphasis on nationalism and enmity with Pakistan by our rulers has ensured that Indians are immediately and unreflectively enraged by the mere mention of azadi. We line up behind our ruling classes, we demonize Kashmir and Kashmiris, and this blinds us to the realities of the situation: promises that were not kept and the disproportionate violent response to protest demonstrations.

Therefore, our fellow Indians experience anxiety and panic at the very mention of resistance in the Valley. We seem to possess a strong sense of ownership over that region of India. The rights of the inhabitants of that piece of land do not find a place in our fevered brains. We are indifferent to the violations of human rights in Kashmir. We are, after all, 'nationalists' committed to the integrity of national sovereignty! Nationalism has proved a progressive force in the fight for independence, but in post-independent India, nationalism has gone a long way to preserving unequal power relations. It has become a drug that truncates autonomy of the will. For these and other reasons, the full dimensions of violence in Kashmir have, since 1989 if not earlier, defied understanding. Part of the problem is that we are unable to understand the reasons for violence. The intricate combination of circumstances that generated violence in the Valley is so complex and so tortuous that it would be rash and foolish to see the violence as the outcome of a one-point causal relationship between factor X and outcome Y. In any case, the Kashmir problem cannot be interpreted as only one of insurgency, or of militants fighting the Indian state for secession, or Pakistan's desire to extract revenge for 1971 and the independence of Bangladesh. Violence is rooted in a complex of causes.

Whatever is the precise mix of reasons that has led to disquiet and conflict in the Valley since 1990, the Kashmir problem has led to four destructive wars between India and Pakistan—in 1947, 1965, 1971, and 1999—and propelled acerbic battles in the United Nations between the two countries. It has posed a problem that besets peaceful relations between the two countries and it is a potential trigger for a nightmarish war between two nuclear powers. Most commentators see Pakistani ambitions to complete the Partition by taking over Kashmir as the only cause of the conflict, when the cause as well as the process defies any simplistic understanding. It is indisputable that Pakistan is involved in fomenting discontent in the region, but it simply could not have done so unless the people were frustrated by their situation in the past and present. We explore that aspect later in this chapter.

Thousands of armed forces comprising the Indian Army, the CRPF, and the Border Security Force, along with the J&K police, are stationed in the region. The conflict has escalated repeatedly, now it is sought to be contained by the demotion of the state into two union territories. Will this quell resistance?

## THE COURSE OF VIOLENCE

Despite the insistent and the massive erosion of the special status of J&K, right up till the late 1980s, few political analysts could predict that the Valley would be overwhelmed by religious fundamentalism and violence. The malpractices that marked the 1987 election to the state assembly provided the proverbial trigger for the outbreak of insurgency. Between 1989 and 1993, the Valley of Kashmir erupted in a series of violent protests that suspended normal life.

For more than four years, protestors on the streets of Srinagar and other cities of the Valley placed one claim firmly onto the agenda—azadi. There is no definite meaning that can be imparted to azadi; as many researchers have shown, the term can be interpreted as the right to self-determination vide regional autonomy within a federal system, or independence through secession. Despite the ambiguity that surrounds the term, it has become the anchor for the struggle in Kashmir since 1990. If the organization leading the struggle, the JKLF, was taken aback at the scale and intensity of anger against the Government of

India, the Indian political establishment had underestimated the depth of resentment in the Valley.

Even as significant political groups were barred from the electoral arena, they turned to other means, particularly to the gun, and to other political agents, particularly to Pakistan. Pakistan had not managed to infiltrate the region or influence the people since 1947. Now, it took advantage of the situation and began to encourage, fund, and train militants and militancy. The objectives of the JKLF that led the protests for azadi were not in sync with the objectives of the Pakistani government—that of annexing Kashmir.[27] The JKLF accepted this as one of the costs of collaboration till the time the leaders found that Kashmiri militants were outnumbered by foreign mercenaries, and that the political ambitions of Islamists replaced the demand for self-determination.

Within the space of a few years the JKLF was replaced by rabid militant organizations wedded to jihad, and the establishment of an Islamic state. The Pakistani government ceased to support the JKLF and transferred support to the fanatical HM, which was ready to follow the orders of the Pakistani government, and particularly of its military intelligence wing, the notorious ISI (Inter-Services Intelligence). Over time, the Pakistani government began to support extremist militant groups such as Lashkar-e-Taiba and Jaish-e-Mohammed, which have been involved in terrorist acts against India, and blacklisted as terrorist organizations by the United Nations in 2002 and 2019 respectively. Pakistan continues to provide sanctuary to a number of terror-dispensing organizations.[28]

Under the influence of Pakistan's ideological onslaught, young Kashmiris left the Valley for training across the border. They left as citizens of India, they came back as implacable foes of the country. Along with them came veterans of the Afghanistan war. In combination, disillusioned Kashmiri youths and foreign militants carried out attacks on civilians and civilian installations. The original demand for azadi took a back seat and jihad took over. The soft Sufi Islam of Kashmir was replaced by a hard and zealous Wahhabi Islam.

---

[27]'Huge Recovery of arms and ammunition in J and K proof of Pakistan's sponsored terrorism', *Zee News*, 16 October 2020.

[28]Bose, *Kashmir*, pp. 142-147.

## THE EXODUS AND THE PEOPLE LEFT BEHIND

A serious fallout of the armed violence was the forced exodus of Kashmiri Pandits from the Valley, which is their home. Major episodes of violence against Kashmiri Pandits by armed groups, fevered slogans of azadi, Islamic declarations painted on the walls of public buildings, and the sheer din created by the banging of utensils inspired fright, dread, and anxiety. Members of the community were murdered in cold blood. Commercial and residential properties were attacked and appropriated. This forced hundreds and thousands of the community to flee Kashmir and seek refuge in the camps of Jammu.

The journalist David Devadas describes the events that led to the exodus. According to him, a crowd led by the brother of one of the leaders of the insurgency, Shabbir Shah, met the Special Commissioner Wajahat Habibullah and the Deputy Inspector General of Police in charge of South Kashmir, Veeranna Aivalli. The delegation requested that the government should do all it could to prevent Pandits from leaving Kashmir. Moderate Muslim leaders personally visited Hindu neighbourhoods to persuade members of the community to stay. But incidents of incredible violence had created an atmosphere of fear and trepidation. Anxiety accelerated as people discovered the dead bodies of several Pandits in the fields. They had been tortured before being brutally killed.[29]

Thousands of Kashmiri Pandits live outside the Valley. They or their parents had left in 1989–90 because of rising militancy. The forced exodus of a people for whom the Valley was their homeland was nothing short of tragic. They had to live out their lives in dark and desolate camps in Jammu and other parts of India. Kashmiri Pandits became refugees in their own country, exiles from their own homeland. Their children grew up in ill-equipped camps. Forced migration shaped a generation of bitter and disillusioned Kashmiri Pandits, living amidst deprivation with only hazy memories of their beautiful ancestral land. The militants did not only kill or force the exile of Hindus. They did the same to moderate Muslims. The exodus changed the demographic and political profile of the Valley. The abnormal politics of violent confrontation took over the normal project of living together, of participation and

---

[29]David Devadas, *The Story of Kashmir: Geopolitics, Politics, Society, Culture, and Changing Aspirations,* New Delhi: David Devadas, 2019, pp. 284–87.

representation, negotiation and compromise, dialogue and contestation.

Till today, the demand for an investigation into the conditions in which the Pandits had to leave has not been met. In 2017, a Kashmiri Pandit group, Roots in Kashmir, petitioned the Supreme Court for investigations of the exodus of their community from the Valley and sought to reopen 215 cases in which 700 Pandits had been killed in 1989–90. The court dismissed the petition on the ground that twenty-seven years had passed since the episode, and it is difficult to find evidence.[30] Later that year, the court rejected a petition from the same organization stating that the July court order should be revisited. This has proved short-sighted because it is widely felt by the exiled Hindu community that its case has not been sympathetically viewed by other Indians, and that the government has not delivered justice. Resentment and anger have created a bitter and angry class of young Kashmiri Pandits, as suggested above.[31]

Ironically, the Valley they had to leave behind did not find peace even after 'ethnic cleansing'. In the summer of 2010, protests once again swept the Valley. It was termed the most severe form of unrest since the early 1990s, marked as it was by a new form of protest—stone pelting.[32] The uprising burst onto the streets to protest random killings of civilians. The protest brought the elderly, women, and teenagers onto the streets. Stones were pelted at security forces, and young men and some women were involved in hand-to-hand combat with armed police and paramilitary forces. These wide-ranging protests were not initiated or led by the separatist leaders, they were unorganized and spontaneous. Leaders of protest movements and separatists had been able to initiate and control demonstrations. It became apparent that a new generation was not willing to accept this leadership. The problem is that a leaderless protest movement cannot be controlled. This is troublesome because such movements can go in any direction.

Demonstrations, stone pelting, curfews, blockades, and attacks on public buildings including hospitals and medical care centres impacted

---

[30]Anusha Soni, 'Supreme Court rejects PIL seeking probe into killing, exodus of Kashmiri Pandits', *India Today*, 24 July 2017.

[31]Ashutosh Bharadwaj, 'Kashmiri Pandit's Return to Valley is a Must for "idea of India". But here are the obstacles', *The Print*, 23 January 2020; Anmol Tikoo, 'What About the Kashmiri Pandits?—Twenty Years Later, Make the Question Count', *The Wire*, 22 January 2020.

[32]'Kashmir's summer of discontent is now an autumn of war', *BBC*, 21 September 2010.

daily lives. People could not travel to their place of work, shops were closed, public services were suspended, and a miasma of gloom descended once again on the Valley. Mothers lost their sons, young people disappeared, others were injured and killed in attacks mounted by the security forces as well as the militants. Young people no longer had access to educational institutions and employment, and their careers suffered a hard knock.

The next seismic protest took place in 2016. On 8 July 2016, Burhan Wani, a twenty-two-year-old leader of a group of HM, was shot dead by the security forces during an armed clash in Bumdoora village in Kokernag district of J&K. The killing set off large-scale and intense protests by Kashmiri citizens in the Valley, and in some districts of Jammu. After 2010, discontent seemed to have ebbed. It broke out six years later in a renewed form. This time, the movement involved large numbers of middle-class educated youth, women, and children. For the first time, women came out in large numbers to join the protest.[33]

It has been reported that in response to the demonstrations that started in July 2016, Indian security forces used excessive force that led to unlawful killings and a high number of injuries. Civil society groups estimate that between 90 to 105 people were killed during the unrest between July and December 2016.[34] Crowds used stones against the security forces. The latter curbed demonstrations using disproportionate force.[35]

The CRPF used a 12-gauge pump-action shotgun that fires metal pellets resembling ball bearings to attack stone pelters. The shotguns contain 500 to 600 pellets made of lead alloy. They are fired at high velocity that disperses metal pellets over large areas. Experts conclude that the trajectory of these shotguns cannot be controlled, and shooting

---

[33]Office of the United Nations High Commissioner for Human Rights, *Report on the Situation of Human Rights in Kashmir; Developments in the Indian State of Jammu and Kashmir from June 2016 to April 2018 and General Human Rights Concerns in Azad Jammu and Kashmir and Gilgit-Baltistan,* 14 June 2018, p. 6. The 2018 report relied on information available in the public domain through the Right to Information Act, findings of research and monitoring carried out by local, national and international non-governmental organizations, and human rights defenders, and documents and statements such as Parliament Questions, court orders, and police reports as reported in the Press Trust of India.

[34]Ibid., p. 17.

[35]Ibid.

becomes random and arbitrary.[36]According to a United Nations Human Rights Commission Report of June 2018, the use of pellet guns resulted in multiple deaths and bodily harm to hundreds of civilians. Civil society organizations tell us that a large number of Kashmiris have lost their vision because of being injured by pellet guns. But security forces continue to use them, even though their use has caused numerous disasters.[37] The post-mortem of one young man showed that a pellet cartridge shot at close range had penetrated and burst in his abdomen, leaving 300 metal fragments in his body.[38] According to human rights groups and medical professionals in Kashmir, apart from physical injuries, many victims of pellet guns face serious mental health issues.[39]

No case of the use of disproportionate violence has been brought to the court. These deaths and injuries are a gross violation of the basic rights of citizens under the provisions of international law. The state must investigate and prosecute infringements of basic rights. Human rights jurisprudence expects the state to conduct swift, thorough, and non-partisan investigations of such violations. It is expected to provide the victims immediate relief and reparations. A growing body of jurisprudence in international law and human rights focuses on the obligations that states have towards their citizens whose basic rights have been trampled upon for reasons that cannot be justified. This bore grim repercussions.

The story of Zuhaib Maqbool, a thirty-two-year-old photojournalist, is particularly harrowing. While he was covering a protest in Srinagar's Rainawari area on 4 September 2016, hot metal balls pierced his left eye and his upper body. From that moment his life changed irrevocably. After that moment he could neither face sunlight nor artificial light. Zuhaib has been condemned, for no fault of his own, to live the rest of his life behind shades. He has undergone six surgeries to reclaim his sight but this has not helped.[40]

Another story dwelt on the findings of a study titled 'Psychiatric Morbidity in Pellet Injury Victims of the Kashmir Valley'. This was

---

[36]Ibid., p. 22.

[37]Ibid., p. 23.

[38]'SC orders CBI to probe into Manipur extra-judicial killings', *The Hindu*, 14 July 2017.

[39]Office of the United Nations High Commissioner for Human Rights, *Report on the Situation of Human Rights in Kashmir*, p. 23.

[40]'The forgotten story: News photographer struggles to save his eyes and his life', *The Citizen*, 4 December 2016.

conducted by the Department of Psychiatry of the Government Medical College, Srinagar. The research team studied hundreds of pellet victims. These victims continue to live with anxiety and depression. According to a 2016 survey by the Geneva-based Médecins Sans Frontières, nearly 1.8 million adults in the Valley experience symptoms of mental distress: 41 per cent exhibit depression, 26 per cent anxiety, and 19 per cent suffer from post-traumatic stress disorder. The study was based on a survey of 380 pellet and pellet-plus-firearm injury patients. The number of victims of the pellet gun (which was introduced in 2010) ranges from 10,000 to 20,000, with many unable to tolerate light. They are forced to live indoors in the shade. Compared to the rest of India, the number of people affected by depression in the Valley is much higher. Psychiatrists fear that depression will affect the next generation as well.[41]

The Valley of Kashmir has seen five waves of unrest: 1989, 2008, 2010, 2016, and 2018. Security forces have confronted hostile populations and often lose their lives in the process. More troublingly, unlike the first protest in 1989 over botched elections and denial of democracy and rights, subsequent waves of discontent have been leaderless and often hijacked by 'new Islamists'. The initial agenda of restoring democracy and rights to the Kashmiris has been submerged in the vocabulary of jihad and dreams of establishing an Islamic state. The new jihadists fight a war in the name of religious fundamentalism, and they are reportedly backed by a myriad of sources in terms of funding, training, and personnel.

In the process, the goals of a people who became restless by coercive laws and mounting violence have shifted from self-determination to, in some circles, the establishment of an Islamic state. Society has become so fragile and precarious that discontent can erupt into violence in an instant. The use of the gun did not quell violence. It brought more Kashmiris out into the streets. Crowds tried to beat back cordons of policemen clad in steel armour. It became common and disturbing to see children who were around ten or eleven coming into the streets, protesting and proclaiming their readiness for martyrdom.

The involvement of young and educated Kashmiris in militancy is

---

[41]Peerzada Ashiq, 'In Kashmir Valley, hundreds of pellet victims face a hazy future', *The Hindu*, 2 June 2019.

cause for alarm. No longer can we attribute violence only to agents from outside the country. On 3 June 2019, *The Hindu* carried a front-page story. Nearly 75 per cent of militants killed in 2019 in the valley were locals. The J&K governor, Satya Pal Malik, reportedly stated that whereas the objective of the security forces was to kill Pakistan-trained terrorists, a large number of locals have been killed because they had joined the ranks of terrorists. Since the beginning of 2019, 101 terrorists have been killed, of which 76 were locals. This is the first time in two decades that more locals died at the hands of the security forces than foreign terrorists. In 2018, of the 246 terrorists killed in encounters, 60 per cent belonged to the Valley.[42]

In sum, a combination of corruption, misgovernance, electoral mismanagement, closing off of the political space to new political agents, and violations both of the Constitution and of the political pact by the Government of India paved the way for the slide into political violence. Initially, the JKLF led the violent uprising in 1990. But Kashmiri organizations lost control over the insurgency in a short span of time, and militants from outside the country practically hijacked the revolt. The entry of third parties into the region was inevitable, given the history of India-Pakistan tensions over Kashmir since 1947. Yet, Pakistan did not succeed in its endeavours till 1989, when citizens of the Valley lost all trust in the political system. Observers suggest that though Pakistan had been trying to destabilize the region for long, its efforts bore fruit only in 1989 because by that time frustration in the Valley had coalesced into deep grievances.[43]

Generalized dissatisfaction, the repression that was launched by the Indian state on the protestors, and the outbreak of violence opened the doors to foreign mercenaries mainly from Pakistan, and increasingly Afghanistan, to enter the Valley, hijack the struggle, and subordinate it to their own ends, notably jihad. How many people of the Valley back them is a question that permits of no ready answers. The situation is troubling.

---

[42]Vijaita Singh, '75% of militants killed in Kashmir Valley were locals', *The Hindu*, 3 June 2019.

[43]Neera Chandhoke, *Contested Secessions: Rights, Self-Determination, Democracy, and Kashmir,* New Delhi, Oxford University Press, 2012, p. 17.

## COERCION AS VIOLENCE

'My gaze,' writes the Kashmiri poet Zarif Ahmad 'Zarif', 'has been silenced, what frenzy is this?'[44] The gaze is silenced not only by the gun but by deterrents such as the draconian Armed Forces (Special Powers) Act (AFSPA), which was also imposed on parts of the Northeast in 1958, as we shall see in the next chapter. A separate version of the Act was introduced in 1990 for Kashmir because of the special status of the Valley vide the now defunct Article 370. The AFSPA grants broad and sweeping powers to the security forces and protects them from accountability. Section 4 of the Act allows any personnel operating under the law to use lethal force for self-defence and against any person who is seen as breaking the law or orders that prohibit the assembly of more than five persons. The security forces are granted virtual immunity from prosecution in civilian courts for their conduct.[45] Any attempt to prosecute members of the armed forces has to get the prior sanction of the central government. Therefore, the victims of random and arbitrary coercion do not have the right to complain if armed personnel are not penalized. In the years the law has been in force, there has not been a single prosecution of armed forces personnel granted by the central government.[46]

Any suggestion that the AFSPA should be modified is met by outrage not only in the Valley but also in the rest of the country. The Act continues to wreck the lives of ordinary people and continues to protect the security forces. But the latter are simply not held accountable for enforced or involuntary disappearances in the Valley. Human rights activists have pointed to sites of mass graves and asked for an investigation, but no initiative to investigate illegal or random killings has been taken. Nor has the government intervened to provide security for women against assault. The general belief seems to be that cases of violence and sexual misconduct are dealt with competently by the military judicial system. This places the onus of justice on organizations whose personnel have committed injustice in the first place.[47]

---

[44]Chinki Sinha, 'Everyone's a poet of loss, memory and madness in Kashmir', *DailyO*, 17 August 2016.

[45]Office of the United Nations Commissioner for Human Rights, *Report on the Situation of Human Rights in Kashmir*, pp. 11, 27–28.

[46]Office of the United Nations High Commissioner for Human Rights, *Report on the Situation of Human Rights in Kashmir*, p. 11.

[47]Ibid., p. 11.

The basic principles of democracy, the rule of law, the basic right to life and liberty, and accountability are infringed by the provisions of the AFSPA and the Jammu and Kashmir Public Safety Act, 1978. Both these highly coercive laws have become the new normal in the Valley. Institutions and processes that protect citizens from the power of the state have been held hostage to strong and sometimes irrational notions of national integrity and security. In the discipline of International Relations, the concept of security has been expanded to protect ordinary individuals from want, from discrimination, and from violence. To place individual citizens at lower levels than the country or count them as less worthy than an abstract notion called the nation or national security is highly undemocratic. It paves the way for authoritarianism.

In 1997, the Supreme Court upheld the validity of the AFSPA, but since then has passed orders challenging prohibitions on the prosecution of security personnel vide section 7 of the Act.[48] In 2005, the Supreme Court had appointed a committee to review the Act. The committee reported that the law had become a symbol of oppression, an object of hate, and an instrument of discrimination and high-handedness. The report was rejected by the Ministry of Home Affairs in December 2015.[49] The Act has been condemned by the National Human Rights Commission, by international organizations, and by international human rights experts.[50] It is generally held that the Act fosters a climate of impunity for perpetrators of violence. Various international human rights bodies have suggested that the courts should decide whether proceedings initiated under the Act are vexatious and abusive. Judicial enquiries should be mandatory in cases of death at the hands of security armed forces. Above all, judges in such enquiries should be empowered to direct the prosecution of armed forces.

In July 2017 the Supreme Court asked the CBI to investigate extra-judicial killings in Manipur.[51] In March 2018, the then union minister of state, Hansraj Ahir, told Parliament that there was no proposal to amend or repeal the Act, but there are attempts to make it more effective and

---

[48]Ibid., p. 12.
[49]Ibid., p. 13.
[50]Ibid., p. 13.
[51]Ibid., p.14.

humane. Doubts remain. Can military courts uphold standards of a fair and free trial? In 2010, three civilians were killed in Baramulla district. Five army personnel were convicted by martial court held by the army in April 2014 and given a life sentence. In July 2017, an Armed Forces Tribunal suspended the life sentence and granted bail to the same five army personnel. The decision of the tribunal was not challenged in any institution. The ruling, in effect, disregarded the fact that the Valley was seething with discontent.[52]

## THE SPIRAL OF VIOLENCE

Matters have come to such a pass that till the lockdown of the state in August 2019, children aged ten to eleven years old were coming into the streets to protest. It is worth asking who they were protesting against—the easily recognizable security forces of the Indian state or the ubiquitous mercenaries who speak a language that Kashmir was unfamiliar with till the 1990s, that of jihad. Even if a political solution is found, the impact of the cloven hoof of the beast, which has erased the shared history of Kashmir, destroyed the people's ability to trust each other, and fomented distrust and hate will not be erased from collective memories. People have been massacred and their living spaces have been devastated by militancy. The Kashmiri Pandits, Sikhs, and moderate Muslims have been forced to leave their homes and their hearths and live out their lives in the barren camps in Jammu and other parts of the country. In 1990 India introduced the AFSPA to manage militancy. A large number of security forces were deployed in the state, resulting in allegations of serious human rights violations, including custodial deaths, rape, enforced disappearances, and extrajudicial executions. At the same time, armed groups commit serious human rights violations including hostage-taking, targeted killings, and indiscriminate attacks against civilians.

Agha Shahid Ali, who died at the young age of fifty-two, powerfully captures this sense of loss and longing in his poem, 'A Wrong Turn':

> In my dream I am always
> in a massacred town, its name
> erased from maps,

---

[52]Ibid., p. 15.

no road signs to it.
Only a wrong turn brings me here...[53]

And the poet Umair Bhat summed up the tragedy with some pain in his
poem, 'The Siege':

In the streets, filled
with impenetrable smoke,
Kashmir is burning again,

...

The lost
children of the sad country
count shadows
on the sun. [54]

This is but part of the story of violence that runs rampant in Kashmir.
Thousands have been killed by militants and jihadi forces, thousands
detained, thousands have disappeared, young children have been
radicalized, and Kashmiris have been tortured. It is difficult to point a
finger at only one agent or set of agents and state that they, and only
they, are responsible for this tragic violence.

The tragedy is that innocent people of Kashmir are caught between
the Charybdis of Indian security forces and the Scylla of armed groups
that have been active in the Valley since the late 1980s. Terrible forms
of violence have engulfed minds and crippled imagination, forbidden
people to think of the future, compelled them to concentrate only on
holding minds and bodies together. Violence has blurred the future by
the smoke that curls upwards from burning homes and villages. Violence
has begotten only violence and led to multiple tragedies.

## CONCLUSION

Critical observers of the problem have to admit that the origins of the
Kashmir conflict cannot be traced solely to the ambitions of Pakistan
to complete the Partition project and appropriate a Muslim-majority
state. We must accept that the causes for the eruption of conflict within
the territory of sovereign India do not emanate from the meddlesome
instincts of neighbours alone. The causes range from what is seen

---

[53] Agha Shahid Ali, *The Half-Inch Himalayas*, Connecticut: Wesleyan University Press, 1987, p. 37.
[54] Quoted in Sinha, 'Everyone's a poet of loss, memory and madness in Kashmir'.

as a violation of the principle of regional autonomy granted by the Constitution to the state, to the failure to hold a plebiscite in the region, to resentment at the denial of democracy, to the ideological commitment of militants to radical Islam, to deprivation, to struggle for control of resources, and to identity politics.

The tale of the Kashmir tragedy could have been foretold as early as 1953. The Government of India, desperate to prevent further balkanization of the country, became embroiled in a war that was not of its own making with Pakistan. Pilloried in the UN by major Western powers that had turned against India and pressured by right-wing forces to integrate Kashmir into the country, it adopted extremely short-sighted policies in the Kashmir case.

In retrospect, it is surprising that the government did not realize that it was not dealing with a population that had been rendered acquiescent under princely rule. It was dealing with a people that had mobilized against the misrule of the monarch since the 1930s. This politically aware population witnessed a series of cataclysmic events in the aftermath of 1947—the terror and the atrocities inflicted by raiders from Pakistan in 1947, the disruption that followed the war between India and Pakistan on Kashmiri soil, and the partition of the community and of the homeland between two, and then three countries. Above all, this population bore witness to the breach of contractual and constitutional obligations by the Government of India. Yet, the Kashmiri people were prepared to give democracy a chance. But it is precisely democracy that has been compromised and denied to them.

Forty-three years after the accession of the state to India, the people of the Kashmir Valley revolted against perceived injustice. The widespread belief that the Indian state could deliver to the people of the state neither democracy nor justice generated immense discontent. 'Though nothing can be immortall, which mortals make; yet, if men had the use of reason they pretend to, their Common-wealths might be secured, at least, from perishing by internall diseases', wrote Thomas Hobbes.[55] But reason has not been a constitutive aspect of the Kashmir policy of the Government of India. The Commonwealth, consequently, could not be properly secured.

---

[55]Thomas Hobbes, *Leviathan*, New York: Prometheus Books, 1651, p. 170.

## Chapter 5

# THE NORTHEAST
# A THOUSAND ARMED REBELLIONS

*'There were dreamers who thought poetry/was about nation, revolution, freedom/They were dreaming in their sleep/Their dreams died as they slept/Poetry became a casualty of armed skirmishes.'*

—Uddipana Goswami[1]

## INTRODUCTION: INDIA'S NORTHEAST

The editor of the *The Oxford Anthology of Writings from North-East India* tells us that the stories, extracts from novels, poems, and essays collected in the volume are historically located in post-independence India. Many of its authors are the children of violence and some of them have grown up in close contact with those who have memories of Partition and its effects on the Northeast. Others have experienced at close quarters the violence of insurgency, as well as the violence of the security forces in different parts of the region. This has changed the character of their society in many ways. Still others live through daily experiences of traumatic violence that disturbs the seemingly idyllic surroundings of the region.[2]

Caught in the crossfire between insurgents and the security forces, civilians in the Northeast of India lead lives that are (with apologies to Thomas Hobbes) uncertain, precarious, desperate and, often, painfully short. Some citizens search for nothing less than divine intervention to resolve their predicament and to relieve their pain. After more than two decades of waiting for a political resolution of political extremism, and

---

[1]Uddipana Goswami, 'Would I be a poet still?' Cited in Rini Burman, 'Guns with Occasional Music: Female Poets from the Northeast', *Kindle Magazine*, 2014.
[2]Tilottoma Misra (ed.), 'Introduction', *The Oxford Anthology of Writings from North-East India: Fiction,* New Delhi: Oxford University Press, 2011, pp. xi–xxxii.

in a bid to neutralize the crackdown of the Indian state on mainly the Isak–Muivah faction of the National Socialist Council of Nagaland, the Nagaland Joint Christian Forum on 6 February 2019 organized a special prayer meeting. The congregation prayed that God would intervene and impart wisdom to the leaders of the conflict and to the Government of India. People offering prayers asked God to ensure that the Indo–Naga political problem would be resolved before the 2019 general elections.

The prayer was held simultaneously across all districts and churches belonging to different Christian denominations. Thousands of Nagas attended church services held specifically for peace. The meeting believed the government, which persists in sidelining crucial issues confronted by the state, had now instigated a non-issue to divert attention from pressing problems. These are things, the statement continued, that we should commit to God, so that with the prayer of believers He will intercede in the slow descent towards chaos. The non-issue referred to was the Citizenship (Amendment) Bill 2016, a piece of legislation that created fear and discontent in the region prior to the 2019 general elections.[3] The bill was bulldozed through both houses of Parliament by the BJP. Thereafter, in December 2019, the CAA evoked large-scale protests and demonstrations across the country including the Northeast. These protests continued in various forms till the outbreak of the pandemic in March 2020.

What are the causes—whether proximate or distant—of the problems of the Northeast? How can they be resolved? Policymakers across the world seem to believe that economic development and the construction of infrastructure and modes of communication ensure compliant populations. These measures might even deter discontent and civil war. In recent years, the Indian government has concentrated on building infrastructure and intensifying communication in the region. Highways and bridges, it is expected, will act as a corridor between India and East Asian countries that have witnessed impressive economic growth. They will also connect the seven states of the Northeast with each other. Communication, the government blithely believes, will lead to the expansion of social transactions, economic growth, and stability in the region.

---

[3]Rahul Karmakar, 'Special peace prayer in Nagaland', *The Hindu*, 6 February 2019.

History, however, informs us that there are simply no neat prescriptions that can effectively address struggles for political power, for control over resources, for dignity, and assured respect for identity. Economic development has not been fully able to address the grievances of the citizens of the Northeast. Some of these conflicts go back to 1947, and they are not easily reducible to readily identifiable causes or simple economic solutions. Some identity politics are undoubtedly connected to economic ambitions, but trajectories of politicized identities tend to outstrip economic grievances and acquire semi-autonomy from the original cause. Defying all prescriptions including that of using coercion, countless violent rebellions—big and small, short-lived and long-lasting, contained and not so easily contained—have occurred and continue to occur since 1947. The roots of discontent of course go back, as cases of many political conflicts in India do, to the colonial period.

## THE GENESIS OF DISCONTENT

The geographical region of the Northeast of India is politically organized into seven states—Arunachal Pradesh, Assam, Manipur, Meghalaya, Mizoram, Nagaland, and Tripura. The region is strategically significant for India because it borders China, Myanmar, Bangladesh, and Bhutan. It was certainly strategically and militarily important for the colonial power. In the late eighteenth century, the East India Company set about consolidating its power in the Northeast for two reasons. It had to secure the borders of an economically productive Bengal, and it had to protect the external frontiers of British India against neighbouring powers, particularly Burma. Towards this end the colonial power restructured the frontier region geographically, administratively, and politically. The project involved the formal and informal subjugation of the princely states of Assam, Tripura, and Manipur. It also involved the pacification of several tribes through treaties, pacts, and the remaking of political geography. The restructuring bred its own set of dynamics that continue to rock the region.

In 1793, the East India Company was provided with a fortuitous chance to intervene in Assam, a crucial region which borders erstwhile Burma on the southeast, is rimmed by the great Himalayan mountain range on the north and the east, and shares a common boundary with Bengal in the south. In 1793, the monarch of Assam confronted internal revolts and the takeover of Guwahati by rebels. He requested the Company for help. The East India Company dispatched infantry battalions to the state to control the internal insurgency. The troops subsequently withdrew. However, the Ahom monarchy in Assam continued to be threatened by insurgents. Political instability weakened Assam and the monarchy came under the control of Burma from 1819 to 1824. The Ahom king once again called upon the British to aid his people who were being tortured and killed. In addition, Cachar and Manipur had been brought under the sway of imperial Burma. The rulers of both territories asked the British for help.

The East India Company intervened militarily in 1823 to save not only the three frontier regions but also Bengal from the imperial ambitions of Burma. On 24 February 1826, after the First Anglo-Burmese War, the Treaty of Yandabo was signed between Burma and the East India Company. The treaty stipulated that Burma would not interfere in Assam. Raja Gambhir Singh was recognized as the ruler of Manipur. In the same year, the British annexed Assam and constituted it as a division within the Bengal Presidency.

On 6 February 1874, Assam became a Chief Commissioners' Province by a proclamation of the British Indian government. Four new districts—Cachar, Garo Hills, Khasi and Jaintia Hills, and Naga Hills—were added to the existing six districts of Assam—Goalpara, Kamrup, Darrang, Nagaon, Sibsagar, and Lakhimpur. In September of the same year, the district of Sylhet was brought under the administration of the newly constituted province. After twenty years, the Lushai Hills District was added to Assam. Different entities in the region were allotted their own political status. Assam became a province of British India. Manipur, Tripura, and Cooch Behar were princely states that were controlled by the colonial power through a series of pacts. The Naga Hills District was constituted in 1867, but the borders of the administrative unit were not settled.

The British government, in its zeal to consolidate power in every part of India, made and remade territorial borders without regard for the ethnic composition of people who were brought into the same administrative units or divided by newly constituted borders. Similar policies had been adopted by European powers in the case of Sub-Saharan Africa. As mentioned in the previous chapter, in 1885,

European powers, participants in the ignoble Scramble for Africa, met in Berlin. The objective of the meeting was to divide Sub-Saharan Africa between European powers and to thus pre-empt the possibility of war between the countries competing for control over the territories and resources of the region. A map of Sub-Saharan Africa was tacked onto the wall, and lines drawn by a pencil across the map partitioned the continent into different political units. Each unit was handed over to a European power. The African people were not consulted and the carving up of the continent was carried out without regard for the ethnic composition of the society that was now constituted into a colonial state. Warring tribes were brought within the ambit of a state, for example, the Ndebele and the Mashona in Rhodesia. And one community, the Somali people, was divided between territories held by the British, French, Italian, and Ethiopians. The reckless splitting up of Africa, an act that will go down in history as one of the darkest phases of European imperialism, paved the way for identity struggles. This took the form of separation, irredentism, or both. Both forms of conflict have bedevilled Sub-Saharan Africa for decades since the 1960s when a majority of countries became independent.

The same phenomenon has marked the Northeast of India. The boundaries of Assam contained a host of ethnic groups, many of which spoke different languages and subscribed to different cultures and traditions. The process laid the grounds, as in Sub-Saharan Africa, for the outburst of tensions and conflicts between these groups in the future. The creation of administrative units—General, Excluded, and Partially Excluded Areas—in the rest of the region changed the political status of groups that had different political histories. Some of these groups had been organized as kingdoms, some were under the sway of chieftains, and some were constituted as autonomous tribal units. A number of measures were taken to protect the autonomy and the culture of tribal areas, notably Scheduled Districts (1874), Backward Tracts (1919), and Partially Excluded and Excluded Areas (1935).

The Constituent Assembly had adopted the Sixth Schedule in 1949 to provide for the administration of tribal areas in the region through the establishment of autonomous district councils, separate regional councils, and autonomous districts within the state. The autonomous district council has the power to legislate on land, forests, fisheries, and public health, subject to the approval of the governor of the state. The autonomous district councils also have jurisdiction over civil and judicial matters. The Schedule was, in effect, devised to provide for some degree of self-rule for tribal communities, and to ensure protection for land, traditions, customs, and identity. In contemporary political theory, the institutionalization of some degree of autonomy to local levels is recommended for multicultural societies but the effects of such devolution at local level is a matter of debate.

Across the world, the problem of balancing regional and ethnic autonomy, on the one hand, and integration into the wider political community, on the other, has troubled academics and policymakers for some time now. They have not discovered any set formulae that will ensure a tension-free integration of autonomous units into a wider federation. The grant of regional autonomy through institutions of self-government can go in any direction, whether integration or separatism.[4] It is this tension that has bedevilled the region of the Northeast since its inception.

For instance, the one administrative measure that has had far-reaching repercussions is the Inner Line, an imaginary boundary framed and implemented under the provisions of the Bengal Eastern Frontier Regulation of 1873. No one could enter the territory that lay behind the line without permission from the district authorities. Tea planters were forbidden from acquiring estates in the area. The objective was to protect tribal communities, often nomadic, sometimes settled, from the depredations of the outside world. Ironically, the line not only established a territorial border, it also instituted a divide between the 'outsider' and the 'insider'. The Inner Line, writes Bodhisattva Kar, drawing upon a communication from A. Mackenzie, junior secretary of the Government of Bengal, to the secretary of the Government of India, Foreign Department, was supposed to demarcate the 'hills' from the 'plains', the nomadic from the sedentary, the jungle from the arable—in short, the tribal areas from Assam proper. '[T]he communities forced to stay beyond the Line were seen as belonging to a different time regime—where the time of the law did not apply; where slavery,

---

[4]Ian S. Lustick, Dan Miodownik, and Roy J. Eidelson, 'Secessionism in Multicultural States: Does Sharing Power Prevent or Encourage It?' *American Political Science Review,* Vol. 98, No. 2, May 2005, pp. 209–29.

headhunting, and nomadism could be allowed to exist. The Inner Line was expected to enact a sharp split between what were understood as the contending worlds of capital and pre-capital, of the modern and the primitive.'[5] In independent India, the States Reorganisation Commission set up in 1953 to examine the formation of linguistic states in India concluded that the Line was responsible for ethnic unrest and the demand for separate hill states.

In 1970, the political geography of the region was restructured once again, and the political map of the region was redrawn. This was in response to the eruption of discontent among various ethnic groups in Assam. The Naga and the Mizo people had openly rebelled. In 1970, the Khasi, Jaintia, and Garo Hills were constituted into a substate, Meghalaya, within Assam. In 1971, the two union territories of Manipur and Tripura were upgraded to the status of full states. Mizo Hills District and the North-East Frontier Agency, now Arunachal Pradesh, were given the status of union territories. Both territories acquired statehood in 1987. In 1972, Meghalaya was upgraded to a full state. Nagaland had acquired statehood in 1963, for reasons discussed below. The political geography of the region was, however, not settled by these means and the region continues to be shaken by unrest and aspirations for more control over resources, power, and protection of culture and language.

## UNREST IN THE NORTHEAST
Except for Mizoram, which opted for peace in 1986, and some parts of Assam after the government signed an accord with the Bodo tribe, the Northeast is a deeply troubled region, a region whose history and geography has been inscribed in violence. If we were to map out conflict zones in India, we will find this part of the country stained with the blood of militants and security forces and disfigured by the wounds of innocent civilians. Between bouts of blood-spattered violence, we witness the eruption of vociferous protests over draconian laws, the threatening presence of the armed forces in some of the states, demands for greater autonomy, attempts to control resources, and even conflict over secessionist demands that reject any kind of compromise, the

[5]Bodhisattva Kar, 'When was the Postcolonial? The History of Policing Impossible Lines', in Sanjib Baruah (ed.), *Beyond Counter-Insurgency: Breaking the Impasse in Northeast India,* New Delhi: Oxford University Press, 2009, p. 51 n 6, 52.

sovereignty of the Indian state, and integration into the country.

Protest takes many forms. It can be articulated through armed struggle. It is expressed by people in Nagaland stripping naked at public meetings. Nagas, writes Dolly Kikon, are no longer naked the way they are often represented by mainstream India documents and art, but they continue to shed their clothes as a symbol of protest and as an affirmation of cultural identities. In many demonstrations and public gatherings, one notices an increasing number of men dressed traditionally as warriors with spears, and women with sarongs wrapped around their chests. Once a sign of barbarism, these bare bodies have become political tools of protest.[6]

Some of the longest conflicts in the country have occurred in this part of India. The Indian government has entered into numerous agreements with militant groups (for instance with the Manipuris and the Nagas, as discussed below), many of which challenge the inclusion of their homelands in the Union of India, want their own states, and demand integration on their own terms. Unfortunately, the overriding impression is that our lawmakers and administrators prefer to see armed conflicts as a law and order problem, rather than a political one. There is, after all, a significant distinction between conflicts occurring over random violations of law and order and political unrest. Political conflicts cannot be resolved through the use of disproportionate force. The resolution of political conflict demands another sort of thinking; it calls for the unleashing of considerable imagination, innovative reflections, and appropriate policies. The task requires the disruption of extant thinking, perspectives, and frameworks of understanding. The use of force merely exacerbates the problem. Political conflicts demand political resolutions.

Perhaps it is easier for governments to see rebellion as a law and order problem and not as a deep challenge to the legitimacy of the Indian state, to state policies, or indeed to the spatial boundaries of the nation state. The histories of Kashmir, Assam, Manipur, Nagaland, and Mizoram, however, tell a different story. Political wars which pursue an agenda not sanctioned by the Constitution, for instance, secession, howsoever chaotic and unspecified the right might be, as the previous chapter has shown, have to be taken with the seriousness they deserve.

---

[6]Dolly Kikon, 'From Loincloth, Suits to Battle Greens; Politics of Clothing the "Naked' Naga"', Baruah (ed.), *Beyond Counter-Insurgency*, pp. 81–100, p. 95.

To see a political war as a law and order problem is not only to gravely misread the issues involved, the perspective also reduces the role of the state to an agency that maintains stability at any cost. The state in a democracy is primarily an upholder of fairness as justice. We cannot think of the state as an institution solely obsessed with stability and order, often without law. If the democratic state is reduced to an agency that enforces only stability, democracy is compromised and justice consigned to the wayside. We only expect and experience violence, not justice, not the institutionalization of the preconditions of a life of dignity, and certainly not peace.

In an evocative poem titled 'When the Prime Minister Visits Shillong the Bamboos Watch in Silence', the poet Kynpham Sing Nongkynrih poetically documents this scepticism:

When Prime Minister Gujral
planned a visit to the city
bamboos sprang up from pavements
like a welcoming committee

But when he came, he was
only the strident sounds of sirens
like warnings in war-time bombings

The bamboos watched in silence.

He came with twin objectives
a mission for peace and progress
but he was a rumbling in the clouds
a prattle in the air...

Only the bamboos watched in silence
too used to the antics of men.[7]

These verses are a damning comment on how political violence has been misinterpreted and mismanaged in India. If people take up arms against the state, can this be neutralized either by sending in armed forces, or by formal visits by heads of government? Political wars demand sustained political intervention; they are not resolved easily,

---

[7]Kynpham Sing Nongkynrih and Robin S. Ngangom (ed.), *Anthology of Contemporary Poetry from the Northeast,* Shillong: NEHU, 2003, pp. 161–63.

and in the absence of intelligent inputs, government policy can foment discontent. Let us look at three instances of the mismatch between government policy and cycles of discontent that illustrate this point.

## VIOLENCE IN NAGALAND

There is no one cause for discontent and armed struggle in the Northeast. In many cases, armed rebellion has been sparked off by what inhabitants see as the unjust incorporation of tribal lands by the Indian state. The original grievance has been exacerbated by the imposition of draconian laws and the entry of new non-state actors, and mutated into a desperate search for peace. As the reputed journalist Patricia Mukhim wrote in 2005, when India became independent, the various tribes of the Northeast were made to sign the Instrument of Accession into the Indian union through coercion. The perception remains that India, with its sheer might, has co-opted smaller principalities into itself.[8]

Take Nagaland of which the poet, Easterine Kire, writes in some despair, 'In the worst of the war years/the horror has taken us beyond poetry/beyond words into silence/the deep silence of inexpressible pain.'[9] The roots of the longest conflict in India go back to the first half of the twentieth century. In 1918, a pan-Naga club (that included members of tribes living in different regions of the Northeast) was formed by ex-soldiers who had fought in World War I. The club quickly became a vehicle of Naga aspirations for cultural autonomy, a right that was protected by the British government. The colonial government, after subduing the Naga tribes in the latter part of the nineteenth century, had proclaimed that the culture and traditions of the people will be defended against any kind of interference.

In 1929, members of the club submitted a memorandum to the Simon Commission that was visiting India to discuss future political arrangements. The memorandum demanded that when the British government decided to leave India, it should ensure that the region is left independent. It should also guarantee that the Naga people would

[8]Patricia Mukhim, 'Where is this North-east?' *India International Centre Quarterly,* 2005, Vol. 32, pp. 177–88.

[9]Easterine Kire, 'Locating Trauma in Mizo Literature: The Beloved Bullet', in Margaret Ch Zama (ed.) *Emerging Literatures from Northeast India: The Dynamics of Culture, Society and Identity,* New Delhi: Sage Studies in the Northeast, 2013 p. 66.

retain their autonomy and that they had the right to form their own political community. The memorandum made it clear that the Naga people had no desire to live under Indian sovereignty.

Under the Government of India Act of 1935, Nagaland was declared an Excluded Area. In April 1945, the Deputy Commissioner of the Naga Hills District established the Naga Hills District Council. This was meant to provide a forum for representation of all groups in the territory. In February 1946, the institution was reorganized to form the Naga National Council (NNC). This council was given the task of negotiating with the Government of India after the British withdrew from the subcontinent.

In 1946, the people of Nagaland submitted a memorandum to the British Cabinet Mission, which had come to India to prepare the ground for the grant of independence. The memorandum reiterated that the NNC stands for the solidarity of Naga tribes and demanded that the Naga Hills should be granted autonomy within Assam. Jawaharlal Nehru, the then president of the Indian National Congress, rejected any independent status for the Naga people. In 1947, the NNC sent a memorandum to the viceroy, Lord Mountbatten. The council requested him to set up an interim government in the territory for ten years. After that, the memorandum stated, the Nagas will choose the kind of government they wished for. After repeated deadlocks on the issue, Nehru sent Akbar Hydari, the governor of Assam, to discuss the matter with the Naga leaders. A nine-point agreement was signed on 29 June 1947 between the Government of India and the NNC.

Point nine of the agreement set the ground for an acrimonious debate. The article stated that the Government of Assam, as the agent of the Government of the Indian Union, will have special responsibility to ensure the due observance of the agreement for a period of ten years. At the end of this period, the NNC will be asked whether it requires the agreement to be extended or whether it would rather opt for a new agreement.

This clause became a matter of dispute between the Government of India and the NNC. The latter maintained that the clause provided enough scope for their people to declare independence and secede from the union at the end of the agreement period, that is, in 1958. The government believed that after ten years when the situation was reviewed, the agreement would be redrafted according to the needs of the people. But it refused to agree to any clause that might spark off secessionist demands.

In the meanwhile, a group of people in Nagaland rebelled against inclusion into the territory of India. A section of the NNC revolted under the leadership of Angami Zapu Phizo, the ideologue of Naga nationalism, and a prominent member of the council. This section declared independence on 14 August 1947. Phizo organized ceremonies in Kohima to celebrate the independence of Nagaland. The faction boycotted India's Independence Day on 15 August 1947.

On 16 May 1951, Phizo, after consulting the representatives of all the tribes, held a plebiscite and asserted that 99.1 per cent of the population had voted for independence.[10] In 1952, the Nagas boycotted India's parliamentary elections. In 1953, the insurgents declared the establishment of the People's Sovereign Republic of Free Nagaland. Anticipating that the Indian Army would use every means possible to suppress the insurgency, Phizo created militant groups and armed them with weapons, most of which were relics of the World War II. In 1955, the Indian state retaliated and sent the army to the area to suppress the insurgency. The army displaced and relocated thousands of villagers into clusters of villages.[11] Forced collectivization was considered indispensable for surveillance and to prevent essential supplies to the guerrillas. The experience of being dislocated from their ancestral villages, many of which had been built around sacred groves, further alienated the Naga people from the Government of India.

Phizo escaped to Britain, reportedly with the help of the Government of Pakistan. He tried to internationalize the issue of Naga independence, but did not succeed. In the meanwhile, war between the underground Naga army and the Indian Army escalated. A small group of moderate Naga leaders, who had distanced themselves from Phizo, decided that it was better to work with the Government of India, which was committed to the protection of customary laws and traditions. The moderate leadership organized a convention of all tribes in August 1957. The convention was attended by 1,765 delegates and 2,000 visitors representing all the

---

[10]'Naga Plebiscite Day by Adinno Phizo', *Nagaland Post*, 7 April 2021.

[11]E. N. Rammohun, 'The Naga Insurgency-Part I', United Services Institution of India, undated.

tribes. A resolution for a negotiated settlement of the Naga issue, and for setting up the Tuensang Frontier Division of the North-East Frontier Agency in the Naga Hills District and placing it under the External Affairs Ministry, was adopted. The Indian government agreed.

The Naga People's Convention (NPC), whose members had opposed the armed movement led by the NNC, intensified activities and organized meetings in 1958 and 1959 despite massive threats from underground guerrillas. In 1960, the Government of India signed an agreement with the NPC. The agreement stated that in three years Nagaland would become a full state with special rights. One of these rights was inserted in the Indian Constitution as Article 371A. The article states that the customary law of the Nagas will not be touched by any act of Parliament, and that laws passed by Parliament will not apply to the territory unless they are ratified by the local legislature. Village and tribal councils, as well as the state assembly, would exercise control over the resources of the area.

The NNC refused to recognize the new state. The guerrilla force split and regrouped a number of times, but there was no let-up in the fighting. Over time, exhaustion set in, and on 11 November 1975, the Shillong Accord was signed. Former militants accepted the Constitution of India, agreed that arms would be deposited, and that leaders of the movement would formulate other issues for discussion and final settlement. The sway of the Unlawful Activities (Prevention) Act over the territory was abrogated. Many groups opposed the accord because they felt that it embodied the spirit of meek surrender to India. They broke away from the NNC to form the National Socialist Council of Nagaland (NSCN-IM). This has split further into numerous groups since 1988. The NSCN-IM or the Isak-Muivah faction, the largest of these groups, declared ceasefire with Indian troops in July 1997 and initiated a long, torturous, and still unfinished process that might lead to peace.

In August 2015, the Naga insurgent groups led by the NSCN-IM signed a peace accord with the central government. There was hope that the accord would mark the end of the longest insurgency in the country. Under the agreement, the Government of India recognized the unique history of the Naga people and the legitimacy of their aspirations, their sentiments, and their demands. In return, the militant group recognized the inalienable sovereignty and legitimacy of the Indian state.

Yet, the hope that the agreement would mark the end of a bitter and protracted conflict that has led to displacement, destruction, devastation, injuries, killings, and war, both formal and informal, proved misplaced.

Negotiations continued, albeit with hiccups. On 1 November 2020, representatives of the NSCN-IM stated that the militant group would sign the deal along with other insurgent groups and confirmed that negotiations with the Government of India were still on. Once the accord is finalized, it was stated, they will sign it.[12] Further, the main stumbling block—the insistence of the group that it will retain its own Naga constitution and flag—will be put aside. Concurrently, the central government has been holding talks with seven Naga rebel outfits organized into the Naga National Political Groups (NNPGs). The grouping has been wary of the framework the NSCN-IM had signed on 3 August 2015 which for long was not made public. In 2017, the governor of Nagaland had included more political groups in the dialogue process and signed a preamble with them. At the same time, other Northeastern states are wary of any accord because the NSCN-IM has been speaking of a Nagalim, or a greater Nagaland, by including Naga dominated areas in neighbouring states—Assam, Manipur, and Arunachal Pradesh—to unite 1.2 million Nagas.[13]

India still awaits a peace accord. The wages of near civil war are articulated poignantly by Easterine Kire who writes in her poem titled 'Kelhoukevira': 'Their hearts too grieved to heed the harvest/Maidens ceased song and mourned the brave ones/And blindly followed a broken people/Who turned their backs/And slowly walked away/From a burning village, a burning village/…they trampled her silent hills/And squeezed life out of her/And washed their guilt in her blood, Washed their guilt in her blood.'[14] The stanza epitomizes the story of violence that tracks people's lives in Nagaland.

## MANIPUR: THE ROAD TO DISCONTENT

Apart from Jammu and Kashmir, another case of contested accession to the Indian Union is that of Manipur. In Manipur, the main conflict

---

[12]'Centre, NSCN-IM to sign Naga peace accord soon', *National Herald*, 1 November 2020.

[13]Vijaita Singh, 'Peace deal on verge of being finalized say Naga groups', *The Hindu*, 11 September 2020.

[14]Kikon, 'From Loincloth, Suits, to Battle Greens', p. 97.

is between the people and the Government of India for a specific historical reason detailed below. Superimposed on the conflict is discord between thirty-three hill tribes and the people of the valley. It is estimated that Manipur possesses more than thirty-five armed non-state outfits that battle with each other more often than they battle with the Government of India. The deaths that have resulted from these tensions are incalculable. 'In recent years,' writes Sanjib Baruah, 'the official count of lives annually lost in insurgency-related incidents in Manipur has been in the hundreds. In addition the role of ethnic militias in inter-ethnic conflicts, such as between Nagas and Kukis and, more recently between Kukis and Paites, have made those conflicts extremely violent.'[15]

The valley of Manipur is inhabited by Meiteis that form 68 per cent of the population. The Meiteis, with a recorded history of 2,000 years, are justifiably proud of their culture, language, script, and their tradition of democracy that predates electoral democracy in India.

Along with a rich literary culture, the Meiteis had instituted a system of kingship, and a religion of their own called the Sanamahi. Over time, a number of travellers from the state went through the Cachar hills into Bengal and brought Hinduism to the region. The cult of Vaishnavite Hinduism took root in the valley and was patronized by the monarchs. Interestingly, in recent times, we see a revival of the ancient cult of Sanamahi as part of the protest against mainland India. At the end of the nineteenth century, the hill people came under the influence of Christian missionaries, mainly American Baptists and Welsh Presbyterians.

The origins of conflict in the region lie in the integration of the state into the Union of India. On the eve of India's partition, Manipur had adopted a Constitution and held an election to constitute a democratically elected government. The Maharaja of Manipur signed the Instrument of Accession shortly after August 1947. Accession was not considered sufficient and the Government of India wanted Manipur to be integrated into the union.

When Sardar Vallabhbhai Patel, who was responsible for the accession of princely states to India, was told of the reluctance of the maharaja to merge his state with India, he asked just one question, 'Is there no

---

[15]Sanjib Baruah, *Durable Disorders: Understanding the Politics of Northeast India,* New Delhi: Oxford University Press, 2005, p. 60.

brigadier in Shillong?'[16] The governor of Assam, Sri Prakasa, and the advisor for tribal areas, Nari Rustomji, had reported that the maharaja was visiting Shillong. It was clear what Sardar Patel meant, wrote Rustomji.[17]

The maharaja did not have the opportunity of consulting his people, his advisers, and his council of ministers. On 15 October, Manipur merged with India in a ceremony dominated by personnel of the Indian Army. There is enough cause for discontent.[18]

## THE COURSE OF VIOLENCE

One of the most gifted theatre directors in India, Ratan Thiyam, lives and works in Imphal. He is known for his evocative and powerful depictions of the tragedies that inexorably track conflict. In his play *Uttar-Priyadarshi*, he imaginatively depicts the bloodshed that followed the ancient Battle of Kalinga. The bloodshed motivates Emperor Ashoka to reflect on the costs of war and he slowly converts to Buddhism. All parties to the conflict should have learnt from the play, should have absorbed the costs of war. The tragedy is that we do not learn the lessons history and the enactment of historical episodes teach us. This is painfully apparent in the case of Manipur and other conflict zones in India and the world.

Much of the discontent and armed struggle in the region has been sparked off by the highly oppressive laws that have been imposed by the Government of India on the people, particularly the notorious AFSPA, which has been discussed in the previous chapter. Take a famous case that illustrates arbitrary killings and speaks volumes about the impunity of the Indian state. On 10–11 July 2004 in Manipur, soldiers of the Assam Rifles broke into a young woman, Manorama's house in Imphal and confined her to a room. She was mercilessly beaten and dragged out of the house.

While she was brutally tortured, the soldiers repeatedly demanded that she give them information about her former comrades belonging to the banned insurgent group, the People's Liberation Army (PLA).[19] The PLA had been fighting the Indian state for over two decades, but

---

[16]Ibid., p. 59.
[17]Ibid.
[18]Ibid., pp. 59–60.
[19]Amala Dasarathi, 'Remembering Thangjam Manorama', *Feminism India*, 9 March 2017.

Manorama had left the militant group and returned home.

The next morning her body was found in a field riddled with gun shots and other injuries.

A few days later, India witnessed a novel and heart-rending form of protest. Several women of all ages marched towards the soldiers guarding the gate of the Kangla Fort. As they neared the guards, the women stripped naked and flourished a banner which read 'Indian Army Rape Us.' The scene was nerve-wracking. The soldiers, it was reported, lowered their eyes at the spectacle of women, some old enough to be their mothers, uncovering their bodies as part of a process of naming and shaming.[20] The Manipuri poet Robin S. Ngangom wrote in anguish of a lost homeland and the brutalities of war:

> Everywhere I go
> I carry my homeland with me…
> And I want to tell my poet-friends
> of the twelve mothers who stripped themselves
> and asked soldiers to rape them.[21]

The conscience of the central government was finally stirred, and Prime Minister Manmohan Singh appointed a committee to examine the hated and reviled AFSPA. The committee was headed by Justice B. P. Jeevan Reddy, the former chairman of the Law Commission of India. The committee held a series of hearings in Imphal amidst vociferous and angry protests. The anguished testimonies of mothers who had lost their sons in encounter killings, of wives whose husbands never came home, of women who had been subjected to sexual assault, and stories of families torn apart overwhelmed the sensibilities of the members of the committee. The committee finally recommended that the law should be repealed.

The AFSPA aroused anger on a scale seldom witnessed in Manipur. The activist Irom Chanu Sharmila went on a fast to protest the draconian law. The fast lasted for almost sixteen years from November 2000 to August 2016. The AFSPA grants immunity, as discussed in the chapter on Kashmir, to security personnel to maintain and restore law and

---

[20]Anubha Bhosle, 'Indian Army Rape Us', *Outlook*, 10 February 2016.
[21]Robin S. Ngangom, 'Everywhere I Go', in Tilottoma Misra (ed.) *The Oxford Anthology of Writings from North-East India*, pp. 46–47.

order. Irom Sharmila was periodically arrested by the government and force-fed.[22] Changing her preferred mode of politics, she called off her fast in 2016. She stood for state assembly elections in 2017, after she had set up a political party, the People's Resurgence and Justice Alliance (PRAJA). Though the people of Manipur supported her during her years of fasting, and though she was widely admired as an icon of courage and resistance, her party lost the elections.

The ubiquity of violence has taken a heavy toll on society. Poets and writers chronicle the dejected faces of mothers of young men and women who have been picked up either by the security forces or by rival armed ethnic groups. Tayenjam Bijoykumar Singh writes of Ratan Thiyam's powerful play *Kurukshetragi Peerang*, that dwells on the futility of war and the endless search for peace. At the end of the play, the actors light oil lamps that symbolize enlightenment. 'Wars bring only destruction…. An enlightened Panchali vows to arm herself with Dharma and wipe away tears from the eyes of the multitude of anguished mothers whose valiant sons had been felled in the battlefield of Kurukshetra.' Pointing out the relevance of the epic to present-day Manipur, Singh draws a parallel between the bereaved mothers of the times of the Mahabharata and the mothers of Manipur whose sons lost their lives at a young age. 'Every day news about the killings of youths in various circumstances flashes in the headlines of local newspapers at Imphal…. Has anyone ever bothered to think about the woes of the bereaved mothers?'[23]

## INTRA-ETHNIC TENSIONS

The struggle for regional autonomy within the federal system, for secession in extreme cases, and protests against draconian laws are exacerbated by intra-ethnic tensions. This has led to the formation of private militias, which wage war against the state and often against each other. A number of these private militias are known for extortion, rape, and violence. Tayenjam Bijoykumar Singh has in a short story, 'The Mauled Cub', poignantly captured the fate of the ordinary citizen caught in a vice—between the violence of non-

[22]'Irom Sharmila re-arrested on charges of attempt to commit suicide', *Mint*, 22 August 2014.

[23]Tayenjam Bijoykumar Singh, 'Kurukshetragi Peerang-Ratan Thiyam's Gift to Mothers', in Misra (ed.), *The Oxford Anthology of Writings from North-East India*, p. 203.

state actors and the violence of the security forces.

One evening, the family of a young woman, Tombi, recounts our storyteller, heard gunshots. Soon after the shooting had died down, heavily armed men in uniform forcibly entered their house and dragged her brother, a student of Class X, out into the road without giving any reason. The parents blocked the way of the uniformed soldiers and pleaded for the life of their young son, but the troops threatened to shoot them down. The father died of grief and the mother and daughter were forced to give sanctuary to three young men who were a part of an insurgent group. These young men came and went as they wished.

Tombi and her mother were helpless against heavily armed strangers; they could neither inform their neighbours nor report them to the police. Both women stayed aloof from the neighbours for another reason. If news of the presence of men in the house of two women became public, Tombi's marriage prospects would be doomed. Still, Tombi felt secure because she had her mother to guard her. Her mother was a lioness looking after her cub.

Tombi, however, could not be protected all the time. One night while she was asleep, a hand was placed on her, and the leader of the three youths 'had his way.... Having had his fill, he soon left, leaving behind a devastated Tombi. The lioness had failed to protect her cub. Tombi, the badly mauled cub, lay awake sobbing the whole night.' The next day, soldiers entered the home for a search operation. Tombi, lying listlessly on her bed, simply did not get the time to hide. Nor did she have the energy. Three men in uniform entered her room. Without a word, and whining like animals, they jumped on her and pinned her to the bed. 'Unable to bear the pain of the brutal force, she fainted almost immediately and lost consciousness. Unhindered, the men changed position to release their pent-up fury on her beautiful form sans clothes.'[24]

Between the violence exerted by the security forces of the state, and the armed militias that represent an identifiable or an unidentifiable agent, ordinary citizens live in a perpetual state of fear. In every case, the person who has the most to lose is the helpless victim of violence.

---

[24]Tayenjam Bijoykumar Singh, 'The Mauled Cub', in Misra (ed.), *The Oxford Anthology of Writings from North-East India,* pp. 183–92.

## THE STORY OF ASSAM

Violence gains traction in specific contexts. Sanjoy Hazarika writes that the collapse of institutions, the inability or the disinterest of officials in tweaking existing systems to improve the quality of life of ordinary citizens, the climate of fear and foreboding, the cloud of anger, suspicion, and despair that has ruled different parts of the region are interconnected. Local governments are unable to deliver basic services at a time when conflicts rage and agitations surface, when street protests erupt and there are repeated crackdowns by military and paramilitary forces. Security forces move around unquestioned and engage in a daily display of power. The prevalence of AFSPA and other coercive laws ensure this will happen again and again.[25] During peacetime, he continues, when the guns are silent but the people are not, they are tense and watchful of each other, of the underground, of the military and non-military, and of the politician and the businessman who are in cahoots with each other.[26]

It is possible to trace many reasons for periodic outbursts of resentment and anger in the region. One set of causes has to do with the perception that tribes and kingdoms were unjustly and forcibly incorporated into the Indian Union. The ubiquitous and threatening presence of security forces and the perpetuation of unjust laws such as the AFSPA that violate every semblance of democracy generates frustration and rage. Armed militias violate the basic rights of their own people in what are considered insurgent zones. The context of insecurity and fear is compounded by unresponsive state governments.

Groups have taken up arms for another reason—pursuit of a state of their own. In the 1980s, a movement that represented the interests of the Bodos, the largest plains tribe in Assam, took up arms against the dispossession of their lands by Bengali and Assamese settlers. The eruption of war bore predictable outcomes: terrorization of citizens caught in a pincer-like situation between government forces and armed non-state militias.

In 1988, the National Democratic Front of Bodoland (NDFB) demanded an independent country of Bodoland. Another insurgent

---

[25]Sanjoy Hazarika, *Strangers No More: New Narratives from India's Northeast,* New Delhi: Aleph Book Company, 2018, p. 27.
[26]Ibid., pp. 27–28.

group, the Bodo Volunteer Force, signed the Bodo Accord in 1993 with the Indian government. However, yet another section of the group rejected it and formed the Bodo Liberation Tigers in 1996. The group demanded independence from India. Another peace accord signed in 2003 proved ineffective. On 27 January 2020, the central government signed a third peace accord with the NDFB and the All Bodo Students' Union. The pact created a Bodoland Territorial Region within Assam, granted political autonomy to the unit, protected culture and language rights, and promised economic benefits. In return, armed militias laid down arms and gave up their demand for an independent Bodoland. But peace was not secured.

The United Liberation Front of Assam (ULFA) is another group that has pursued secession, though it has been progressively weakened. The group was born on 7 April 1979 in Rang Ghar in Sibsagar following the anti-foreigner agitation led by the All Assam Students' Union (AASU). The objective of the group was to establish a sovereign, socialist Assam free from the exploitation of the Indian Union. This state, it was declared, would be inclusive and give equal status to minority communities and smaller tribes. Unlike the narrower objective of other movements, the ULFA focused on the exploitation of Assam's vast resources, underdevelopment, unemployment, and on the unfair treatment meted out to the state by the central government, compared to other states of India. The ULFA was welcomed by many right-thinking groups as a progressive organization that focused on unity, progress, development, regional autonomy, and inclusiveness. Many young people, frustrated by joblessness and the economic backwardness of their state, took up arms in support. In the long run, the path of unimaginable violence adopted by the ULFA leading to extortion, kidnapping, and murders alienated the people of Assam. Ultimately, it also has had to negotiate with many of its leaders surrendering to the government.[27]

It is, however, interesting that ULFA had succeeded in shifting the focus from migrants and religious minorities to exploitation, economic backwardness, cultural alienation, and neglect of the literary and linguistic achievements of the people. After the leadership entered into negotiations with the Indian government, the power of the organization seemed to

[27]Karishma Hasrat, 'ULFA-I faces survival test after deputy chief's surrender. All about the rebel outfit in Assam', *The Print*, 19 November 2020.

fade away. Resistance to the CAA gave the armed group a new lease of life.

## ARMED RESISTANCE IN THE NORTHEAST

In sum, some armed groups in the Northeast want to secede from India, others wish to dominate other ethnic groups, and yet others lay more modest claims. War against the Government of India has quickly translated, in some cases, into strife with other groups within the state or the region, whether ethnic or religious or linguistic. One author suggests that any analysis of the security situation in Northeast India is characterized by all-round frustration. Inhabitants of the region have endured decades of conflict, at times smouldering and at times active, that has kept most of the region militarized, subjected to restrictions on civil rights and political activity, and economically depressed. Yet, violence persists. The centre argues that it is doing the right thing, whereas human rights activists, academics, and civilians complain that people in the region remain impoverished and insecure, and there is limited understanding at the centre of the region and its grievances.[28] The eruption of violence at the metaphorical drop of the hat scars the face of one of the most beautiful regions of India.

Baruah writes that murders, bombings, kidnappings, extortion by militants, and killing of militants by security forces in actual or staged encounters has become a routine part of news from the Northeast. The irony, he seems to suggest, is that there is also news of elections, of ceasefires, and talks with militias. 'But the two kinds of news and images co-exist with disturbing ease.'[29]

Though the Government of India has tried to negotiate with insurgent groups, on various occasions without completely lifting laws that the groups have protested against, the problem might well defy management. Because no sooner does the Indian government sign an agreement with one group than another group starts a cycle of violence or continues the battle of self-determination. This is most explicit in the case of Nagaland. The region might see some peace after the occasional ceasefire, but the situation is precarious and brittle. The net result of the

---

[28]Bethany Lacina, 'Rethinking Delhi's Northeast Policy: Why neither Counter-insurgency nor Winning Hearts and Minds is the Way Forward', *Beyond Counter-Insurgency*, p. 329.
[29]Baruah, *Durable Disorders*, p. 61.

proliferation of armed groups is that some groups endure and reproduce their agendas centred on conflict, and others collapse within months or years after their formation. India's neighbours have been dragged into the conflict, sometimes unwillingly, because various insurgent groups establish bases in these countries.

The geography of the region presents a pattern of shifting alliances and allegiances, breakaways, mergers and splits, agreements and disagreements and, in general, a picture of conflict amidst a degree of uneasy coexistence. The creation of unease, of fear, and of trepidation, the reinforcement of suspicion and of distrust nurtures another sort of violence—one that can break into bloody riots without substantive cause. In some cases, the powerful continue to exert control and the weak bend before this open exercise of domination.

Harekrishna Deka writes of a subtler domination of the promise of freedom, of groups that promise freedom but render you unfree. 'You'll come with us/We will take you by the hand/Don't look at the road/We will cover your eyes/We will build the road for you/And we will tie up your hands/We will take you to the freedom ground/And uncover your eyes/.... *You will come with us/You will smile our smile/You will dance our dance/You will cry our tears*'.[30]

## MIGRATION AND VIOLENCE

There are other pressing reasons besides regional autonomy or separatism that lead to violence in the Northeast. The most notable cause that has emerged onto the political landscape since the beginning of the twentieth century is migration into the region, particularly Assam, for more than a century. Migration to Assam from Bengal was encouraged by the British colonial power. In the nineteenth century, the British discovered the resource-rich state of Assam, known for coal, tea, and oil. Hindu residents of Bengal were imported to work in the offices of the tea gardens, the government, and the oil and coal industry. At the same time, the colonial government encouraged Bengali Muslim peasants, who were experienced in the art of riverside farming, to settle along the river and cultivate land. This resulted in waves of settlement by Bengali-speaking people.

---

[30]Harekrishna Deka, 'Towards Freedom', Translated from the Assamese by Bibash Choudhury, in Misra, (ed.), *The Oxford Anthology of Writings from North-East India*, p.16.

By the beginning of the twentieth century, the non-Assamese formed a substantial part of the population in the state. As a result, Assamese Hindus launched a series of initiatives to recapture their linguistic and cultural inheritance. In 1903, the formation of the Assam Association became the fulcrum of Assamese identity and nationalism among the middle classes. The association gave voice to the middle classes and effectively articulated their aspirations and their grievances. Other organizations that were to prove politically significant in Assam later were set up, for example, student associations. The first students' association, the Asom Chatra Sanmilan, was formed in 1916. The other landmark in the formation of cultural politics was the establishment of the Assam Sahitya Sabha in 1917. Intellectuals began to write and speak in Assamese. The net result was the consolidation of resentment against the Bengali language. Linguistic assertion over time became the linchpin of Assamese identity.

Inter-community tensions were worsened by the census of 1931 that created considerable panic among the population. It carried a report by the Census Commissioner of Assam, C. S. Mullen. He reported that one of the most important events in Assam in the last twenty-five years, a phenomenon that would in all likelihood affect the future of the people and destroy society more surely than the Burmese invasion of 1825 had done, was migration. The whole structure of Assamese culture and civilization has been the invasion, he wrote. 'It is sad but by no means improbable;, he continued, 'that in another thirty years, Sibsagar district will be the only part of Assam in which an Assamese will find himself at home.'[31] This sentence, which was part of a larger and highly inflammatory paragraph, contributed to the construction of a siege mentality among the Assamese. As suggested in earlier chapters, historians have argued that census reports issued by the British, exemplifying the strong tendency of colonial officials to see Hindus and Muslims as two antagonistic communities always at war with each other, were the underlying reason for Partition and recurrent communal riots in India. The paragraph authored by Mullen bears witness to the argument.

Throughout the first half of the twentieth century, antagonism marked the relationship between Assamese and Bengali speakers. In

---

[31]G. Seetharaman, 'National Register of Citizens in Assam: Issue of illegal foreigners continues to be a major political one', *Economic Times*, 14 June 2015.

1947, the problem was exacerbated. During Partition, Hindus migrated from East Bengal, the eastern wing of Pakistan, to southern parts of Assam. This added to the litany of grievances of the Assamese. After 1947, the economic condition of Assam declined, for it had lost access to the Chittagong Port that became a part of Pakistan. The Assamese literary and cultural elite concentrated on defining the state as Assamese, labouring to ensure that Assamese became the official language of the state, and that it was also the language of instruction. In 1960, despite linguistic diversity, Assamese became the official language of the state.

The process of migration from East Pakistan accelerated in 1971 when the Government of Pakistan clamped down on East Bengal. The Citizenship Act, 1955, for the Northeast had fixed the date of citizenship as 26 January 1950. But after the war in 1971, the date for legalizing immigrants and granting them citizenship was fixed as 25 March 1971. The Indian prime minister, Indira Gandhi, agreed with the prime minister of Bangladesh, Sheikh Mujibur Rahman, that Bangladesh would not take back immigrants who had come to India before the independence of the country. India committed that it would accept them as citizens.

The new cut-off date catapulted major protests by various organizations, prominent among them being AASU, the Assam Sahitya Sabha, a regional party called the Purbanchal Lokha Parishad, and a social group which called itself the Asom Jatiyatabadi Yuba Chatra Parishad. By 1979, the cauldron of generalized discontent, with what was seen as the cynical politics of the central government, boiled over. The immediate cause was the by-election in Mangaldoi parliamentary constituency where the sitting MP, Hiralal Patwari, had died. In February 1978, the Election Commission discovered that large numbers of immigrants were included in the electoral rolls in Mangaldoi, a constituency that had substantial number of settlers from East Bengal. The Chief Election Commissioner decided that migrants would be included in the voters' list. When the Election Commission announced that polls would be conducted on the basis of the 1976 electoral rolls, four student organizations met, formed the Asom Gana Parishad (AGP), and announced the commencement of the anti-foreigner agitation in Assam.

On 6 November 1979, a large rally was convened in Guwahati and, four days later, large numbers of people courted arrest. Schools and colleges were closed and office staff also struck work and courted arrest. Political parties were asked to boycott the elections. Though the movement ostensibly spoke of the values of constitutionalism and citizenship, the subtext carried highly volatile and combustible terms such as 'foreigners' and 'Bangladeshi immigrants'.

The leaders of the movement claimed that though 31 to 34 per cent of the population in 1971 were foreigners, they were still included in the electoral rolls. The AGP demanded that all immigrants from East Pakistan, now Bangladesh, should be deported and a National Register of Citizens should be updated based on the Indian Citizenship Act for the Northeast. Two constituents of the coalition of organizations spearheading the movement spoke of secession—the Asom Jatiyatabadi Yuba Chatra Parishad and Purbanchaliya Loka Parishad. The former would later develop into the United Liberation Front of Assam, or ULFA.

On 8 June 1979, the AASU sponsored a twelve-hour general strike in the state and along with the Asom Gana Parishad, which was a coalition of political and cultural organizations, asked the authorities to detect, disenfranchise, and deport foreigners. The two organizations proceeded to coordinate resistance across the state. The initiative was backed by unprecedented support from society. Protestors picketed government offices and went on strikes as a form of civil disobedience. The movement called for a boycott of the forthcoming parliamentary elections in 1980 and the assembly elections in 1983. A series of negotiations with the central government followed.

Over time, the movement resorted to everyday violence, and bomb blasts became the order of the day. AASU refused to accept the new cut-off date of 1971 as agreed upon by Indira Gandhi and Sheikh Mujibur Rehman. In 1982, elections to the state assembly were declared by Indira Gandhi's government despite massive resistance from the AASU and other student groups. Activists asked the people to boycott the elections because the electoral rolls had not been revised. AASU leaders were arrested and the people decided to boycott the elections. With the announcement of the elections to the state assembly, the movement escalated and swelled. Large contingents of paramilitary forces were dispatched to Assam. Violence, however, did not abate. Bridges over the river Brahmaputra and its tributaries were burnt, schools were set on fire, people were killed in police firings, and the election became a battle between the police and the people, and between different religious groups in the state.[32]

## NELLIE: A SYNONYM FOR VIOLENCE

One of the deadliest communal riots in the country took place in the state in 1983 over this issue. At this time, student-led movements against 'foreigners' had gained traction. A massacre took place in a cluster of fourteen villages around Nellie situated in the central Assam district of Nagaon. Estimates hold that 1,600 to 2,000 people were brutally murdered. Unofficial estimates tell us that the figures were much higher. Over a period of six hours, 1819 Muslims were killed.[33] In 1947, a referendum had been held in Mymensingh to determine whether the residents wanted to go to Pakistan or stay in India. A substantial number of people voted to join Pakistan, but a slice of Mymensingh remained part of Assam.

Though large numbers of Hindus had migrated from the region to India in 1947, Muslims who had migrated even before Partition were identified and killed in Nellie. The immediate cause for the massacre was the refusal of the people living in the cluster of villages surrounding Nellie to boycott state elections in 1983.

Huge numbers of people in the state had been targeted as migrants from the region of formerly undivided Bengal, subsequently East Pakistan and Bangladesh. Therefore, the only way members of a beleaguered community could establish their credentials as citizens of India was by protecting their documents of residence, and by ensuring that their name was on the voters' list. In 1983 in Nellie, thousands of people were murdered in the most gruesome ways because they were identified as illegal immigrants and because they refused to accept the boycott.

The immediate cause was defiance of the boycott, but a larger historical issue that stalks collective life in the state formed the background to the massacre. Without understanding the issue that has shaped history and bred tensions between people, the immediate provocation and mass murder simply do not make sense. We will return to the historical build-up in a moment; here, let us register the enormity of what is called

---

[32]A comprehensive account of the movement has been authored by Manash Firaq Bhattacharjee, 'Decades of discord; Assam against itself', *The Wire*, 11 August 2018.

[33]Chandrima Bannerjee, '36 years on, survivors of Nellie massacre remember India's bloodiest election', *Times of India*, 17 April 2019.

the Nellie massacre. Nellie was one of the few incidents of communal violence in rural India. The victims as well as the perpetrators were simple peasants. Reports hold that the main attackers belonged to a plains tribe, the Tiwas. The tribe resented migrants, claiming that the latter had appropriated land and resources. Other attackers belonged to the Hira and the Koch tribe. Some of the attackers were caste Hindus.[34]

The immediate provocation has been touched on above. Elections were slated to be held in Nellie and neighbouring villages inhabited by Muslims. These villages were surrounded by Tiwa, the Lalung, and other ethnic villages. On 14 February 1983, residents of the surrounding villages met, and decided that any Muslim who was in favour of the election should be socially and economically ostracized. Any violation of the diktat carried severe penalties. Amidst rumours of a communal clash in neighbouring villages between the Assamese and the Bodos, and the discovery of bodies of children belonging to groups that were either in favour of or against the poll, tension and anxiety prevailed in the cluster of villages around Nellie. On 17 February, the second phase of the poll took place amidst rumours of Muslim attacks on Assamese villages across the river. Residents of Nellie were forcibly prevented from voting in the polls. The elections heralded the onset of one of the most shocking bloodbaths in Indian history.

On 18 February, a howling mob surrounded Nellie armed with guns, spears, swords, and daos. Cries of 'joi ai Asom' rent the air as residents of the villages ran to escape the murderers. When the Muslim groups began to retreat, they were set upon by dao-wielding attackers from the rear. The killings redoubled in ferocity. Heart-rending stories about how every member of extended families of the village was killed, of how throats were slashed, little babies were knifed, and women holding onto their children were massacred, did the rounds. The carnage went on till the morning of the next day but no one came to their aid. Some 200 survivors huddled in refugee camps, the dead were disposed off through mass cremations, rotting corpses lined the villages, houses were gutted, and as the sound of wails and mourning resounded in the sky, the rivers ran red with blood.

The Assamese poet Uddipana Goswami asks a heart-rending question

---

[34]A detailed account of the massacre is found in Makiko Kimura, 'Agency of Rioters: A study of Decision-making in the Nellie Massacre, Assam, 1983', *Beyond Counter-insurgency*, pp.188–206.

in her poetry. 'How does a river die, a river like Rangi?/Do you have to dam her, drain her, dig her/In order to kill her?/Do you need to tell her she is no more/Your mother, lover, sister, friend? Or do you like the ancient king choke her/With the blood of a thousand foes?'[35] Goswami subverts the romance of the river, she makes it bear the burden of innumerable bodies, of those who were dead simply because they wanted to live and work on a piece of land into which they mixed their blood and sweat, the land that others lusted after. Land around which identities are constructed and harnessed is the paramount bone of caste and communal contention in modern India.

A survivor, Khairruddin, recounted his experience of that time in vivid detail. He recollected the way in which the mob set fire to his house while he tried to escape with both his sons on his back. As he ran away from the carnage, he came across his daughter's lifeless body. He was unable to grieve even for a moment. He was trying to get his other children to safety. Khairruddin was injured when someone hit him on the head and he collapsed moments after. He watched in helpless silence as his younger son was hacked to death. He lost his older son when he swam away from the mob across the river Kopili. The CRPF rescued him and his wife, but she succumbed to her injuries in the police station. Khairruddin lost two sons, a daughter, his wife, his parents, and four of his brothers along with their families. His tragic story does not allow him to sleep till date. 'Whenever I close my eyes,' he said, 'I see the faces of my dead children.'[36] This is only one account of the horrendous killings in Nellie.

Indira Gandhi and President Giani Zail Singh visited refugee camps and promised compensation and an investigation into the violence. The compensation was a pittance of ₹5,000 for the next of kin of the deceased, ₹3,000 for the injured and two bundles of tin sheets to rebuild their burnt homes. The compensation reached the intended beneficiaries much later. A total of 688 cases were filed; the police issued charge sheets in only 310 cases. These cases were closed and not a single perpetrator was punished.[37]

---

[35]Rini Burman, 'Guns with Occasional Music: Female Poets from the Northeast', *Kindle Magazine*, 22 July 2014.

[36]Subasri Krishnan, 'Thirty-two years Later, the Nellie massacre remains all but forgotten', *The Caravan*, 18 February 2015.

[37]Ratnadeep Choudhary, 'Nellie massacre and "citizenship", when 1800 Muslims were killed in Assam in six hours', *The Print*, 18 February 2019.

In July 1983, the Commission of Inquiry on the Assam Disturbances (The Tewary Commission) was set up to investigate the matter. It submitted its 600-page report to the state government in May 1984. The report was never tabled in the assembly. Some civil society organizations and sections of the media managed to access the report, which reportedly held that the government had information about an impending attack on Muslim villages. Subsequently, criminal cases were filed in the high court and the Supreme Court, but they were dismissed.[38] Nellie symbolized one of the most barbaric acts of violence in India, perpetrated upon victims for reasons that are completely unjustifiable. These deaths could have been avoided. Avoidable deaths are one of the most serious tragedies of humankind.

## A TRANSITORY PEACE
In 1985, the Assam Accord crafted by Prime Minister Rajiv Gandhi's government established the criteria, strategy, and structure for the foreigner issue. The parties to the agreement were the central government, the Assam government, and the AASU. The accord sought to address the immigrant issue from Bangladesh, establish constitutional safeguards for citizens, and provide economic incentives for growth. The accord between the AASU and the Rajiv Gandhi government established that migrants coming to India from East Pakistan before 1 January 1966 would be formally made citizens, those who came after this date till 24 March 1971 would be disenfranchised for ten years, and those who came after 25 March 1971 would be expelled and their names deleted from the electoral rolls.

The negotiations were carried on in the shadow of disruptions, strikes, and civil disobedience, all of which bore testimony to the power of the AASU. The students' movement reflecting a broader strain of Assamese subnationalism fetched support from the society and various cultural organizations, but it tended towards chauvinism. In the process, all Bengali Muslims, whether from India or from Bangladesh, were seen as Bangladeshis and foreigners and subjected, on occasions, to violence. Assam's ethnic diversity was held hostage to the politics of cultural nationalism.

---

[38]Ipsita Chakravarty, 'Why was Assam's Nellie massacre not prevented, despite intimation of violence', *Scroll.in*, 18 February 2017.

In 1986, India's Citizenship Act was amended to include the provisions of the Assam Accord. Elections were held and the movement was transformed into a political party which won a majority of seats and formed the new state government. The Indian Parliament had passed the Illegal Migrants (Determination by Tribunals) Act, 1983, wherein tribunals were to be established to determine fairly the question of whether a person was an illegal immigrant, so that the government could expel them. The date for establishing citizenship was set as 25 March 1971, when the Pakistani Army had cracked down on East Pakistan, propelling major migration. Therefore, all migrants before the date are held to be citizens of India because Bangladesh does not take responsibility for people who were citizens of erstwhile East Pakistan. Those who came after 25 March 1971 will be treated as non-citizens. This tribunal was scrapped in 2005.

In 1951, a National Register of Citizens for the Northeast had been enacted by the Government of India. It was revived after the Assam Accord in 1985. In December 2014, several petitions before the Supreme Court sought implementation of the main clause of the Assam Accord, that is, the detection of foreigners and the deletion of their names from the electoral rolls of Assam. A two-judge bench of the Supreme Court consisting of Justices Rohinton Fali Nariman and Ranjan Gogoi ordered that the National Register of Citizens (NRC) be updated and began to monitor the process of updating the register. The state coordinator for the NRC, Prateek Hajela, was appointed to keep the court informed of the progress of the exercise that involved 3.29 crore people. They had to fill in forms and submit elaborate documentation to establish citizenship.

The problem is that the principle of detection and detention was being implemented after almost three decades, and people were asked to produce papers that they might not possess. Most of the people called upon to prove citizenship are poor and non-literate. They have often lost their papers during natural calamities such as floods that hit their homes and workplaces. Above all, the updating of the NRC has bred fear. Some people committed suicide, some were harassed by the border police, and others were held in detention centres that lack basic amenities. What is more troubling is that the reinvention of the NRC unleased another wave of hatred and violence in Assam.

On 7 April 2019, Shaukat Ali, a sixty-eight-year-old Muslim man in the Bishwanath Chariali area of Assam, which is part of the Tezpur constituency. He was surrounded and thrashed by a mob. The mob forced him to eat pork, which is against his religious beliefs. His only crime, if could be called that, was that he was selling beef. The crowd kept haranguing him, asking him whether he was Bangladeshi, and whether his name was or was not in the NRC.[39]

This is what the alignment of the rights of citizens with the majority, and the non-alignment of these rights with minority religious identities, has done to our own people. Though for the Assamese people all Bengali-speaking people are illegal immigrants, irrespective of their religion, increasingly the notion of an illegal migrant seems to focus on Muslims.

The bias against the community has reached unspeakable proportions now in the form of visible and invisible violence. Finally, when the updated NRC was finalized, out of the 19 lakh people who could not establish citizenship, 16 lakh were Hindus. The BJP moved rapidly to set aside the NRC.

## CONCLUSION

It is by now well known that Assam has seen much violence over the issue of who is and who can be a citizen of India. In the process, the contribution of migrants to the productivity of Assam, the cultural and linguistic resources of the region, and to ethnic diversity and the making of a plural society are forgotten. They are seen only as migrants, as alien. The main and the deep divide is linguistic, but increasingly it has become religious. When this divide is triggered off and translates into incidents of violence, people turn on each other and draw lines between themselves and those who might have been neighbours, lovers, friends, fellow citizens, and sharers in a collective fate. The lines are drawn on the shifting sands of identity. The struggle for identity permeates armed struggles within the region, aspirations for a state of their own or for more autonomy, and resistance to the imposition of coercive laws.

Violence is also experienced through fear of the future, through trepidation that the nightmare will not end, and through terror that the gunshots will not cease. The Naga journalist and poet Monalisa

---

[39]'Assam police arrest four in Shaukat Ali's mob attack case: Hunt on to nab the rest', *The Wire*, 11 April 2019.

Changkija poignantly narrates the constant unease that haunts lives in the Northeast in her poem 'Aftermath':

> The silence of the sunlit summer afternoon
> has just been shattered by gun shots across the town
> I stand rooted to the ground waiting for the echoes
> to die down in my mind...
> I am desperately searching for an answer
> to my daughter's question, when will the gun shots end?[40]

'I cannot', she says in desperation in another poem, 'Stop This Nightmare', 'make myself write/Another word of another shot dead.'

This is the story of some of the states of the Northeast of India—this beautiful region of mists and forests, of myths and of stories of resistance to power. It is a saga of violence inflicted by people on the security forces, by security forces on the people, and by people on each other. The causes of violence may be determinate, but the trajectory of violence is unpredictable, it sweeps away everyone and everything in its way. The social sciences tend to flatten the enormity of the human condition and reduce human fatalities to statistics. Can numbers capture the pain of loss or the anxiety of waiting for the next bout of violence? Perhaps it is only the literary and the poetic form that can come to grips with the tragedy of the human condition.

---

[40]Monalisa Changkija 'Northeast outside the newspaper pages', Zama (ed.), *Emerging Literatures from Northeast India*, p. 141.

## Chapter 6

# MAOIST VIOLENCE

*The moon*
*The river*
*The flower*
*The stars*
*The birds*
*We can look for them later*
*But today,*
*In this darkness*
*The last battle is yet to be fought*
*What we need now in our house is—fire*

—Murli Mukhopadhyay, 'Fire'[1]

## INTRODUCTION

The history of violence in the areas that the Maoists (also known as the Naxalites) have made their own is once again a story of ordinary villagers and tribals buffeted by storms of violence unleashed by both the Maoists and the security forces of the Indian state. The causes for and the nature of armed struggle is, however, different from other narratives of violence mapped in this volume. In this case, we have on our hands a revolutionary armed struggle that challenges the basic claim of the Indian state—that it is democratic. The struggle points relentlessly to the failure of the state in delivering justice to the poorest and the most marginalized of Indian citizens. The ideology of the Maoists puts forth a vision of a society based on liberation, equality, and justice. The Naxalites do not want to secede from India. Nor do they want to claim special

---

[1]Sumanta Banerjee (ed.), *Thema Book of Naxalite Poetry,* Kolkata: Thema Books, 2010, pp. 54–55.

privileges from the state. Their intent is to secure emancipation for the poorest, the most neglected, and the voiceless. The Maoists give the most vulnerable sections of Indian society a voice. Have they succeeded? Perhaps yes, perhaps no.

The problem is that the Maoists, completely and utterly sceptical of the ability of the democratic state to respond to the misery that follows inequality, speak the language of violence. They unabashedly engage in violent means to achieve their ends. The second problem is that—what can be termed 'revolutionary politics'[2]—targets not only the emissaries and the agents of the Indian state, but also innocent citizens. Admittedly a clear, consistent, and coherent ideology distinguishes the Maoists from other insurgent groups. And deep commitment to the basic values of class equality makes them distinctive in a landscape where violence is used sometimes indiscriminately, and often for ignoble causes. Yet, the use of violence, even in the cause of what counts as justice, has borne terrible consequences. Innocents are swept up in the maelstrom caused by uncontrolled force. This compromises the claim of the Maoists that they deliver justice to the poorest and the most marginalized. The indiscriminate use of violence can actually lead to further injustice because it causes great harm. Finally, as the concluding section will argue, when violence is not, or cannot be, controlled by transformative politics, it defeats the very purpose of revolutionary politics.

## A SHORT HISTORY OF MAOIST VIOLENCE

The central government claimed in 2018 that its National Policy and Action Plan, adopted in 2015 to cover security and development, has fetched tangible results. The policy has succeeded in reducing the sway of the Maoists over large parts of central, eastern, and southern India.[3] According to the report, the number of districts affected by left-wing extremism had risen to 217 in 2017 but then declined. The Ministry of Home Affairs, claiming that Naxalism is no longer the biggest internal security threat to the country, redrew the geographical map of what is called the 'Red Corridor'. Remapping brought down the number of districts affected by Naxal violence from 106 to 90, spread across 11 states. Out of the 90 districts that have been identified, 30 are the

---

[2]Neera Chandhoke, *Democracy and Revolutionary Politics*, London: Bloomsbury, 2015.
[3]Rahul Tripathi, 'The contours of the new Red map', *Indian Express*, 27 November 2020.

worst affected. The states that are the most affected are Chhattisgarh, Jharkhand, Odisha, and Bihar. West Bengal, Maharashtra, and Andhra Pradesh are partially affected. Uttar Pradesh and Madhya Pradesh are slightly affected, according to the MHA.

The report also noted that Maoists have rapidly penetrated states that were not affected earlier—Karnataka, Kerala, Tamil Nadu—in order to link the western and the eastern Ghats. Naxals have also made their presence felt in Northeastern states such as Assam and Arunachal Pradesh.[4]

Ironically, the report on the reduction of the domain of Maoism followed an outburst of intense violence by Naxal cadres. In the latter part of 2018, armed cadres of the Maoist movement masterminded vicious attacks on political leaders, security forces, and civilians. In September 2018, in the Araku Valley of Andhra Pradesh, Naxalites killed an MLA of the Telugu Desam Party, Kidari Sarveswara Rao, as well as his predecessor Siveri Soma.[5] A number of people and security officials lost their lives in a series of attacks in Chhattisgarh on the eve of elections to the state assembly. One BSF sub-inspector was killed in Kanker district in a Maoist strike.[6] Five persons, including one CISF jawan, were killed in Dantewada in a blast.[7] On 11 November 2018, a day before the assembly elections, people living in the interior areas of Dantewada, Bijapur, and Sukma districts reported to the press that Maoist groups had asked them to boycott elections. Notices of the Election Commission hoisted at voters' booths in schools were vandalized or pasted over with slogans, flags, and warnings asking government officials to leave the area.[8] This cast a pall of fear and trepidation on the local population.

This was not the first time the Naxals had wreaked violence, often on innocent civilians, during election time. On 26 May 2013, in the days leading to the state elections, the Maoists ambushed a string of cars ferrying the leaders of the Congress Party in the Bastar forests of Chhattisgarh. Mahendra Karma, a Congress leader who had

---

[4]Ibid.

[5]Sumit Bhattacharya, 'TDP MLA, leader shot in Visakapatnam', *The Hindu*, 24 September 2018.

[6]Ritesh Mishra, 'BSF officer killed in 6 serial blasts by Maoists in Chhattisgarh', *Hindustan Times*, 8 November 2018.

[7]S. Kareemuddin and Ritesh Mishra, '5 persons killed in Maoist Strikes before P.M., Rahul campaign in Chhattisgarh', *Hindustan Times*, 8 November 2018.

[8]Rashmi Drolla, 'Under a shadow of Maoist threats Chhattisgarh goes to the polls on Monday', *Times of India,* 11 November 2018.

masterminded the formation of an anti-Naxalite group, the Salwa Judum, was brutally killed. Reports of the attack sent shock waves throughout the country. V. C. Shukla, a prominent leader of the Congress, was injured, some Congress workers lost their lives, and others were kidnapped.[9]

In April 2019, on the eve of the General Elections in the Bastar region of Chhattisgarh, the sitting MLA, Bhima Mandavi, and four security personnel were killed in an attack by the Maoists. Mandavi belonged to the ruling party at the centre, the BJP. The attack took place even though security during the elections had been fortified considerably.[10] As a report on the killings put it, '[t]he Naxals in the region have repeatedly check-mated the police and paramilitary personnel, sending out a loud message that not only does their war with the Indian State continue, but they are very serious about it, and will do everything to guard their supremacy in the region...the Naxals are ahead of the security forces.'[11]

This indiscriminate use of violence has to be condemned unabashedly. Still, let us tarry for a moment and glance briefly at the context in which some of these brutal and senseless killings have occurred. The intent is not to exonerate the killers but to understand the intricate ways in which violence breeds violence. Take the context of the killing of the Congress leader Mahendra Karma, known as the Bastar Tiger. Karma had represented Bastar in the Lok Sabha and represented Dantewada in the state assembly. He was responsible for the founding of two anti-Maoist forces in the state of Chhattisgarh: the Jan Jagran Abhiyan in the 1990s and the infamous Salwa Judum in 2005. Salwa Judum, a notorious vigilante group reportedly supported by the state government and funded by the central government, forcibly moved thousands of tribals from their homes and relocated them in camps, ostensibly for the purposes of protecting them against the Maoists.

Though this state-funded but privately armed group was represented as a people-backed struggle against Maoism, writes Jason Miklian, we cannot ignore the fact that some of the leaders of Salwa Judum were

[9]Joseph John and Rashmi Drolla, 'Maoists kill Salwa Judum founder Mahendra Karma along with other Congress leaders', *Times of India*, 26 May 2013.

[10]Debobrat Ghose, 'Dantewada MLA Bhima Mandavi killed by Naxals: Intelligence failure, non-adherence to SOP's and leaks to blame', *Firstpost*, 10 April 2019.

[11]Ibid.

little but warlords. It was reported that they proceeded to divide the territory and the forest resources of Dantewada amongst themselves, and control camps which sheltered displaced persons. In exchange for protection services, they received funding, food, and arms from the Chhattisgarh government. Criss-crossing Dantewada in convoys of trucks, and supported by automatic weapon-wielding plainclothes and security personnel, members of the vigilante group recruited young men as special police officers to man a supplementary force. It was alleged that the organization had been contracted by corporate houses, which were intent on appropriating mineral-rich land. The Salwa Judum provided protection and ground clearing services for excavation and mining.[12] The vigilante project bore a bitter harvest. Villagers were displaced, villages were stripped bare, vast stretches of cultivable land lay fallow, collection of forest produce was disrupted, people had no access to weekly markets, schools were turned into police camps, and basic rights were trampled upon.[13]

A petition was filed in the Supreme Court by concerned scholars and human rights activists. They requested the court to ensure that the state government should discontinue support for the vigilante group consisting of more than 5,000 tribal youths. On 5 July 2011, the Supreme Court ordered that both the Chhattisgarh government and the central government should desist from arming callow youth, allotting to them the status of Special Police Officers, and expecting them to perform police functions. Raw recruits had neither been given basic training in the use of arms, nor rudimentary knowledge of human rights law. And these hurriedly conscripted young men had been let loose on villagers in the name of fighting Maoism by any means possible.[14]

It is possible to recount endless stories of the competitive violence unleashed by the government, the Maoists, and vigilante groups on the inhabitants in the Red Corridor in central and eastern India. We can of course join into the official discourse that the Maoists are terrorists and that they aim to take over the state for the sake of wielding

---

[12]Jason Miklian, 'The Purification Hunt: The Salwa Judum Counterinsurgency in Chhattisgarh India', in Alpa Shah and Judith Pettigrew (eds.), *Windows into a Revolution: Ethnographies of Maoism in India and Nepal,* New Delhi: Social Science Press and Orient BlackSwan, 2012, pp. 282–308.

[13]Ibid., p. 302.

[14]J. Venkatesan, 'Salwa Judum is illegal says Supreme Court', *The Hindu,* 5 July 2011.

power. This would mean that we do not explore the context in which armed struggle broke out. Nor do we look at what is distinctive about revolutionary politics. Why do people pick up the gun, or support gun-wielding guerrillas in a democracy when rulers can be changed through elections? They know that the act of picking up guns to achieve political goals will have terrible consequences for lives and livelihoods. The Indian state has declared war on the Maoists, and vigilante groups further this agenda by infiltrating villages and fostering suspicion among the residents. Violence is inflicted by all parties on the citizens of India, and it is difficult to name one as the perpetrator and one as the victim. What is clear is that innocent citizens are harmed.

It cannot be disputed that Maoists have let loose a fury of violence on innocent citizens who travel in trains that are blown up, who inadvertently walk or drive over landmines placed by guerrilla bands of the revolutionary party, who are caught fatally in the crossfire between the armed guerrillas and the security forces of the state, and who live in constant fear that they will be targeted as informers or police agents and executed by kangaroo courts.

Maoist attacks on security forces and kidnapping of policemen have bred serious consequences. For every attack and every kidnapping, security forces extract vengeance on villagers who are not at fault. Their only crime is that they are forced to give shelter, food, water, and sometimes render taxes to Maoists, as well as to vigilante groups and security forces. They have become helpless pawns in the hands of the Maoists on the one hand, and the security establishment and its proxies on the other.

The leading of a life that is bare and stark is the context of deprivation. Adivasis lead lives marked by tremendous hardship and lack of access to basic preconditions of sustenance; they are wracked by fear of displacement from homes and hearths by multiple projects of the state and dominant groups, and shiver in trepidation at the prospect of harassment by moneylenders, contractors, and middlemen. A difficult and bare life dodges their heels. It almost appears that their voice is neither heeded nor even heard in the corridor of power. This becomes clear when we pay even a brief visit to the Red Corridor.

## THE CONTEXT OF DEPRIVATION

In the Red Corridor, little babies die of malnutrition and preventable diseases like diarrhoea; women endure life threatening diseases such as anaemia and malnourishment; poverty relentlessly stalks the lives of inhabitants; and disease, illiteracy, and hunger are their constant companions. It is this place, marked by multiple disadvantages, that the Maoists have made their base.

The Human Development Report 2011 brought out by the erstwhile Planning Commission held that poverty is concentrated in regions of a few states in the central and eastern parts of the country: Bihar, Jharkhand, Odisha, Chhattisgarh, Rajasthan, Madhya Pradesh, and West Bengal, along with some parts of Uttar Pradesh. According to the report, these states, with the exception of West Bengal, have been at the bottom of the Human Development Index (HDI) ranking list since 1999–2000.

The HDI takes into account three indicators: life expectancy at birth, education indices based on literacy and mean years of schooling, and monthly per capita consumption adjusted for inflation and inequality. On this basis, the report concluded that poverty is concentrated in mainly two communities, the STs and the SCs, and some groups of the Other Backward Classes (OBCs).[15]

The United Nations Human Development Report 2019 has ranked India 129 out of 189 countries in terms of human development indicators, up one rank since the 2018 report. At the same time, 28 per cent of a total of 1.3 billion absolute poor live in India. Over the years, all reports show that poverty is concentrated in groups that have been ranked low in the social hierarchy of the country. The 2010 UNDP Human Development Report had affirmed that 81 per cent of STs, 66 per cent of SCs and 58 per cent of OBCs belong to the category of multi-dimensionally poor. The ST and SC populations in these regions suffer from a double disadvantage—that of material deprivation and social discrimination. The report held that 56 per cent of the SC and 55 per cent of the ST population of the entire country lives in Bihar,

---

[15]*India Human Development Report 2011 Towards Social Inclusion*, Planning Commission, Government of India and Institute of Applied Manpower Research, New Delhi: Oxford University Press, pp. 3, 17, 18. An update to the report was released by the Institute in 2014. See Aarti Dhar, 'Human Development indicators are on the upswing in Bimaru States,' *The Hindu*, 14 March 2014. The report included Uttarakhand in the category of poorer states and excluded West Bengal.

Chhattisgarh, Jharkhand, Odisha, and parts of West Bengal and Andhra Pradesh.[16]

The UNDP Human Development Report 2010 pointed out that large numbers of Indian citizens possess very little access to primary goods such as food, health, education, and shelter. Compared to other social groups in the country, a majority of the SCs and STs in the conflict regions belong to the category of the absolutely poor, and are condemned to live a life much below the threshold of what is considered to be human.

And they are so condemned because of the contingent, and hence purely arbitrary, factor of birth. The overlap between absolute poverty and birth in a particular community is not mere happenstance. Notably, people are not poor because they do not possess the basic skills that enable them to participate in profitable transactions; they are poor because they have been born into a community that has been historically stigmatized by the deplorable caste system as the (former) untouchable, or the 'polluting'. The highly iniquitous caste system banished the SCs to the social margins of society. The STs have always been regarded as outsiders, inhabiting as they did the social and the spatial margins of India.

Both communities have been prevented by an intricately designed system of social sanctions from accessing opportunities that were readily available to other members of society, such as education, development of skills, remunerative employment, and participation in social transactions, let alone participation in the public sphere as well as the personal sphere of social interaction. Children born into these two social categories have been for centuries handed down nothing but deprivation, social discrimination, rank indignities, and performance of menial tasks as their patrimony. It is this segment of the population—which continues to suffer from a double disadvantage: of social stigma and material deprivation—that forms the bulk of the inhabitants in the region run over by Maoism.

Deprivation in tribal areas has been intensified by massive land appropriation from populations that depend on land, forests, and rivers for their livelihood. This is not entirely new. Tribals have been, for years,

---

[16]UNDP Human Development Report, *The Real Wealth of Nations: Pathways to Human Development*, p. 99, available at <http://www.hdr.undp.org/sites/default/files/reports/270/hdr_2010_en_complete_reprint.pdf>.

stripped of their land by moneylenders and forest officials, displaced by mining and infrastructure projects, the establishment of Special Economic Zones (SEZs), or wildlife conservation efforts. Projects that tap invaluable resources such as mines, forest produce, and water have displaced millions of Indians, and a majority of these Indians are Adivasis.

In the beginning of the twenty-first century, a qualitatively different project of appropriation appeared on the scene: seizure of natural resources such as minerals and forest produce backed by industrialists and governments. The process, it could be said, practically re-enacts Karl Marx's depiction of primitive accumulation, a process by which populations were alienated from the resources that enable them to lead a sustainable life. These resources are then harnessed to the accumulation of capital. Unbridled appropriation of non-renewable resources such as iron in Chhattisgarh, Jharkhand, and Madhya Pradesh; bauxite in Odisha; and diamonds in Bastar has taken place through legal as well as illegal mining, establishment of SEZs, setting up of hydroelectric plants and industrial units, and the use of open cast-mines.

The Dandakaranya region, a forest area which borders the four states of Andhra Pradesh, Chhattisgarh, Maharashtra, and Odisha, and which covers three districts—Bastar, Kanker, and Dantewada—has become one of the main sites for land grabs by state governments acting on behalf of the corporates. Reportedly, this region possesses an estimated 70 per cent of coal reserves, 80 per cent of iron ore, 60 per cent of bauxite and most of India's chromite reserves.[17] The craggy and bleak terrain is inhabited mainly by Adivasis whose livelihood depends upon the resources of the forest.

Jaipal Singh, who represented the STs in the Constituent Assembly, had made a powerful case for the recognition of historical injustice that had been wreaked on tribal populations. In a speech made on 19 December 1947 about the Resolution on the Aims and Objectives of the Constitution, he had said: '[i]f there is any group of Indian people that has been shabbily treated it is my people. They have been disgracefully treated, neglected for the last 6,000 years.... I take you all at your word that now we are going to start a new chapter, a new chapter of

---

[17]Nitin Sethi, 'As Forests Feed Growth, Tribals Given the Go-by', in Santosh Paul (ed.), *The Maoist Movement in India: Perspectives and Counterperspectives,* New Delhi: Routledge, 2013, pp. 131–33.

Independent India where there is equality of opportunity, where no one would be neglected.'[18] Ironically, it is precisely this section of the Indian people that has been exploited because they inhabit a land rich in mineral and agricultural resources.

## THE WAR AGAINST DEPRIVATION

The regions in which the armed guerrilla squads of the Maoists operate dovetail neatly into areas in which the tribals, arguably the poorest of the poor, live and eke out a living. Maoism has erupted in a hilly and thickly forested region that runs from the north of India through Bihar, Jharkhand, and Chhattisgarh in the centre, down to Odisha, Andhra Pradesh, Tamil Nadu, and some parts of Madhya Pradesh, Uttar Pradesh, Karnataka, and West Bengal. Intensive armed engagement has taken place in the southern part of Chhattisgarh—Dantewada, Bastar, Kanker, Rajnandgaon, and Narayanpur. The Naxalites have drawn on and drawn out the grievances of the local populations against upper-caste landlords, moneylenders, and governments, all of which have, in combination or individually, succeeded in exploiting them and divesting them of resources that sustain livelihoods and belief systems.

It is the expropriation of land that has helped build a support base for Naxalites who entered the region from Andhra Pradesh in the 1980s. Into the political vacuum created by systemic social injustice, the Maoists stepped in with their ideology, rhetoric, and dreams of a new world geared towards the interests of the poor and the oppressed; their strategy of a People's War; their long term objective of taking over state power; and their immediate project of ameliorating the needs of those who have been subjected to extreme deprivation and social stigma through armed struggle.

It is true that tribal communities, which for long have been subjected to double injustice, have revolted against landlords, usurious moneylenders, revenue and forest officials, and other sundry people in positions of power that seek to extract mileage from the poor and the vulnerable, for at least a century. The Maoist struggle marks a new phase in the fight of the poor and the most disadvantaged, or more precisely, the fight *for* the poor and the most disadvantaged. Firstly, isolated and

---

[18]*Constituent Assembly Debates: Official Report*, New Delhi: Lok Sabha Secretariat, 1989, pp. 143–44.

often sporadic or random struggles have been located in a specific ideology and strategy. Secondly, struggling people have been shown visions of a new world where discrimination is banished and where a new society based on justice is secured through armed struggle. The aim of the Maoists is the replacement of the existing power structure by a state that secures justice for all people.

Maoist armed struggle can be distinguished from other armed insurgencies that fight for the rights of a language group, an ethnic group, or a religious group within the state, and secession from the state. The Maoists perceive the existing state as incapable of delivering justice to the poor and the struggling. The state is wedded to the interests and the ideologies of the rich and the powerful. The vision of Maoism is justice for all. But the strategies deployed to secure this vision are ethically and politically flawed because they are wedded to violence. This becomes evident when we survey the biography of revolutionary violence in India.

## ARMED STRUGGLE IN INDIA

Sumanta Banerjee, who calls himself a 'one-time Maoist activist', divides the Maoist movement in India into three phases. The first phase lasted from 1967 to 1975, the second from 1980 to 1990, and the third and the current phase from the 1990s onward. The periods might overlap; what is important, as Banerjee suggests, is the present third phase which has taken place in a very specific set of circumstances.

The saga of armed struggle in post-Independence India was inaugurated in March 1967 in a district in West Bengal—the Naxalbari area in Darjeeling. Sharecroppers and landless labour, armed with the slogan of 'land to the tiller', revolted against local landlords and other exploitative agents. Over the years, the Naxalbari uprising spread over West Bengal and spilled over into Andhra Pradesh, Odisha, Bihar, Madhya Pradesh, Uttar Pradesh, Punjab, and Kerala. Some of these states, or rather regions within these states, continue to be wracked by armed struggle waged by the Maoists.

A number of analysts have traced the origins of the armed uprising to the deep ideological divide in the relationship between the Communist Party of the Soviet Union (CPSU) and the Communist Party of China (CPC). Both parties vehemently disagreed on ideology, strategy objectives, and agents of revolution. For the CPSU, the main agent of revolution had to be industrial workers in the context of a capitalist society. For the CPC, it was the peasantry that had to lead the revolutionary upsurge in a semi-imperial and semi-feudal economy. The conflict deeply affected the internal communist movement. It escalated into a diplomatic crisis and ruptured relations between the Soviet Union and China. In 1969, armies of the two countries clashed on the border.

The breach in the international communist movement impacted the Communist Party of India (CPI) in 1964. The CPI split and a new party, the Communist Party of India (Marxist), or CPI (M), emerged onto the horizon of Indian politics. Despite superficial divisions on the line each party wanted to pursue—the one established by the CPSU or the one mandated by the CPC—both parties remained committed to elections and parliamentary democracy. In a short span of time, another split within the CPI (M) generated a third communist formation, the Communist Party of India, Marxist-Leninist (CPIML).

The split was catalysed by a group led by Charu Mazumdar, who challenged the CPIM's ideology, analysis of Indian society, and strategy of revolutionary transformation. In eight essays published between 1965 and 1967, Mazumdar attacked the CPI (M) for rescinding on Marxist ideology and for its commitment to electoral democracy. The breakaway faction, taking its inspiration from Mao Zedong, declared that the chief contradiction in a semi-feudal and semi-imperialist India is between the peasantry and the landlords. This seemingly irreconcilable divide can only be resolved through armed struggle, the overthrow of the state, and the establishment of a 'People's Democracy'. Power, Charu Mazumdar argued, reiterating the slogan of revolutionaries across the world, flows from the barrel of a gun. He was expelled from the CPI (M) in 1967.

Mazumdar was familiar with revolutionary politics from his early days. He had participated in a violent peasant uprising in 1946 in Bengal. The Tebhaga uprising was anchored in the demand that the share of the landlord in the produce should be reduced from half to one-third. Spearheaded by the undivided CPI, Tebhaga catapulted the crucial issue of the right of the worker over the product of her labour. This could only be achieved by destroying the power of the landlord over the bodies and the labour of the peasant. Destruction of this power had to be wrought through violence. The movement collapsed, but it left a legacy that stirred the political consciousness of later peasant movements against exploitative landlords, usurious moneylenders, and forest and revenue officials.

Mazumdar subsequently turned his attention to the Jalpaiguri district of Bengal, where two communist workers, Kanu Sanyal and Khokan Majumdar, had begun to organize peasants and workers into Kisan Sabhas. He joined the efforts of other activists in motivating landless labourers, sharecroppers, small peasants, and tea garden workers to rise against the exploitation of landowners.

In 1967, armed struggle broke out in Naxalbari and other regions. Naxalbari, which lies in the Terai region of Darjeeling district, was known for tea plantations that had been established by British and Indian companies. Labour from the tribal areas of Jharkhand and Madhya Pradesh had been brought to work on low wages amidst highly exploitative conditions. The uprising generated the terms 'Naxalbari' and 'Naxalites', the first referring to the process of armed struggle and the second to armed revolutionaries known in China as Maoists.

Twenty years after Independence, the democratic state had failed to deliver the basic preconditions of life to the Indian people. The ruling party, the Indian National Congress, had become power-hungry, corrupt, and insensitive to the needs of the people. The two Left parties had adopted the electoral route to democracy and the leadership of the Naxalites attacked them for whittling down the agenda of revolutionary transformation: the raison d'être of the Communist movement. In 1947, the great poet Faiz Ahmad Faiz had written the epitaph of the moment of independence, the other face of which was the partition of the country. He had spoken of the loss of hope and yet he instilled hope in the defeated masses: 'let us once again reassemble and struggle for liberation, let us continue; our work is not yet over' (Chale chalo keh voh manjil abhii nahin aayi).[19] It is precisely this unfinished task of delivering to the people justice and deliverance from oppression and exploitation that the Naxalite movement took up.

The strategy of armed struggle adopted by the Naxalite movement was motivated by the ideology of guerrilla war fashioned by Mao Zedong. The victory of the Chinese Communist Party in 1949, and the defeat

---

[19]Translation provided by the author.

of French forces by Vietnamese guerrilla forces at Dien Bien Phu in 1954, had amply vindicated this ideology and strategy. In Mozambique, armed struggle by Frelimo under the leadership of Samora Machel, the liberation war in Angola, and the guerrilla war waged by the Partido Africano para a Independencia de Guinea e Cabo Verde (PAIGC), or the African Party for the Independence of Guinea and Cape Verde, under the leadership of Amilcar Lopes Cabral in Guinea Bissau, vindicated the case for unconventional warfare.

In India, the outbreak of armed struggle in Naxalbari inspired a generation of young people who had become disillusioned with the state of the economy, the polity, and society. They left prestigious universities and well-paid jobs to join the struggle. They were not alone. The late sixties and early seventies were a time of great upheaval across the globe when the youth revolted against the establishment. Revolutionary romanticism and a passionate desire for a new order that could deliver justice and eliminate injustice exploded across the globe at the turn of the 1970s, firing minds and sparking off imaginations. Campus revolts broke out in the 1960s in the US, Germany, France, Italy, Japan, Mexico, and other countries of the West. Young people rejected the ideas, institutions, and visions of a liberal capitalist order that had been forged in the aftermath of World War II.

In the United States, campus revolts against US involvement in the Vietnam War articulated a generalized ethos of rebellion against the established order. The civil liberties movements, gender struggles for equality, the struggle for the right to sexual preferences, and rebellions in ghettos of American cities dissipated expectations that the American way of life would provide a luminous model for the rest of the world to follow. Hundreds of thousands of African Americans participating in urban protests mounted a formidable challenge to practices of discrimination and racism, as well as poor housing, dismal schooling, unemployment, and police brutality.

May 1968 is remembered as the time when university students launched a political, cultural, and sexual revolution. And the world recollected the words of the English poet William Wordsworth who, in *The Prelude*, wrote of the 1789 French Revolution thus. 'Bliss was it in that dawn to be alive, But to be young was very heaven! O times…When Reason seemed the most to assert her rights.' Wordsworth was perceptive.

The vision, the energy, and the languages invented by rebellious young people injected a breath of fresh air into jaded and bankrupt political discourses. If the young do not struggle for emancipation, who will?

In India, young people joined the revolution. Many of them were quickly disillusioned for two reasons: one, the movement lacked a coherent ideology; and two, it was committed to the use of violence. If some students fought along with the Naxalites, others were terribly disappointed with the call to annihilate class enemies and with Charu Mazumdar's injunction that their hands had to be stained with the blood of the class enemy. Till date, Charu Mazumdar is slammed for his insistence that the annihilation of class enemies is a higher form of class struggle and his emphasis on the need to physically liquidate feudal classes in the countryside—landowners, moneylenders, and their agents.

But some young people continued with the struggle. Red Guard squads were formed in schools and colleges to serve as a precursor to the formation of an Indian People's Liberation Army. The period of discontent saw the instigation of workers by romantic revolutionaries to rise against capitalists, denouncement of class enemies, desecration of statues of revered leaders, raids on government offices, gheraos, strikes, attacks on police personnel, hoisting of flags hailing Chairman Mao on the rooftops of prominent universities, and damage to public property. In rural areas, peasant militias armed with bows and arrows seized grain from the kulaks. The escalation of violence led to deaths in police firing, killing of landlords, and snatching of arms. It was a movement that was based on romantic visions of the end of exploitation and the inauguration of an era of equality. But it was destined to dissolve for a number of reasons.

## EVALUATING NAXALBARI

With the benefit of hindsight, what are we to make of the first phase of the Naxalite revolt against institutionalized injustice inflicted upon the tribals and the Dalits, and the wider objective of taking over state power? Naxalites were attacked for what was perceived as revolutionary adventurism. The party was not well organized, it had not disseminated its ideology adequately and, as Manoranjan Mohanty argued, the movement was pre-organizational. It mechanically applied formulations of the Chinese revolution in India and concentrated more on violence and less on politicization of the constituency it spoke on behalf of.[20] More significantly, the struggle sparked off state repression and catapulted the expansion of paramilitary forces. In other words, Naxalbari was premature and more romantic than revolutionary in its programme and objectives. More significantly, it sparked off state repression. Thus was written the rather sad epitaph of a movement that had gripped the political imagination of many a young student who sought to liberate India from the ills of the human condition the post-Independence leadership had consigned the country to.

Within two years, the armed struggle in West Bengal and Andhra Pradesh was put down ruthlessly by the state. Top leaders and cadres were arrested. Charu Mazumdar was arrested on 16 July 1972 and died twelve days later in police custody. The police did not hand over his body to his family and he was given an unceremonious burial by the security forces. His comrade, Jangal Santhal, turned into an alcoholic and headed towards a disgraceful end in 1981. Kanu Sanyal disowned violence and opted for the parliamentary route to politics. In 2010, he committed suicide.

Post-Naxalbari, the second phase of Naxalism inaugurated a series of splits in the movement along personal rather than ideological lines. Consequently, the movement divided and proliferated like the proverbial amoeba. In Bihar of the 1980s and the 1990s, it was possible to find at least twelve to fourteen Naxalite groups, each professing copyright over the ideology, the strategy, and the objectives of Naxalism, and often locked in deadly battles with each other. The second phase was also marked by the degeneration of revolutionary struggle and rapid descent into mindless acts of violence, which scarred not only the bodies of landlords, but also those of small farmers, petty government employees, members of rival political parties, and anyone suspected of being a police informer, including former comrades who had dissented from the line of the leadership.

Sumanta Banerjee concludes that the history of the last four decades of the Naxalite movement in India is a painful record of attempts, both heroic and loutish, to bring about revolutionary changes in the benighted

---

[20]Manoranjan Mohanty, 'Challenges of Revolutionary Violence: The Naxalite Movement in Perspective', *Economic and Political Weekly*, Special issue on Maoist Movement in India, Vol. XLI, No. 29, 22–28 July 2006, pp. 3,163–68.

economic and social living conditions of the poor. Courageous battles against vicious state machinery, followed by self-sacrifice by thousands of guerrillas and patient efforts by dedicated cadres to initiate land reform and bring about changes in their areas of control, were marred by lumpen acts of extortions from petty traders and contractors and ruthless killings of people suspected to be police informers.[21]

The third phase of the movement was inaugurated at the turn of the twenty-first century, more precisely in 2004. Two features marked the third phase as significant. The first was land grab by corporates backed by state governments. The second was the unification of two major factions of the Naxalites. The regions which form part of the Red Corridor are rich in minerals and agricultural and forest produce. The corporates and the state have confronted resistance because communities have not only a material but a sacred relationship to the land, forests, and rivers.

Consider the sanctity that the Niyamgiri Hills in Odisha hold for the resident communities, or the mythology around the river Narmada. In these regions, conflict over appropriation of land took on serious proportions. In August 2013, a plan by the British corporate Vedanta to mine bauxite in the Niyamgiri Hills was rejected by twelve village councils, or gram sabhas, of the region. Forest produce from the hills provides livelihood for the members of the community, they graze their cattle there, and worship the hills as the abode of their God. The 8,000-strong Dongria Kondh tribal group had been agitating against the project for almost ten years. In 2014, the Government of India rejected Vedanta's project to mine in the hills.[22]

The vote on the issue whether the project should be allowed followed a Supreme Court ruling in April 2013.[23] The villagers decided that the decision of the court should be respected, particularly since the mining project affects their rights to worship their deity known as Niyam Raja who resides in the hills. The court had ruled that the religious rights of the community have to be protected. Therefore, the ban levied in 2010 on mining bauxite for the Lanjigarh Alumina Refinery by the

---

[21]Sumanta Banerjee, 'Beyond Naxalbari', *Economic and Political Weekly*, 22 July 2006, pp. 3,159–63.

[22]Neha Sethi, 'Government rejects Vedanta's bauxite mining plans in Niyamgiri', *Mint*, 11 January 2011.

[23]Priscilla Jebaraj, 'Court directs gram sabhas to take a call on Vedanta', *The Hindu*, 16 April 2013.

Environment Ministry could be lifted depending on the will of the local people. (Under the Right to Fair Compensation and Transparency in Land Acquisition, Rehabilitation and Resettlement Act 2013, local populations have the right to accept or reject projects.)

The special relationship tribal communities have towards the land on which they reside, with the rivers and the forests, a relationship that is both sacred and material, makes the region their habitat. This habitat is often sought to be taken away by capital in alliance with the government for purely private purposes. Nehru saw dams and big projects as the temples of modern India. He was criticized for his policy of appropriating natural resources. We have to recollect, however, that whatever land was taken over was utilized for public purposes such as irrigation and power. Today, land can be seized by the state on behalf of the corporates for purely private gains.

The Maoists led the resistance against the wholesale grab of land by corporates, a process that stripped people of access to resources and to their sacred places. The struggle was launched by a combination of the two most significant groups in the movement. The first group, People's War (PW), was the outcome of a 1998 merger between People's War Group (PWG) and CPI(ML) Party Unity—the former dominant in Andhra Pradesh, Southern Chhattisgarh and parts of Maharashtra, Madhya Pradesh, Karnataka, and Tamil Nadu, and the latter dominant in Jehanabad and Gaya districts of Bihar. The upshot of the merger of PW and MCC was the formation of the Communist Party of India (Maoist) and the formation of the People's Liberation Guerrilla Army (PLGA) that has an estimated 9,000 to 10,000 trained fighters and which owns sophisticated weapons.

Renouncing the parliamentary path to democracy, a form of government viewed as corrupt and corrupting, the party declared war on the Indian state in order to establish the people's power. No elections, no participation, no representation, no accountability of the rulers to the ruled will do. In the mode of guerrilla struggle made famous by Mao, liberated zones in the rural hinterland have to be expanded to encircle the cities and overwhelm the rest of the country. Power must be seized through the barrel of a gun.

## WHAT HAVE THE MAOISTS ACCOMPLISHED

The Naxalites launched armed struggle in 1968. India changed as its economy transformed and was liberalized, people lost faith in revolutions that devour their own children, new generations were more interested in securing well-paid jobs instead of joining the struggle for their fellow citizens, and the advent of civil society put an end to revolutionary imaginaries. But the Naxalites continued to fight for the rights of the poor and the dispossessed with violence.

Has the use of violence against the forces and the institutions of the Indian state succeeded in achieving the objectives of the Naxalites? There can be no clear answer to the question.

First, we have to recognize that guerrilla war against the colonial power is qualitatively distinct from war against a government that has been democratically elected. Armed struggle in India, where democracy, howsoever imperfect it might be, is accepted as legitimate, is difficult if not impossible. Sumanta Banerjee suggests that India, a parliamentary republic, despite large-scale corruption and criminality, still enjoys democratic legitimacy among wide sections of the people and major contending social groups find democracy useful for their own ends. 'The system apparently has not yet exhausted all its potentialities of exploiting the hopes and aspirations of the Indian poor and underprivileged sections.'[24] The sophisticated bourgeois Indian state, skilled in evoking and harnessing loyalties to its own cause, is even more skilled in neutralizing challenges and upping the ante.

Second, the Maoists have had to face the armed might of the state. The Government of India has used formidable military force to wipe them out. At the same time, it has invested funds for infrastructure and welfare programmes in the districts most affected by Maoism. The introduction of a number of measures designed to reverse legacies of underdevelopment, ameliorate poverty that was fuelling the conflict, and embark on development in poverty-stricken areas has contributed to strengthening the democratic credentials of the state. Bureaucrats concentrate energies on the most neglected districts in which armed struggle prevails, try to establish secure access to education, organize camps on preventive and curative healthcare, repair infrastructure,

---

[24]Banerjee, 'Beyond Naxalbari', pp. 3,159.

and improve the channels of distribution of foodgrains. The central government has given financial support to the state governments for the purpose of instituting long-term development projects as well as provision of social goods. In sum, the 'clear, hold, and develop' strategy uses the 'magic mantra' of development to win back tribal populations.

Third, the focus on building infrastructure, roads, highways, and bridges has helped government officials to penetrate thick and inaccessible forest areas which provide bases for the armed struggle. The parallel with the strategy deployed by the former ruler of Cuba, Fidel Castro, is striking. After having waged a successful guerrilla war against the government, Castro proceeded to build modern highways in the till then inaccessible Sierra Maestra region of Cuba to reward inhabitants for their support. It also ensured that in the future, guerrilla onslaughts would not be repeated. Modern means of communication and information technology have managed to neutralize the potential of guerrilla war to fight an army that is technologically superior in many ways. The Maoists have had to retreat further into the forest areas of central and south-central India. But they are encircled relentlessly by the security forces.

Fourth, admittedly the Maoists have carried out certain social and economic reforms. They have, in pockets of the Dantewada region, transferred land to the tiller, extended aid to poor farmers, established cooperatives, ensured that peasants get just prices for their agricultural commodities and minor forest produce, disbursed knowledge about modern techniques of agriculture, distributed better quality seeds gathered from elsewhere, and encouraged voluntary labour to construct tanks with canal systems.

Yet, as analysts of the movement tell us, the Maoists also deploy the indiscriminate use of coercion to herd people to the fold of their ideology. We simply do not know whether the tribals and the SCs in the Red Corridor have been persuaded, coaxed, or coerced into sharing the goals of the party. Neither do we know whether they prefer immediate solutions to pressing problems, compared to the long-term objectives of seizing state power. It is also debatable whether villagers line up behind cadres of the party out of fear, or whether they are genuine converts to the ideology of the party. Is the party characterized by the use of force rather than mobilization? Reports from the field suggest that the former is more prevalent.

Bela Bhatia, who has carried out fieldwork in Bihar and Andhra Pradesh, suggests that a movement that promises liberation can actually end up making people feel less free. It is also problematic that members of mass fronts pay the price for actions taken by the underground party. These actions, again ironically, are taken on behalf of the people but without their knowledge or consent. The use of violence has taken a heavy toll, she concludes.[25]

Fifth, a series of studies tell us that the development schemes inaugurated by the Naxalites are precisely the ones that the government is promoting to stave off the threat of Maoism. Nirmalangshu Mukherji has made an interesting point in this context. Even if wages in the region have increased because of the bargains the Maoists have finalized with the contractors, he suggests, these are far less than the minimum wages paid in other parts of the country, for example, Kerala.[26] The irony is that the initiatives taken by the Maoists have but a pale resemblance to development projects in other parts of the country, projects initiated by the same state they wish to overthrow. Nandini Sundar makes roughly the same point. The Maoists have established mass organizations in Dandakaranya guerrilla zone and carried out development work. But these initiatives simply cannot match what the government could have done for the villagers, if only it had the political will to do so.[27] Indisputably, every political party focuses on development in its political manifestos and in rhetoric. Maoist attempts to ameliorate the plight of the poor bears an uncanny resemblance to its enemy—the Indian state. The reverse is equally true; the Indian state completes the agenda of Maoism. This is the supreme irony of what is called revolutionary violence.

What is it then that Maoism has accomplished? The scholar John Harriss holds that the Maoists have tapped into, and to some extent at least, have articulated the long-standing grievances of Dalits and landless peasants against high-caste landowners and the grievances of the tribal people against the state for what is has done, notably displacement and

---

[25]Bela Bhatia, 'On Armed Resistance', *Economic and Political Weekly*, Special issue on Maoist Movement in India, Vol XLI, No. 29, 22–28 July 2006, pp. 3,179–82.

[26]Nirmalangshu Mukherjee, 'Arms Over the People: What Have the Maoists Achieved in Dandakaranya?' *Economic and Political Weekly*, Vol. XLV, No. 25, 19 June 2010, pp. 16–20.

[27]Nandini Sundar, 'Bastar, Maoism and Salwa Judum', *Economic and Political Weekly*, Special issue on Maoist Movement in India, Vol. XLI, No. 29, 22–28 July 2006, pp. 3,187–92.

sanctioning of repressive policies, as well as what it has not done i.e., provision of basic necessities.[28]

It is possible that the Maoists have succeeded in maintaining the agrarian demands of the rural poor through continuous struggles. They have dramatically foregrounded the interests of the poorest of the poor, an agenda that had been marginalized in the obsession with economic growth and focus on India's ability to become a major power. The foregrounding of development concerns through armed struggle is a sad commentary not only on the ability of the Indian state but also that of the Maoists. Does our democratic government come alive to the needs of the triply oppressed only when they take recourse to violence? Are the Maoists fighting a people's war at great costs to themselves and to their constituency only to implement the agenda of mainstream parties?

Sixth, the political fault lines of the Maoist agenda are more than obvious. They are surrounded by security forces trained in the art of guerrilla war, so they lack the time and the space to spread their programme and convince people of the benefits of their strategies. Resultantly, we have on our hands violence without political mobilization. Maoist cadres have undertaken some development activities such as distribution of land and training in techniques of agriculture and irrigation, but there is nothing in this agenda that does not find space in the agendas of political parties. Moreover, the Indian state, after decades of criminal neglect of the poorest regions of the country, has now set in place the beginnings of a development agenda. Will these initiatives go a long way in reducing the appeal of the Maoist agenda and making it redundant? Perhaps.

It is true that armed struggle has succeeded in several countries. History bears witness to this. But in these cases, the movement could mobilize local populations because they fought colonial powers and not democratically elected governments. Whether it was the liberation war in Algeria, the first Indo–China war, Guinea–Bissau, Mozambique, Angola, and even China, the overriding dimension of the project was that of nationalism. We have an interesting and a somewhat troubling phenomenon on hand in India—the use of extreme violence as a mode

---

[28]John Harriss, 'What is Going on in India's "Red Corridor"? Questions About India's Maoist Insurgency', in Robin Jeffrey, Ronojoy Sen, and Pratima Singh (eds.), *More Than Maoism: Politics, Policies and Insurgencies in South Asia,* New Delhi: Manohar, 2012, pp. 25–46.

of protest and as a mode of creating a new society, and inadequate or weak opportunities for politicizing the people and inviting them to make their own history through sustained mobilization. What is more troublesome is that these two objectives run into tension.

The use of violence suppresses political objectives, and the demands of creating a better life for the Indian people requires mobilization of people towards the cause of establishing a society that will be less exploitative, less oppressive, and more just. This can be achieved only if the revolutionaries form an alliance across the class spectrum. The forging of a coalition seems like a remote dream. Experience of revolutionary war in India has, however, shown that a major contradiction stalks the Maoist agenda: the tension between reformative measures in areas in which the party has established a base and the long-time objective of seizing power.

We have to conclude that in democratic India, the chances of success of violence to achieve justice is difficult. Mobilization by the revolutionaries can be outmatched by the democratic state employing all the resources as its command to 'win hearts and minds'. The outbreak of violence is also outmatched by the democratic state employing deadly weapons against its own citizens. Democratic governments have succeeded in legitimizing torture, illegal detentions, encounter deaths, and imposition of draconian laws that take away civil liberties by invoking national unity and security. But it is the notion of the 'national' that helps in consolidating public opinion against revolutionaries. In turn, revolutionaries confronted by the legitimating strategies of a democratic state, as well as intense coercion, have to focus their energies on guarding their flanks.

## CONCLUSION

The historian Simon Schama asks rhetorically in his magisterial *Citizens: A Chronicle of the French Revolution:* What were the gains of the French Revolution of 1789? If we had to look for one indisputable story of transformation, it would be the creation of the juridical entity of the citizen. But no sooner had this hypothetically free person been invented than his liberties were circumscribed by the police power of the state. Just as Mirabeau and Robespierre had feared, liberties were held hostage to the authority of the state.

Violence was not an unpleasant aspect of the revolution, nor did it distract from the accomplishments of the revolution, concludes Schama; it was the motor of the revolution. All the headlines in newspapers, revolutionary festivals, songs and street theatre, regiments of little boys waving their arms in the air swearing patriotism, all the paraphernalia that was designated as the political culture of the revolution were the products of the same macabre preoccupation with the just massacre and the heroic death.[29] The lesson is clear. Violence begets only violence.

The net outcome is that we have violence without political mobilization of the constituency that will give to dispossessed people awareness of injustice, the need to break inflexible bonds of oppression, and the need for a new society that does not tolerate injustice and that respects the dignity of all. If revolutionaries have few chances in a democracy to pursue the agenda of political awareness and mobilization, both of which give to the dispossessed a voice, we witness violence as theatre. To put the point across starkly, democratic states are not the best contexts in which to pursue a revolutionary agenda. In democratic countries, we find the phenomenon of revolutions sans politics. This leaves only violence, which converts people into consumers rather than citizens who have recovered a voice through struggle.

Without politics in command, violence not only goes berserk, it reduces prospects that the marginalized will be able to confront an unjust system in a sustained manner or that they will be able to stand up and speak back to history. The mandate of Maoist or revolutionary violence is not only violence, the mandate is to transform society and to show the way to a better one, to a society in which little babies will not die of neglect and in which people will not be diminished because the preconditions of a life of dignity have been denied to them. But without sustained mobilization, we get only violence. What we do not get is revolutionary politics that can transform entire societies.

---

[29]Simon Schama, *Citizens: A Chronicle of the French Revolution,* London: Penguin, 1989, pp. 858–60.

# THE CASE AGAINST VIOLENCE

## INTRODUCTION TO A CONCLUSION

The poet Amreeta Syam scripts an imaginary conversation between Subhadra, one of the wives of the hero of the Mahabharata, Arjun, and Lord Krishna in the poem 'Kurukshetra'. The great war of the Mahabharata has generally been understood as a war of the just against the unjust, a war of the righteous against the unrighteous. Nevertheless, the human costs of the war were unimaginable. Generations were wiped out as two branches of a family confronted each other, determined to kill or be killed. Subhadra, whose young son, Abhimanyu, was brutally killed in the war, asks Krishna to account for the losses.

> The war was after all a fight for a kingdom
> Of what use is a crown
> all your heirs are dead
> When all the young men have gone
> …And who will rule this kingdom
> So dearly won with blood
> A handful of old men
> A cluster of torn hopes and thrown away dreams.[1]

The passage forces us to think through the question: what is society left with after the grisly play of violence is exhausted? In the twelfth episode of the Mahabharata, Yudhishthir, the eldest brother of the Pandavas, is convulsed with grief. He has lost his brother, Karna, his sons, and his nephews in the course of the war. What, he wonders, is

---

[1]Amreeta Syam, 'Kurukshetra', in P. Lal (ed.), Vyasa's *Mahabharata: Creative Insights*, Calcutta: Writers Workshop,1992, pp. 13–17.

the value of power if the path to this goal is drenched with the blood of his own people? 'Indeed', he ruminates, 'the whole Earth hath been subjugated by me…. This heavy grief, however, is always sitting in my heart, viz., that through covetousness I have caused this dreadful carnage of kinsmen.'[2]

He is advised to seek the guidance of the patriarch of the clan, Bhishma, a skilled exponent and even more accomplished practitioner of the art of statesmanship, who has lain on a bed of vertically planted arrows on the battlefield, waiting for an appropriate time to order his own death. Yudhishthir, approaching the great hero and his paternal great-uncle with some trepidation, utters these words: '[P]ersons conversant with duty and morality say that kingly duties constitute the highest science of duties…. Do thou, therefore, O king, discourse on those duties.'[3] Bhishma teaches him the craft of statesmanship in the Shanti Parva. The king should nurture his people; he should hold his people together but, more importantly, he should practice non-violence or ahimsa.

In Indian philosophy, the notion of violence is closely connected to ignorance about our own nature, and of our relationship to others and to the world. Enlightenment dissipates violence and enables us to choose between our propensity to violence and non-violence. When they choose non-violence over violence, human beings make ethical choices. In the aftermath of the war that caused suffering on an unprecedented scale, the Shanti Parva places great importance on non-violence as the highest form of rajdharma. Power is meant to protect the weak. The ruler should restrain from exploiting the weak, for the eyes of the latter can scorch the earth. 'In a race scorched by the eyes of the weak, no children take birth. Such eyes burn the race to its very roots…. Weakness is more powerful than even the greatest Power, for that Power which is scorched by Weakness becomes totally exterminated. If a person, who has been humiliated or struck, fails, while shrieking for assistance, to obtain a protector, divine chastisement overtakes the king and brings about his destruction. The divine rod of chastisement falls upon the king. If he practices injustice, a great destruction comes upon the state.'[4]

---

[2] *The Mahabharata of Krishna-Dwaipayana Vyasa,* translated by Kisari Mohan Ganguly, Vol. 8, Shanti Parva, Part I, New Delhi: Munshiram Manoharlal, 1998, pp. 1–2.

[3] Ibid., Section 56, p. 113.

[4] Ibid., Section 91, pp. 199–200.

Modern political theory has moved beyond the notion of a monarch and his subjects to an abstraction called the state, a form of government we know as democracy, to citizens who are the bearers of rights, and to justice as the paramount principle of a democratic order. The principles of democracy—right to freedom, equality, and justice—can only be realized when society enjoys a measure of peace and stability. According to the social contract theory in Indian political texts, people opt for a state because in a pre-political state of nature the only principle that regulates social relations is that of force and coercion. People live in fear because their lives can be diminished at any time because, according to the law of nature, the big fish eat the small fish.

People can hardly pursue their projects if they are likely to be killed, maimed, dismissed, insulted, and humiliated for reasons that are arbitrary—such as poverty or being born into a caste or a religious community that has been stereotyped in perverse ways. Therefore, people in a pre-political and pre-social state of nature opt for a state that will ensure peace and stability. This is an essential precondition for life itself. This was the hope that independent India started its political life with in 1947, but the legacies of history are not so easily dismissed.

We have not learnt from our own experience of violence in the pre-Independence period, that of communal violence. The Partition of India, the division of territory, the loss of homelands and livelihoods, the experience of being torn away from the locus of memories and imaginations, and general insecurity sparked off the kind of violence seldom seen in the otherwise violent history of the world. We did not learn from Partition and we have not come to terms with our own history.

Nationalist leaders defied the logic of Partition, that is, the splitting up of territory on religious grounds. The Constitution of India incorporated the spirit of secularism and the principle of minority rights. Yet, the history of communal violence continues to bedevil the country. We recognize that political leaders and all kinds of entrepreneurs spark off violence for their own narrow and partisan ends. We see with unease a transition from communalism to communal riots. But we also must address an uneasy question—how is it that people are so readily moved by politicians who engage in rabid communal rhetoric? Do we have violence in our bones even if it is for the most part unrealized and unexpressed?

The other two forms of violence explored in this work stem from exploitative ideologies. The Indian state has passed a number of laws to stem the onslaught of hate crimes against women, children, and the lower castes, but the implementation of protective legislation has been tardy and even negligent at times. The shades of patriarchy and caste discrimination loom large over our horizon. They shape sensibilities, attitudes of the rulers, and the perspective of citizens on how women and the lower castes should be treated.

The chapters on violence in Jammu and Kashmir and the seven states in the Northeast again focus on the role that histories of political institutions play in the continuation of violence. The one institution that can be held responsible for the mess much of the world finds itself in is the nation state. In India, the creation of a nation state out of a welter of disparate territories bred its own consequences. The monarch of Jammu and Kashmir acceded to India on certain terms and conditions, notably that of regional autonomy. It was precisely regional autonomy that began to be whittled away in a short period of time. By the turn of the 1990s, the Valley rose in protest and since then we have seen repeated bouts of violence. Though the special status of the state was taken away by the BJP government in August 2019, violence continues to dodge the heels of people of the region. In Manipur, the monarch acceded to the Indian Union but he was forced to merge his state with India, without consulting his elected government. In both states (J&K has now been split into two union territories), violations of the terms of accession have bred discontent. Across the region, the imposition of draconian laws that cast a pall of fear over the citizens has led to insurgency. Insurgency has proliferated and we see that armed non-state groups fight each other more than they fight the Indian State.

Violence in these two cases of J&K and the Northeast has been the product of violations of certain conditions agreed upon when princely states that were technically not a part of British India acceded to the Indian Union. Other factors—aspirations for autonomy or a state of one's own, ethnic rivalries, resentment that cultural and linguistic rights of tribal communities are being infringed upon, and above all, migration that changes the demographic and linguistic profile of the region—play an important role in the eruption of bouts of violence.

The case of Maoist violence falls into a different category altogether.

In the late 1960s, a section of the Communist movement broke away from the parent party, the CPI (M), and took up arms to fight for the rights of the most underprivileged sections of society—the Adivasis, Dalits, and poor peasantry. The Indian state clamped down on what was termed insurgency but the movement persisted in one state or another. The case of political violence falls into the category of class struggle. Though cadres of various Maoist factions have taken up arms against the state in pursuit of social and economic justice, they have also inflicted tremendous violence on the same people they claim to be fighting for. In all cases of political violence, ordinary citizens are caught in a pincer-like situation between the security forces and armed non-state actors.

Violence should have no role to play in a representative democracy but in India, violence is an integral part of politics. We have realized that violence and democracy are not strangers to each other. The important point is that governments should take care to keep the beast of violence on the margins through the realization of the basic rights to life, liberty, equality, justice, and, above all, dignity. If governments show lack of imagination, if they interpret political wars as law and order problems, and if they respond with coercion and intimidation, we will have more and not less violence on our hands.

What does violence do to both the perpetrators of this mode of power politics and to audiences? It might accomplish the objectives of the wielders of violence but at great cost. It damages society and diminishes people: the perpetrators, the victims, and those who watch, irremediably. Violence is ultimately counterproductive. This was the lesson M. K. Gandhi taught us, not as the Mahatma but as a political philosopher. He not only instructed us to observe the tenets of ahimsa, he also told us why violence is not a desirable option for societies and for states. And he did so in a particular context, the first decade of the twentieth century when violence had become the accepted currency of politics.

Once again, we have to visit Gandhi's arguments against violence— sane, rational, and, above all, astute, arguments. We must take them seriously after mapping different sorts of violence that beset our country. We can perhaps understand why citizens opt for violence as a form of politics. Yet, the suffering and damage this form of politics entails causes terrible unease. Invoking images of brutality, of predators and of hapless victims, of savage violations of the body and damage to the mind, of crime, of dismemberment, of decapitation, of assault, of rape, of mutilation, of murder, of genocide, of ethnic cleansing and of other acts designed to maim and harm, violence, not surprisingly, is burdened by a great deal of terrible connotations. Violence is wrong; it can never ever be justified. Let us see why it cannot be justified.

## NEGATING VIOLENCE: THE GANDHI WAY

At a meeting of the Indian National Association held at the Imperial Institute in London on 1 July 1909, a murder was committed. The assassin was a young Indian student, Madan Lal Dhingra, and the victim was the political aide-de-camp to the Secretary of State for India, Sir William Hutt Curzon Wyllie. Hailing from a propertied and an influential Hindu family living in Amritsar, Punjab, Madan Lal Dhingra had travelled to England for further studies in 1906. He had practically completed his course in engineering and was due to return to India in October 1909. But a number of events intervened to frustrate his return. In London, he had come to be closely associated with the India House radicals. In particular, Dhingra came under the sway of Vinayak Damodar Savarkar (1883–1966), who at that period of his life tended to glorify the cult of violence.

Savarkar argued strenuously for a guerrilla war against the colonial government on the same lines as the 1857 uprising, which he termed the First War of Independence. He was a prominent member of India House, which had been set up by Shyamji Krishna Varma, and become a centre of radical politics practiced by Indian students in London. Savarkar reportedly cast a spell on the young men in India House. He certainly influenced Dhingra greatly. In his recollections, *Six Glorious Epochs of Indian History*, Savarkar wrote that Dhingra was 'converted to our revolutionary views through my principles and guidance'.[5]

Though several young men dedicated their lives to the glorification of violence, in the period following 1857, there was no one to rival Savarkar. Savarkar wrote into the history of the Revolt of 1857 a cynical justification of revenge, retaliation, and retribution. His attitude to violence was captured in his work. Describing in unsettling detail

[5]Cited in Vishwa Nath Datta, *Madan Lal Dhingra and the Revolutionary Movement*, New Delhi: Vikas Publishing, 1978, p. 51.

the horrors that the Indian soldiers had wreaked on British women and children, Savarkar termed these acts as holy ritualistic sacrifices. Without violence, he was to insist, early man could not have survived and militarily weak nations would have been destroyed. The only option to destruction was to develop military qualities in the Hindus. This they could do by giving children airguns instead of cricket bats.[6]

The approach mirrored the development of the cult of violence that swept many Indian students into its intricate and overlapping coils in London. The anti-British campaign culminated on 10 May 1909. Indians abroad organized the annual celebration of honouring the martyrs of the 1857 Revolt against British colonialism. The emotionally laden and vengeful tone of the speeches made on these occasions, and some charged denunciation of colonial brutality, stimulated, or so it appears, a young Indian student to take a life, apparently his very own gesture of political protest against the hounding of patriots in India in the post 1857 period. The British judiciary later sentenced Dhingra to death.

News of the assassination reached Gandhi who was then travelling to London as part of a deputation from Transvaal in South Africa. Gandhi was acquainted with Curzon Wyllie, but his reaction to the murder outstripped grief at the death of an acquaintance. Violence, he had come to believe by 1909, was not only utterly futile, it was corrupt, corrupting, and sterile. Nothing came out of violence but violence; nothing ever could. This deep conviction had shaped his choice of political strategy—satyagraha against the racist regime in South Africa.

After hearing the news of the murder, Gandhi wrote to Lord Ampthill on 29 July. Lord Ampthill was the former governor of Madras and acting viceroy of India (1900–06). Subsequently, he became the president of the South Africa British Indian Committee, established to discuss issues of racial discrimination with Gandhi's deputation. Gandhi wrote that the movement in the Transvaal, with which he had identified, was an eloquent and standing protest against violence. The only way to counter violence was self-suffering and not the infliction of suffering on others.[7]

Gandhi's rejection of violence was grounded in familiarity with the arguments made in support of using violent means against the colonial power. Whenever in London, he had made it a point to connect

---

[6]Jyotirmaya Sharma, 'Savarkar's Justification of Himsa', Book Extract, *Outlook*, 2 October 2015.

[7]Cited in James D. Hunt, *Gandhi in London*, New Delhi, Promilla and Co., 2012, p. 118.

with Indian groups who had embraced the politics of violence, attend their meetings, and hold extensive discussions on various issues. Their dedication to the cult of violence dismayed Gandhi. At a meeting to honour Dhingra, the chief spokesperson of the India House radicals in London, Savarkar thundered: '[t]he only lesson required for India at present is to learn how to die, and the only way to teach it is by dying ourselves. Therefore I die, glorying in my martyrdom.'[8] And Gandhi despaired. This despair motivated him to intellectually address and thereby make efforts to negate political violence.

*Hind Swaraj*, written on board the ship that carried Gandhi from London back to South Africa in 1909, was, as he remarked in 1921, his answer to the Indian school of violence and its prototype in South Africa. 'I', wrote Gandhi in *Young India*, 'came in contact with every known Indian anarchist in London. Their bravery impressed me, but I feel that their zeal was misguided. I felt that violence was no remedy for India's ills, and that her civilization required the use of a different and higher weapon for self-protection.'[9]

He thereupon set himself to the task of elaborating the nature of this higher weapon. The task was undeniably difficult. Although violence was no solution to the problems posed by colonialism, undeniably it *was* the violence of the colonial state that had triggered off this outcome. Gandhi, therefore, not only had to negate violence, he had to show what could take its place in the struggle against colonialism. Accordingly, he saw his mandate as one of exploring the many ramifications of violence, reflecting on the circumstances in which the use of force was ethical, and, in general, trying to transcend violence. The referent point of his argument against violence was the early decades of the twentieth century, but the argument holds valid till today.

Interestingly, Gandhi's answer to the problem of violence was culture specific. Holding fast to his belief that India's civilization required the use of a 'higher weapon for self-protection', he drew upon Hindu and Jain traditions to argue against violence and for non-violence. This was necessary because the revolutionary terrorists had legitimized violence

---

[8]Ibid., p. 134.
[9]M. K. Gandhi, '"Hind Swaraj" Or The "Indian Home Rule"', *Collected Works of Mahatma Gandhi*, New Delhi: Publications Division, Ministry of Information and Broadcasting, Government of India, November 1920–1921, Vol. xix, pp. 277–78.

by invocation of the message of the sacred text, the Bhagavad Gita—
do whatever your station and your duty asks of you. Gandhi intended
to rescue the Hindu tradition from the frankly instrumental uses to
which it had been put. His alternative to violence was not only culture
specific, it was based on the binary opposition he drew between the
materialistic West and a spiritually-inclined India. Gandhi's response to
the glorification of violence was of enormous importance given the
political context of the cult of violence.

## THE POLITICAL CONTEXT OF VIOLENCE IN INDIA

In the period that followed the suppression of the 1857 Revolt, the
colonial state embarked on a ruthless policy of reprisals clearly designed
to humiliate an entire people, to hammer them into submission, and
to strip them of any vestige of self-respect. In his work on the Indian
Rebellion of 1857 and Victorian trauma, Christopher Herbert writes
of the 'sternly pious' Colonel (later Brigadier General) James Neill
who came to be known for the 'ferocious retribution he had inflicted
elsewhere upon mutineers and their suspected sympathizers'. Neill, who
commanded Cawnpore, one of the centres of the revolt, was to invent
degrading forms of punishment for the Indian sepoys who had taken
part in the revolt and who had been implicated in the massacre of
British men, women, and children in 1857. 'Before being taken to the
gallows, each was forced to clean up with his own hands or to lick up a
small square of blood from the courtyard pavement where the prisoners
had been slaughtered—an appalling pollution for a high-caste Hindu, as
most of the sepoys were.'[10] This incident, writes Herbert, was only one
of the most publicized cases of merciless punishment that was visited
by British authorities upon Indian combatants and civilians during the
fierce campaign to restore British supremacy in India.

In the post-1857 period, colonial policies were clearly arbitrary,
discriminating, and frankly contemptuous and disparaging of Indians. A
backlash was, expectedly, on the anvil. During the late 1870s, resentment
built up against the arrogance of British officials and the policies of
reprisals. In the process, colonial practices, now stripped bare of rhetorical
frills and flourishes such as bringing civilization to the colonized, were

---

[10]Christopher Herbert, *War of No Pity: The Indian Mutiny and Victorian Trauma*, Princeton:
Princeton University Press, 2009, p. 4.

revealed as starkly brutal and essentially dehumanizing.

Young men in India began to believe that the only weapon they had against the depredations of the colonial power was violence. Colonialism is inherently violent because it strips the colony of economic resources, political sovereignty, and sense of historical understanding because it deprives the colonized of their identity. Without a sense of who she is, the individual is rendered vulnerable; she is deprived of confidence that she can counter the oppressions of the colonizer. The only way in which the colonized individual can regain confidence and reclaim identity is through the adoption of violence as a counter to oppression.

A number of groups in India in the late nineteenth century were converted to the idea that the only way to deal with subordination and humiliation was violence. Brought up amidst chilling tales of colonial brutality, educated and often unemployed youth came to believe that they could wipe out dishonour and regain a sense of who they are if they were to pick up a gun and train the barrel at the colonial power. Several organizations dedicated to violence, such as akharas or wrestling rings and gymnasiums that provided training in the martial arts, were established in Bengal, Maharashtra, Punjab, and the United Provinces.

The trajectory of retributive violence was initiated in June 1897 in Maharashtra when two brothers, Damodar Hari Chapekar and Balkrishna Hari Chapekar, assassinated Walter Charles Rand, the plague commissioner of Poona, and Lieutenant Charles Egerton Ayerst, an officer of the administration. Both officials were seen as responsible for the administrative excesses committed in the course of checking the plague in Poona. Even as the administration invaded private spaces in complete disregard of rules of privacy and taboos on entry into the inner domain of family life, acute desire for revenge took hold of many a young man.

Penning his biography in jail, Damodar wrote bitterly of the way the sixtieth anniversary of the reign of the Queen of England was celebrated in the midst of plague in the Bombay Presidency, earthquake in Calcutta, and a terrible famine all over India. Instead of trying to rescue her subjects from the severe misery that had afflicted them, the monarch heaped further financial burdens on them. According to the Hindu shastras, he wrote, a king and his subjects are in the same relationship as a father and son. On this principle, the Queen who can be seen as the mother of her subjects, has devoured her progeny. The two brothers were sentenced to death and hanged in the summer of 1899.

Intense dedication to the shedding of blood and deep commitment to notions of sacrifice marked the political climate in India as young people revolted against the sort of treatment the colonial power had inflicted on them. Psychiatrists tell us that the use of violence is closely associated with anxiety about impotence and the recovery of 'masculinity'. A song composed by Damodar Hari Chapekar for the Ganapati festival in Bombay reflected this worry: 'Fools, what is the use of your being men? Of what use are your big moustaches? Alas, you are not ashamed to remain in servitude; try, therefore, to commit suicide. Alas, like butchers the wicked in their monstrous atrocity kill calves and kine. Free her (the cow) from her trouble, die (but) kill the Englishman. Do not remain idle and (thereby) burden the earth.... Rise, rap your upper arms (like a wrestler in a wrestling bout) encounter (the enemies). May you succeed in slaughtering the wicked.'[11]

Similar sentiments prevailed in influential circles. Bal Gangadhar Tilak, the tallest leader in western India, sought to counter colonial violence by creating a muscular macho culture in the region. A redoubtable warrior for independence and national regeneration, Tilak was given the status of the 'father of Indian unrest' by Valentine Chirol of *The Times*. Love and the willingness to die for the motherland resonated in Punjab as well. Lajpat Rai declared, 'calls for blood, world history was written in letters of blood, let us crown our national movement with martyrdom'.[12] Aurobindo Ghosh of Bengal argued that Indians had to be taught to valorize power. He was to argue that violence by a courageous and committed few was the only way to regain the lost sense of self.

Matters came to a head in 1905. Viceroy Lord Curzon, known for the enactment of several aggressive imperial policies from 1899 onwards, decided to partition the province of Bengal in 1905. The stated reasons for the partition were ostensibly administrative. However, a darker plan was in the making. The idea was to separate the eastern districts of Bengal, which were, in Curzon's words, a hotbed of a Bengali movement resentful of the colonial government, from the rest of the region. The

---

[11]Bimanbehari Majumdar, *Militant Nationalism in India and Its Socio-Religious Background*, Calcutta: General Printers and Publishers, 1966, pp. 86–87.

[12]Daniel Argov, *Moderates and Extremists in the Indian National Movement 1883-1920*, Bombay: Asia Publishing House, 1967, p. 108.

underlying idea was to separate the Muslim majority districts from Hindu majority districts of the province.

The intensity and scale of the anger that swamped Bengal in 1905 was extraordinary. On the one hand, the Indian National Congress mobilized protest in every district of the province on the twin planks of swadeshi (boycott of British products) and swaraj (self-rule). On the other hand, revolutionary terrorists hyped up violence across Bengal. Selective assassinations of British officials and of collaborators, arson, and looting of stockpiles of arms and ammunition marked the political climate of the time. The division between Indians who advocated a middle path and others who argued for immediate independence was formalized in 1907.

The Congress split into the moderate wing which sought self-rule within the empire, and the extremist wing that insisted on demanding political, cultural, and economic independence. The partition of Bengal was undone in 1912, but in the few years between the making and the unmaking of the partition the language and the practice of violence had been upgraded into a common currency of resistance politics. The only route to the achievement of selfhood was violence.

## FRANTZ FANON AND VIOLENCE

These arguments in defence of violence as a mode of the recovery of selfhood were echoed many years later in the famous work *The Wretched of the Earth* authored by Frantz Fanon during the Algerian struggle for independence.[13] Born in the Caribbean in the French colony of Martinique in 1925, Fanon was greatly influenced by his celebrated teacher, Aimé Fernand David Césaire. Césaire's volume of essays, *Discourse on Colonialism*, had quickly attained the status of a classic, and he became famous as the founder of the intellectual and ideological movement Negritude that celebrated blackness.

At a very young age, Fanon was exposed to the savage racism of the French army stationed in the island. At the age of eighteen, he left Martinique and fought with the Free French Forces in World War II. After the end of the war, he stayed on in France to study medicine and psychiatry in Lyons. The intellectual atmosphere in France in that

---

[13]Frantz Fanon, *The Wretched of the Earth,* translated by Constance Farrington, Harmondsworth: Penguin Books, 2001.

period was shaped by the existentialism of Jean-Paul Sartre and the phenomenology of Merleau-Ponty, by Georg Wilhelm Friedrich Hegel and by Karl Marx. These intellectual streams of thought deeply impacted Fanon.

In 1952, Fanon took up the position of chief of staff of the psychiatric ward in Blida-Joinville Hospital in Algeria. In 1954, the series of attacks launched against military and civilian targets by the Front de Liberation Nationale (FLN) heralded the Algerian War of Independence. Within a period of four years, Fanon, deeply critical of French policy towards Algeria, resigned from his job and dedicated himself to the cause of the FLN. Algeria was liberated from French rule in July 1962, seven months after Fanon's death from leukaemia. *The Wretched of the Earth* was published posthumously.

It is seen as a classic that dwells not only on the production and reproduction of violence under colonialism, but also on the violence of the post-colonial elite, and resultant loss of hope. In this much acclaimed work, Fanon brings out in fine detail the subtleties and the power of violence, as well as its waywardness. 'The violence of settler colonialism hammers the colonised into submission. Logically the only way "natives" can speak back to a history that has enslaved their minds and bodies is to use the weapon of the coloniser against him. This may even be advantageous because violence enables the "native" to shrug off the crippling inferiority complex produced by colonialism. Violence rescues natives from inertia, restores their self-respect, and enables men to recover "manhood" translated as agency. For the colonised individual violence is a cleansing force. It frees the native from his inferiority complex and from his despair and inaction; it makes him fearless and restores his self-respect. Even if the armed struggle has been symbolic, and the nation is demobilised through a rapid movement of decolonisation, the people have the time to see that the liberation has been the business of each and all and that the leader has no special merit.'[14] The form of violence adopted by the colonized is reactive but nevertheless beneficial. Violence develops consciousness of a common cause, of a national destiny, and of a collective history.[15]

The theme of violence as liberation was highlighted in the Preface

---

[14]Ibid., p. 74.
[15]Ibid.

to *The Wretched of the Earth* written by Jean-Paul Sartre. When the peasants lay hands on a gun, the old myths fade, and one by one the taboos are overturned; a fighter's weapon is his humanity. For in the first phase of the revolt killing is a necessity; killing a European is killing two birds with one stone, eliminating in one go oppressor and the oppressed; leaving one man dead and the other man free, for the first time the survivor feels a national soil under his feet.[16]

Fanon too is clear about the advantages that violence delivers into the hands of the colonized, notably the recovery of the self. The self has been buried under the burden of colonialism, the only way to extricate oneself from this swamp was through the use of violence. Yet, as we shall see, Fanon has deep reservations about violence. These reservations had been expressed fifty years earlier by Gandhi who negated and countered violence.

## HOW IS VIOLENCE TO BE NEGATED?

Gandhi begins his negation of violence by unsparingly condemning the culture of violence embraced by 'misguided patriots' like Dhingra in *Hind Swaraj*. This was in response to a 'reader's' suggestion that India could win independence by random acts of violence. In the middle of the twentieth century, this mode of resistance was to be termed the Foco theory in South America. In an essay written in 1960, Che Guevara argued that in contrast to the Marxist-Leninist theory of revolution, which had to wait for the maturing of capitalism and the mobilization of the working class by a vanguard party, an elite few could catalyse the revolution with force.[17] Confronted by violence, the government would, in all probability, intensify oppression of the largely rural masses. The people would be left with no choice except to join the guerrillas. This, by itself, would ignite a revolution, validating the proposition that violence is the midwife of history.

About half a century earlier, the reader in *Hind Swaraj* proposed that isolated and indiscriminate violence would likely precipitate a freedom struggle. A quarter of a million men may be lost, but the land would be regained. The partner to the dialogue, the 'editor' (who

---

[16]Jean-Paul Sartre, 'Preface', *The Wretched of the Earth*, p. 19.
[17]M. K. Gandhi, *Hind Swaraj* or *Indian Home Rule*, Ahmedabad: Navajivan Publishing House, 1960.

but lip syncs Gandhi's words and beliefs) responds with outrage: '[d]o you not tremble to think of freeing India by assassination?'[18] In these few words are contained the core of Gandhi's philosophy on the nature of swaraj, the nature of truth, and the philosophy of Advaita or non-dualism. Above all, Gandhi's reflections on violence problematized the relationship between the objectives of the struggle and the political strategies employed towards that end.

Gandhi's arguments against violence can be summed up in three interconnected propositions. One, howsoever urgent may be the need for violence, it is neither pragmatic nor productive. Violence for all its seeming heroism and daredevilry is a lazy way of doing politics because it eschews transformation of either the body politic or of its members. Spectacular acts of violence reduce people into an audience or bystanders. In the process, nothing changes; nothing ever could. Two, Gandhi's rejection of violence originates from a powerful argument on the nature of truth. The production and reproduction of violence follows the absolute conviction that we and only we are in possession of the truth, and that other's truth is necessarily false.

Violent acts seek to inscribe the perpetrator's version of the truth on the body of the recipient, thereby causing harm. But truth, according to Gandhi, is as elusive as the proverbial will-o'-the-wisp. It escapes us the moment we think we have accessed it. It follows that if all known truths are partial, the use of violence cannot be justified. Three, Gandhi's rejection of violence is grounded in his belief in the philosophy of Advaita or non-dualism. In contrast to the Biblical injunction—do unto others as you would have others do unto you—Gandhi asks possible perpetrators of violence to reflect on the following. Since the 'other' is a part of you, any act that causes harm to others injures you as well. The normative argument, the epistemological argument, and the ontological argument build up a formidable case against violence.

## THE LIMITS OF VIOLENCE

Gandhi's argument against violence is grounded in pragmatism. The violence of colonialism is likely to precipitate violence as resistance, but history shows us that the second category simply does not work.

---

[18]Ibid.

In 1920, at a public meeting in Calcutta, Gandhi asked the audience to ponder on the history of British rule in India. Did this, he demanded, not demonstrate that Indians have never been able to either resist, or counter violence with violence? 'Whilst therefore I say that rather have the yoke of a government that has so emasculated us, I would welcome violence, I would urge with all the emphasis that I can command that India would never be able to regain her own by methods of violence.'[19] The approach of violence, Gandhi feels, is simply not practical, because Indians would never be able to arm themselves on the same scale as the colonizer. To adopt violence in such circumstances would be to commit political hara-kiri.

Yet, at the same time, Gandhi expressed sentiments that Fanon was to articulate much later. Fanon wrote elegantly and powerfully of the crippling effects of settler colonialism on the collective psyche of the colonized. The reach of violence, he theorized, is widespread, timeless, and enduring. Footprints of the cloven hoof of violence are practically ineradicable. It is perhaps not surprising that the postcolonial elite cannot but be cast in the mould of the same violence it had led the struggle against. The colours of violence do not wash out quite so easily. Violence, theorizes Fanon, is double edged, it is liberating but also lethal.

Gandhi has presented this argument in another way. But even if this were to happen, even if India could be freed at the cost of torn feet and bloodied hands, her people would never be able to realize what is rightfully theirs or come into 'their own'. The phrase 'their own', which indicates that something is historically due to India, was related to his core concept of swaraj and his belief in the unique civilization of India that made the realization of swaraj or substantive freedom possible.

When violence becomes the architect of history, Gandhi suggests, it can only replace one sort of oppression with another sort of oppression. Those who rise to power by murder, he said, will certainly not make the nation happy. 'Those who believe that India has gained by Dhingra's act and other similar acts in India make a serious mistake. Dhingra was a patriot, but his love was blind. He gave his body in a wrong way; its

[19]M. K. Gandhi, 'Speech on Non-Cooperation, Calcutta, 22 December 1920', *Collected Works of Mahatma Gandhi*, Vol. 19, New Delhi: Government of India, Publications Division, 1966, pp. 102–03.

ultimate result can only be mischievous.'[20]

Roughly half a century later, Frantz Fanon was to theorize decolonization and the new regime that it gives birth to as a mirror image of the oppressive colonial regime. At whatever level we study it, he argued, whether it is in the form of relationships between individuals, or new names for sports, national or private banks, decolonization simply replaces a certain 'species' of men with another species of men. As a historical moment, decolonization, theorized Fanon perceptively, does not come about as a result of magical practices. It cannot be understood, nor can it become intelligible except in the way we study it and give it form and content. Colonialism is violent; if the anti-colonial movement is also violent, it will not be surprising that the new regime will also be violent.

Gandhi had earlier recognized the enduring power of colonial violence. He also understood the attraction that violence holds for a people frustrated and exhausted by the depredations of colonialism. But Gandhi believed that it was possible to negate violence. If only we knew, Gandhi seemed to suggest, what violence is about, we would willingly forswear it.

He warns us that the power of violence over human beings must not be underrated. It is not a weapon that we can pick up and discard at will. It can best be likened to a quagmire that relentlessly sucks people into its murky depths. From here there is no escape. In other words, when violence holds individuals and groups in thrall, moral disintegration follows. For we cannot control violence; violence controls us. Returning to Dhingra, Gandhi suggested that, '…in my view Dhingra was innocent. The murder was committed in a state of intoxication. It is not merely wine or bhang that makes one drunk; a mad idea can do so. That was the case with Dhingra.'[21]

It follows that even if independence is won through violence, people remain in the grip of violence, and those who have committed violent acts become the rulers. Nothing changes, and nothing ever can change when violence is used to craft historical transitions from colonialism to freedom. If 'we' followed the logic that brute force should be used to get what we want, because the English used this sort of force to get

---

[20]Gandhi, *Hind Swaraj*, p. 60.
[21]Datta, *Madan Lal Dhingra*, p. 72.

what they wanted, then we 'can get only the same thing that they got'.[22]

More significantly, Gandhi seems to suggest that though spectacular acts of political violence may appear courageous and praiseworthy, they belong to the realm of illusion. The masses might admire and acclaim the terrorists for personal bravery, but they will remain untouched and steeped in passivity. Acts of violence are isolated from political movements. They reduce people to merely an audience. After the Revolt of 1857, if the colonial state had tried to browbeat Indians into submission through efforts to create compliant subjects, the revolutionaries had converted them into spectators. These enervating effects on popular energies had to be neutralized, and people brought to realization that the attainment of swaraj requires an enormous amount of hard work, courage, commitment to the truth, steadfastness, and, above all, a system of public ethics. It is only then that millions could be motivated to struggle together for freedom and reinvent both themselves and society. Swaraj, for Gandhi, cannot be won by the actions of a few; it demands collective efforts and transformation.

Interestingly, Gandhi's rejection of the Foco theory of violence runs along Marxist lines. The prime precondition of revolutionary transformation is political mobilization. It is not as if subjected people do not have the capacity to struggle and speak back to a history not of their own making. But isolated struggles have to be brought together, energies pooled, and political imaginations sparked through an ideology that gives them both a vision and an objective. This task must be undertaken by a cadre of committed people, who have taken care to prepare themselves for the task of readying others for struggle. Having undergone rigorous training, the activists then proceed to inspire people and transform individual consciousness.

There is a reciprocal relationship, between collective action and individual sensibilities, that of awareness of the issues involved and that of the need to transform oneself or radicalize oneself in and through the process of struggle. Struggle educates, motivates, and transforms. No person, once he or she has been radicalized, can ever be the same. And no society, once it has been radicalized, can ever be the same. Of course, there is the danger that a politicizing agency will politicize

---

[22]Gandhi, *Hind Swaraj*, p. 61.

people the wrong way, in a majoritarian direction, for example. This trend has to be corrected through debate and informed critique in civil society, that space that permits associational life outside the sphere of party politics. To assume that party politics is always correct is to engage in irresponsibility.

Gandhi's rejection of irresponsible acts of violence as a catalyst for change was based on the same lines because the cadres he sent out to politicize people had to abide by the basic principles of satyagraha. The small body of men and women who had prepared themselves for satyagraha through rigorous training, who intended to challenge all manners of wrong, and who were prepared to face the consequences, would awaken intelligent public opinion. The satyagrahi, or those who held steadfastly to the truth, must first mobilize public opinion against the evil which he has aimed to eradicate by means of a wide and intensive agitation. The success of the satyagrahi's efforts must necessarily depend not merely on the appeal to his own conscience *but even more on the awakening of the slumbering conscience of a large number of people.*[23] Much like the vanguardist party, the satyagrahi has to tap and mobilize public opinion through clarifying the issues at stake, emphasizing that injustice is a violation of the basic rights of human beings, and highlighting the need for struggle. And much like the vanguardist party that is expected to have studied history, sociology, political economy, psychology, crowd behaviour, collective action and strategy, the satyagrahi prepares himself or herself through rigorous training. But precisely at this point, Gandhi departs from ideologies of revolution.

Iyer writes that in his appeal to public opinion, and to the concept of truth and non-violence, the satyagrahi differs from methods of violent action by emphasizing self-suffering. We have to go, Gandhi suggested, beyond reason to appeal to people who have settled views. Their eyes are opened not by rational argument but by the suffering of the satyagrahi through fasting, and willing acceptance of consequences of their action or civil disobedience. The satyagrahi as a moral exemplar awakens collective conscience first through rational argument and persuasion, and then by appealing to emotions. As people begin to reflect on and analyse the nature of injustice to which they have been subjected and that needs

---

[23]Raghavan Iyer, *The Moral and Political Thought of Mahatma Gandhi,* New Delhi: Oxford University Press, 2000, p. 286, (italics added).

to be battled, they also come to think about the methods that should be used to battle these injustices. In the process, they are politicized and motivated to act. And this, according to Gandhi, was revolutionary because public opinion becomes a vital force and develops the real sanction which is satyagraha.

Distinguishing satyagraha from passive resistance and other forms of civil disobedience, Gandhi suggested that philosophy is not a weapon of the weak. It demands tremendous moral strength and fortitude because it commands that we relentlessly *battle injustice* with steadfastness, commitment, fearlessness, and willingness to accept punishment. The philosophy of satyagraha enlightens the mind, but more importantly, gives to us a theory of action. In the process, the agent makes people aware of the distinction between what is right and what is wrong, encourages sensitization to injustice, and emphasizes the need to fight for justice and against abuse of power. In the process, the masses become aware of the virtues of non-violence. They make the transition from an audience to an agent. It is only then that the attainment of swaraj, which is in tune with the uniqueness of India's civilization, becomes possible. Swaraj in a restricted sense is identified as self-rule or independence, but in a wider sense implies that citizens can only rule themselves when they learn to discipline their senses, their greed for possessions, and their will to dominate. It is only then that people 'come into their own', in accordance with the historical legacy of India.

Much as the philosopher Plato in ancient Greece theorized, Gandhi sees society as the individual writ large. A free society is an essential precondition for living a life that we consider worthwhile, but unless we strive towards the realization of personal freedom by trying to conquer ignoble and base passions, such a society cannot possibly come into existence. This is made clear when he argues that the relationship between the individual and the community cannot be seen in terms of two discrete entities entering into a relationship with each other. Nor can we see the individual as completely embedded in her community. Each person is distinctive in her own right, but she is constituted as a self-conscious moral being by society. In turn, society is what it is because of its members.

Connecting his rejection of violence with the need to go beyond the concept of mere independence, which will, in all probability, turn out empty and devoid of any further possibility, Gandhi moved towards the concepts of non-violence and swaraj. Violence can only befuddle the mind and obscure issues at stake. It is only non-violence that illumines our minds and our sentiments. For this, the pitfalls of political violence need to be spelt out. Because it is only then that people will be transformed from being spectators to being participants in the struggle for swaraj.

Gandhi rejects violence for another reason. Violence, according to him, stems from the conviction that we, the perpetrators of violence, are right, or that we know the truth. Our notion of truth has to be imposed on others who must necessarily be short of the truth or even wrong. Violence, in other words, is a product of certitude—we know the truth, whether this truth is what the world is about, what the position of different individuals in this world should be, how the world should be organized, how relationships in this world should be patterned, or how the world should be perceived. Such a stance kills the very possibility of respecting others as persons who bear a moral status, because it admits of no other version of the truth but ours. The logical corollary of this premise is that the 'other' appears before us as a lesser human being or as not fully human. We can proceed to imprint their bodies with signs of violence.

At this point, Gandhi introduces a twist in the tale. What is truth? We do not know. Socrates had elaborated this perspective in Plato's *Apology*, which Gandhi had translated into Gujarati. 'Chaerephon,' said Socrates at the trial before which he stood as an accused, 'had asked the Oracle at Delphi whether anyone was wiser than Socrates. The Oracle's reply was in the negative. When I heard the answer,' Socrates continued, 'I was puzzled because I knew that I have no wisdom small or great. The only way of establishing that my knowledge was far less than the knowledge possessed by other men was to find someone who knew more than I did, then I might go to the god with a refutation in my hand. But when I began to speak with men who had a reputation for knowledge,' said Socrates, 'I realised that I was wiser than them only because these knowledgeable men did not even know that they lacked knowledge. I am better off than he is, for he knows nothing and thinks he knows, I neither know nor think that I know. In this latter particular, then I seem to have slightly the advantage of him.'[24]

Gandhi comes to the same conclusion when he begins to examine the nature of truth. 'I,' he was to write, 'have been striving to serve the truth and have the courage to jump from the Himalayas for its sake. At the same time,' he confessed, 'I know I am still very far from that truth. As I advance towards it, I perceive my weakness ever more clearly and the knowledge makes me humble.'[25] Evoking the parable of the seven blind men who had only limited access to knowledge about the elephant they were asked to describe, Gandhi suggests that since human beings are in the position of these seven men, we must therefore be content with believing the truth as it appears to us.

But this does not mean that we stop searching for the truth, because truth or in Hindi, 'satya', means a state of being. Our status is connected to our knowledge of the truth. Nothing is or exists in reality except truth. Where there is no truth, there can be no true knowledge. Yet, different sorts of truths can only approximate the ultimate truth. What appears as the truth to one person often appears as untruth to another person. But that need not worry the seeker, because different truths are like different leaves of the same tree. There is nothing wrong in human beings following their own truth, provided, as Gandhi warns time and again, that we be certain that we know only the partial truth. We are all seekers after the truth. If this is so, none of us have the competence to punish other people through violent words, deeds, or even thoughts.

Above all, Gandhi argued that we harm a part of ourselves when we allow harm to others because they are 'ourselves in a different form'. If others represent us in a different form, then their welfare is bound up intrinsically with ours. Gandhian ethics goes further than the Christian belief that we should treat others the way we want others to treat us. Gandhi tells us what we do to others we also do to ourselves.

Gandhi's rejection of violence moves to a negation of violence and then a transcendence of violence and the embrace of non-violence. Gandhi negated violence because he saw it as incapable of bringing about substantive freedom, because it presupposes a flawed conception of the

---

[24]Plato, *The Apology*, translated by Benjamin Jowett, Chicago: William Benton, Encyclopedia Britannica, reprinted by Oxford University Press, 1952, p. 205.

[25]M. K. Gandhi, 'What is Truth', 20 November 1921, *Collected Works of Mahatma Gandhi*, Vol. 21, New Delhi: Government of India, Publications Division, 1966, p. 474.

truth, and because it ultimately harms the perpetrator. The alternative to violence is, therefore, non-violence, which is a companion concept to Gandhi's theory of truth and swaraj.

## GANDHI'S DESPAIR

Gandhi was forced to accept an unpalatable truth towards the end of his life. He was forced to accept that Indians had followed his injunctions of non-violence when they fought some significant campaigns against the colonial power, such as the Salt Satyagraha. They were ready to peacefully break the law and go to prison because that was the punishment they had opted for. But they could not make non-violence an integral part of their social relations, particularly between the Hindu and the Muslim communities. The death and destruction that accompanied the Partition of India had revealed this clearly. Gandhi refused to participate in the victory celebrations of the independence of India. A sad and lonely figure, he trudged through the killing fields of northern and eastern parts of India, a tragic prophet of peace persuading people not to kill and destroy and visiting refugee camps. The Partition should have been the testing ground for ahimsa; it proved to be the graveyard of Gandhian non-violence. The freedom struggle adopted non-violence, but the moment of transition to independence in the country took place in the context of the blood-drenched Partition.

Gandhi is a beloved memory, he is an icon, because he told us what was wrong with violence and why we should adopt non-violence. We cannot opt for violence because our knowledge is imperfect. We cannot use violence as a tool that hammers vulnerable people with a blunt weapon because it is against our ancient texts and against the philosophy of non-dualism in the Advaita. Gandhi told us that when people use violence to inflict harm on women, on minorities, on the so-called lower castes, to pursue a political goal, and above all, to repress and to dominate, society is reduced to a consumer. We cease to be actors, we may not like these acts of violence, we may be repulsed but we are as vulnerable as the victims of lynching in today's India. Sadly, Gandhi, who taught us that since violence is in our bones we should take even more care to replace it with non-violence, has become politically irrelevant.

Ahimsa remains an aspiration and a moral ideal. Ahimsa is often defeated at the bar of real politics. But we must remember that the notion of non-violence or ahimsa as the first of the many virtues that human beings should possess and exercise was not invented by Gandhi. It is found in ancient texts, in Patanjali's Yoga Sutras, for instance. The Mahabharata is about fratricidal war, but throughout the epic, resounds the phrase 'ahimsa paramo dharma', or that non-violence is the prime dharma or normative order.

But for long we have been confronted with violence against our own people by our own people. Violence not only is a part of relations between citizens and the state, but also relationships between citizens. How do we deal with this? It is time to reflect on what these everyday incidents of violence do to us. It is time to reclaim the space of non-violence that has been under relentless attack by lynchers who take the name of Lord Ram to kill, photograph, and celebrate killings. It is time to ask what exactly violence does to a society. Why is violence bad politics? Violence is the spectacle; we are the consumers of these nauseating acts. Today, these acts have become our world. And we have become as defenceless as the victim.

We have to reinvent Gandhi; we have to make him relevant not as the Mahatma but as a political philosopher who guides us in our struggle against the senseless violence that has crushed our sentiments and our solidarities. We have to abjure violence; we have to adopt the path of ahimsa in our dealings with each other based on mutual respect and obligation to our fellow citizens.

# ACKNOWLEDGEMENTS

I wish to thank Pujitha Krishnan for suggesting that I write a 'big book' on 'violence in our bones'. Her suggestions on the academic content and style of argument, as well as her editorial guidance have been most helpful. A big thank you to the editorial team of Aleph for doing such an excellent job of identifying and correcting, hopefully, inadvertent mistakes in the language, and in the referencing of this work. I have had long conversations with Praveen Priyadarshi on the way the argument should be structured, and what should be and should not be included. My deepest gratitude to Praveen, once my student, and now a colleague in the university system. I wish to express my gratitude to Irfan Habib for academic support. Many thanks to Apoorva Anand for his invaluable help with the translations of various Hindi/Urdu poems cited in this work, and to Partho Dutta for sharing his extensive knowledge of modern Indian history with a political scientist whose academic world begins in 1947. This work was researched and written in the wonderful library provided by the India International Centre, Delhi. Many thanks to the young men and women who look after the library, and who generously cater to the demands of often irate readers.

# BIBLIOGRAPHY

Ajmal, Zaheer, 'Modi's India slips in Democracy Index from 27th rank to 41 now', *National Herald*, 18 January 2019.

Ali, Agha Shahid, *The Half-Inch Himalayas,* Connecticut: Wesleyan University Press, 1987.

Ambedkar, B. R., *What Congress and Gandhi have done to the Untouchables,* Mumbai: Thacker, 1946.

Anandhi, S., and M. Vijayabaskar, 'Where buying a motorcycle can spark a riot', *The Hindu*, 7 January 2013.

Arendt, Hannah, *On Violence*, London: Allen Lane and Penguin, 1970.

Argov, Daniel, *Moderates and Extremists in the Indian National Movement 1883-1920*, Bombay: Asia Publishing House, 1967.

Ashiq, Peerzada, 'In Kashmir Valley, hundreds of pellet victims face a hazy future', *The Hindu*, 2 June 2019.

Aslam, Saira, 'India drops 10 ranks in Democracy Index, *The Hindu,* 23 January 2020.

Auden, W. H., *The Collected Poetry of W. H. Auden*, New York: Random House, 1945.

Banerjee, Sumanta (ed.), *Thema Book of Naxalite Poetry*, Calcutta: Thema Books, 2010.

Bharadwaj, Ashutosh, 'Kashmiri Pandits, Return to Valley is a Must for "idea of India"' *The Print*, 23 January 2020.

Bannerjee, Sumanta, 'Beyond Naxalbari' *Economic and Political Weekly,* Special issue on Maoist Movement in India, Vol. XLI, No. 29, 22–28 July 2006.

——, 'Reflections of a One-Time Maoist Activist' in Robin Jeffrey, Rononjoy Sen and Pratima Singh (eds.), *More than Maoism Politics and Insurgencies in South Asia*, New Delhi: Manohar, 2012.

Bano, Asifa, 'The child rape and murder that has Kashmir on edge', *BBC News*, 11 April 2018.

Baruah, Sanjib, '*Durable Disorders*: *Understanding the Politics of Northeast India*, New Delhi, Oxford University Press, 2005.

——(ed.), *Beyond Counter-insurgency*: *Breaking the Impasse in Northeast India*, New Delhi: Oxford University Press, 2009.

Bedi, Rajinder Singh, 'Lajwanti', in *The Greatest Urdu Stories Ever Told,* selected and translated by Muhummad Umar Memon, New Delhi: Aleph Book Company, 2007.

Bhasin, Avtar Singh, *India and Pakistan: Neighbours at Odds*, New Delhi: Bloomsbury, 2018.

Bhatia, Bela, 'On Armed Resistance', *Economic and Political Weekly*, Special issue on Maoist Movement in India, Vol. XLI, No. 29, 22–28 July 2006.

Bhattacharjee, Manash Firaq, 'Decades of discord; Assam against itself', *The Wire*, 11 August 2018.

Bhattacharya, Sumit, 'TDP MLA, leader shot in Visakapatnam' *The Hindu*, 24 September 2018.

Bhosle, Anubha, 'Indian Army rape us', *Outlook India*, 10 February 2016.

Bose, Sumantra, *Contested Homelands: Israel-Palestine, Kashmir, Bosnia, Cyprus and Sri Lanka*, New Delhi: HarperCollins and India Today Group, 2007.

———, *Kashmir: Roots of Conflict, Paths of Peace*, New Delhi: Vistaar, 2003.

Brass, Paul, *The Production of Hindu-Muslim Violence in Contemporary India*, Seattle: University of Washington Press, 2015.

Breman, Jan, *The Making and Unmaking of an Industrial Working Class: Sliding Down the Labour Hierarchy in Ahmedabad*, New Delhi: Oxford University Press, 2004.

Burman, Rini, 'Guns with Occasional Music: Female Poets from the Northeast', *Kindle Magazine*, 22 July 2014, available at <http://kindlemag.in/guns-ocassional-music-female-poets-northeast>.

Campbell-Johnson Alan, *Mission with Mountbatten*, London: Robert Hale Ltd, 1952.

Canetti, Elias, *Crowds and Power*, New York: Farrar, Strauss and Giroux, 1984.

Carrol, Lewis, *Through the Looking Glass*, Project Gutenburg, Gutenburg Fulcrum Edition, 1991, available at <https://www.gutenberg.org/files/12/12-h/12-h.htm>.

Chakrabarty, Dipesh, 'Modernity and Ethnicity in India', in John McGuire, Peter D. Reeves and Howard V. Brasted (eds.), *Politics of Violence: From Ayodhya to Behrampada*, New Delhi: Sage Publications, 1996.

Chakravarty, Ipsita, 'Why was Assam's Nellie Massacre Not Prevented, Despite Intimations of Violence?' *Scroll.in*, 18 February 2017.

Chakravarty, Uma and Nandita Haksar (eds.), 'Introduction' in *The Delhi Riots: Three Days in the Life of a Nation*, New Delhi: Lancer International, 1987.

Chandhoke, Neera, *Democracy and Revolutionary Politics*, London: Bloomsbury, 2015.

———, *Contested Secessions*, New Delhi: Oxford University Press, 2012.

———, *Rethinking Pluralism, Secularism and Tolerance; Anxieties of Coexistence*, New Delhi: Sage Publications, 2019.

———, Silky Tyagi, Neha Khanna, and Praveen Priyadarshi, 'The Displaced of Ahmedabad', *Economic and Political Weekly*, 27 October, Vol XLII, no 43, 2007, pp. 10-14.

Changkija, Monalisa, 'Northeast Outside the Newspaper Pages', in Margaret Ch Zama (ed.), *Emerging Literatures from Northeast India: The Dynamics of Culture, Society and Identity*, New Delhi: Sage Publications, 2015.

Chendvankar, Pralhad, 'Asmitadarsh', translated by Jayant Karve, Veena Deo and Eleanor Zelliot, cited in Veena Deo and Eleanor Zelliot, 'Dalit Literature-Twenty-five Years of Protest? Of Progress?', *Journal of South Indian Literature*, Vol. 123, 1994, pp. 41–67.

Chowdhry, Ratnadeep, 'Nellie Massacre and "Citizenship", When 1800 Muslims were killed in Assam in Six Hours' *The Print*, 18 February 2019.

Chughtai, Ismat, *My Friend, My Enemy: Essays, Reminiscences, Portraits*, translated and introduced by Tahira Naqvi, New Delhi: Women Unlimited, 2015.

*Constituent Assembly Debates: Official Report*, New Delhi: Lok Sabha Secretariat, 1989.

Cooper, James M., 'Therapeutic Jurisprudence and the Rights of Self Determination' in Burton M. Leiser and Tom D. Campbell (eds.), *Human Rights in Philosophy and Practice*, Dartmouth: Ashgate, 2001.

D' Mello, Bernard, 'Spring Thunder Anew: Neo-Robber Baron Capitalism vs "New Democracy" in India', *Monthly Review*, 21 March 2010, available at <http://monthlyreview.org/commentary/spring-thunder-anew>.

Dangle, Arjun (ed.), *Poisoned Bread*, Hyderabad: Orient Blackswan, 2009.

Dalmia, Vasudha and Heinrich Von Stietencron (eds.), 'Introduction' in *Representing Hinduism: The Construction of Religious Traditions and National Identity*, New Delhi: Sage Publications, 1995.

———, 'Introduction' in *The Oxford India Hinduism Reader*, New Delhi: Oxford University Press, 2009.

Dalmiya, Vrinda, 'Care Ethics and Epistemic Justice: Some Insights from the Mahabharata', in Arindam Chakrabati and Sibaji Bandyopadhyay (eds.), *Mahabharata Now: Narration, Aesthetics, Ethics*, New Delhi: Routledge, 2014.

Das, Suranjan, *Communal Riots in Bengal 1905-1947*, New Delhi: Oxford University Press, 1993.

Dasarathi, Amala, 'Remembering Thangjam Manorama #Indian Women in History', *Feminism in India*.

Datta, V. N., *Madan Lal Dhingra and the Revolutionary Movement*, New Delhi: Vikas Publishing, 1978.

Deka, Harekrishna, 'Towards Freedom', translated from Assamese by Bibash Choudhury, *The Oxford Anthology of Writings from North-East India, Volume II: Poetry and Essays*, New Delhi: Oxford University Press, 2010.

Deogharia, Jaideep and B. Sridhar, 'Jharkhand lynching: 5 villagers held, 2 cops suspended', *Times of India*, 25 June 2019.

Desai, I. P., *Untouchability in Rural Gujarat*, Mumbai: Popular Prakashan, 1976.

Desai, Sonalde, 'Squandering the gender dividend', *The Hindu*, 12 June 2019.

Deshpande, Ashwini, *The Grammar of Caste: Economic Discrimination in Contemporary India*, New Delhi: Oxford University Press, 2011.

Deswal, Deepender, 'Bhagana Dalits convert to Islam for "dignified life"', *The Tribune*, 9 August 2015.

Devadas, David, *The Story of Kashmir: Geopolitics, Politics, Society, Culture, and Changing Aspirations,* New Delhi: David Devadas, 2019.

Drolla, Rashmi, 'Under a shadow of Maoist threats Chhattisgarh goes to the polls on Monday', *Times of India*, 11 November 2018.

Erikson, Erik H., *Gandhi's Truth: On the Origins of Militant Nonviolence,* New York:

W.W. Norton and Company, 1993.

Fanon, Frantz, *The Wretched of the Earth,* translated by Constance Farrington, Harmondsworth: Penguin Books, 2001.

Fraser, Bashabi, (ed.), *Bengal Partition Stories: An Undisclosed Chapter*, London: Anthem, 2006.

French, Patrick, *Liberty or Death: India's Journey to Independence and Division*, London: Flamingo, 1998.

Gandhi, M. K., 'Speech on Non-Cooperation, Calcutta, 22 December 1920', *Collected Works of Mahatma Gandhi*, Vol. 19, New Delhi: Government of India, Publications Division, 1966.

———, 'What is Truth', 20 November 1921, *Collected Works of Mahatma Gandhi*, Vol. 21, New Delhi: Government of India, Publications Division, 1966.

———, 'Speech on Fundamental Rights', *Collected Works of Mahatma Gandhi*, Vol. 45, New Delhi: Ministry of Information and Broadcasting, Publications Division, 1971.

———, *Hind Swaraj or Indian Home Rule*, Ahmedabad: Navajivan Publishing House, 2006.

Ganguly, Sumit, *Conflict Unending: India-Pakistan Tensions Since 1947,* New York: Columbia University Press, 2001.

Gatade, Subhash, 'Waiting for Swach Bharat: A Close Look at the Question of Caste, Sanitation, and Policy Approaches in India' in Kalpana Kannabiran and Asha Hans (eds.), *India Social Development Report 2016: Disability Rights Perspectives*, New Delhi: Council for Social Development and Oxford University Press, 2016.

Ghose, Debobrat, 'Dantewada MLA Bhima Mandavi killed by Naxals: Intelligence failure, non-adherence to SOP's and leaks to blame' *Firstpost*, 10 April 2019.

Goldsmith, Belinda and Meka Beresford, 'India most dangerous for women with sexual violence rife', Thomson Reuters Foundation, 26 June 2018.

Gopal, Ram, *Lokmanya Tilak*, Mumbai: Asia Publishing House, 1965.

Gopal, Sarvepalli, 'Nehru and Minorities', *Economic and Political Weekly*, Special Issue, Vol. 23, Nos. 45–47, November 1988.

Goswami, Uddipana, 'Would I be a poet still?' Cited in Rini Burman, 'Guns with Occasional Music: Female Poets from the Northeast', *Kindle Magazine*, 2014, available at <http://kindlemag.in/guns-ocassional-music-female-poets-northeast>.

Guevara, Ernesto Che, *Guerrilla Warfare*, New York: Monthly Review Press, 1961.

Gulzar, '"Faith is trapped in the teeth of fire": Two poems by Gulzar on India today', translated by Rakhshanda Jalil, *Scroll.in*, 2 December 2020.

———, *Footprints on Zero Line: Writings on the Partition,* translated by Rakhshanda Jalil, New Delhi: Harper Perennial, 2017.

Gupta, Tilak D., 'Maoism in India: Ideology, Programme and Armed Struggle, *Economic and Political Weekly,* Special issue on Maoist Movement in India, Vol. XLI, No. 29, 22-28 July 2006.

Habibullah, Wajahat, *My Kashmir: Conflict and the Prospects of Enduring Peace,*

Washington DC: United States Institute of Peace, 2008.

Harriss, John, 'What is Going on in India's "Red Corridor"? Questions About India's Maoist Insurgency' in Robin Jeffrey, Ronojoy Sen, and Pratima Singh (eds.), *More Than Maoism: Politics, Policies and Insurgencies in South Asia*, New Delhi: Manohar, 2012.

Hasrat, Karishma, 'ULFA I faces survival test after deputy chief's surrender. All about the rebel outfit in Assam', *The Print*, 19 November 2020.

Hazarika, Sanjoy, *Strangers No More: New Narratives from India's Northeast*, New Delhi: Aleph Book Company, 2018.

Heater, Derek Benjamin, *Citizenship: The Civic Ideal in World History, Politics, and Education,* Manchester: Manchester University Press, 2004.

Herbert, Christopher, *War of No Pity: The Indian Mutiny and Victorian Trauma*, Princeton: Princeton University Press, 2009.

Honneth, Axel, *The Struggle for Recognition: The Moral Grammar of Social Conflicts*, translated by Joel Anderson, Cambridge: Polity,1995.

Housman, A. E., *The Collected Poems of A. E. Housman*, New York: Henry Holt and Co., 1940.

Hunt, James D., *Gandhi in London*, New Delhi: Promilla and Co., 2012.

Hussain, Intizar, 'The City of Sorrow', translated from the Urdu by Vishwamitter Adil and Alok Bhalla, in Alok Bhalla (ed.), *Stories about the Partition of India*, Vol. 2, New Delhi: Indus, 1994.

Ignatieff, Michael, *Blood and Belonging: Journeys into the New Nationalism,* London: Vintage, 1994.

*India Human Development Report, Towards Social Inclusion*, New Delhi: Planning Commission, Government of India and Institute of Applied Manpower Research and Oxford University Press, 2011, 2014.

Iyer, Raghavan, *The Moral and Political Thought of Mahatma Gandhi*, New Delhi: Oxford University Press, 2000.

Jadhav, Narendra, *The Outcaste: A Dalit's Life*, translated from the Hindi by Arun Prabha Mukherjee, Kolkata: Samya, 2003.

Jaffrelot, Christophe and Sharik, Laliwala, 'Insider Ahmedabad's Juhapura: What's it Like for Muslims to Live in a Ghetto' *The Wire*, 12 September 2018.

Jagtap, Baburao, 'This Country is Broken,' translated by Vikas Sarang in Arjun Dangle (ed.) *Poisoned Bread*, Hyderabad: Orient Blackswan, 2009.

Jamil, Ghazala,' Night of Terror: The Dust Kicked Up Before the Babri Demolition' *The Wire*, 9 August 2020.

Jay, Anthony, *The Oxford Dictionary of Political Quotations,* Oxford: Oxford University Press, 2012.

Jennings, Ivor, *The Approach to Self-Government*, Cambridge: Cambridge University Press, 1956.

Jhadav, Narendra, *Ambedkar: Awakening India's Social Conscience*, New Delhi: Konark Publishers, 2014.

Jodhka, Surinder S, 'Caste and Untouchability in Rural Punjab', *Economic and Political Weekly*, Vol. 38, No. 19, 2002.

—— and Prakash Louis, 'Caste Tension in Punjab: Talhan and Beyond', *Economic and Political Weekly*, Vol. 38, No. 28, 2002.

John, Joseph and Rashmi Drolla, 'Maoists kill Salwa Judum founder Mahendra Karma along with other Congress leaders', *Times of India*, 26 May 2013.

Kakar, Sudhir, *The Colors of Violence*, New Delhi: Viking, 1995.

Kalyan, Das, 'Dalit youth thrashed for sitting on a chair, eating at wedding, dead', *Hindustan Times*, 5 May 2019.

Kar, Bodhisattva, 'When was the Postcolonial? The History of Policing Impossible Lines', in Sanjib Baruah (ed.), *Beyond Counter-Insurgency: Breaking the Impasse in Northeast India*, New Delhi: Oxford University Press, 2009.

Kareemuddin, S. and Ritesh Mishra, '5 persons killed in Maoist Strikes before P.M., Rahul campaign in Chhattisgarh', *Hindustan Times*, 8 November 2018.

Karmakar, Rahul, 'Special peace prayer in Nagaland', *The Hindu*, 6 February 2019.

Kaur, Inpreet, 'Warring Over Peace in Kashmir' in Waheguru Pal Singh Sidhu, Bushra Asif, and Cyrus Samii (eds.), *Kashmir: New Voices, New Approaches*, Boulder: Lynne Reinner, 2006.

Kaushik, Martand, 'Dalit literature goes global', *Times of India*, 5 April 2015.

Kikon, Dolly, 'From Loincloth, Suits to Battle Greens; Politics of Clothing the 'Naked' Naga', in Sanjib Baruah (ed.), *Beyond Counter-Insurgency: Breaking the Impasse in Northeast India*, New Delhi: Oxford University Press, 2009.

Kimura, Makiko, 'Agency of Rioters: A study of Decision-making in the Nellie Massacre, Assam, 1983' in Sanjib Baruah (ed.), *Beyond Counter-insurgency: Breaking the Impasse in Northeast India*, New Delhi: Oxford University Press, 2009.

Kire, Easterine, 'Locating Trauma in Mizo Literature: The Beloved Bullet' in Margaret Ch Zama (ed.), *Emerging Literatures from Northeast India: The Dynamics of Culture, Society and Identity,* New Delhi: Sage Publications, 2015.

Koul, Sudha, *The Tiger Ladies*, Boston: Beacon Press, 2002.

Krishnan, Subasri, 'Thirty-two years later, the Nellie Massacre remains all but forgotten', *The Caravan*, 18 February 2015.

Kunnath, Georg, 'Smouldering Dalit Fires in Bihar' in Alpha Shah and Judith Pettigrew (eds.), *Window Into a Revolution: Ethnographies of Maoism in India and Nepal,* New Delhi: Social Science Press and Orient Blackswan, 2012.

Lacina, Bethany, 'Rethinking Delhi's Northeast Policy: Why neither Counter-insurgency nor Winning Hearts and Mind is the Way Forward' in Sanjib Baruah (ed.), *Beyond Counter-insurgency: Breaking the Impasse in Northeast India*, New Delhi: Oxford University Press, 2009.

Lakshman, Shriram, U.S. Report takes note of CAA, NRC', *The Hindu*, 11 June 2020.

——, 'U.S. report expressed concern on communal violence in India', *The Hindu*, 23 June 2019.

Lenin, Vladimir N., *Questions of National Policy and Proletarian Internationalism*, Moscow: Foreign Languages Publishing House, undated.

Limbale, Sharankumar, 'The White Paper', translated by Priya Adarkar, in Arjun Dangle (ed.), *Poisoned Bread*, Hyderabad: Orient Blackswan, 2009.

Londhe, Baban, 'Shroud', in Arjun Dangle (ed.), *Poisoned Bread*, Hyderabad: Orient Blackswan, 2009.

Lustick, Ian S., Dan Miodownik, and Roy J. Eidelson, 'Secessionism in Multicultural States: Does Sharing Power Prevent or Encourage It?' *American Political Science Review*, Vol. 98, No. 2, May 2005, pp. 209–29.

Lynch, Allen C. 'Woodrow Wilson and the Principle of National Self-determination; As Applied to Habsburg Europe' in Henry Huttenbach and Francesco Privitera (eds.), *Self- determination from Versailles to Dayton, Its Historical Legacy*, University of Bologna: Angelo Longo Editore, 1999.

Mahmood, Saif, 'The secular agenda of humorist Urdu poetry', *Sabrang India*, 1 April 2016, available at <https://sabrangindia.in/column/secular-agenda-humourist-urdu-poetry>.

Majumdar, Bimanbehari, *Militant Nationalism in India and Its Socio-Religious Background*, Calcutta: General Printers and Publishers, 1966.

Mallapur, Chaitanya, 'Crimes against women up 83% but conviction rate hits 10-year low; Delhi reports highest crime rate in India', *Firstpost*, 12 December 2017.

Mallapur, Chaitanya, 'Communal violence rose by 28 % from 2014 to 2017, but 2008 remains year of highest instances of religious violence', *Firstpost*, 9 February 2019.

Manish, Sai, 'Babri Demolition, 25 years on: BJP's transition from Ram to reform to Ram' *Business Standard*, 6 August 2019.

Matilal, Bimal Krishna in Jonardon Ganeri (ed.), *Epistemology, Logic, and Grammar in Indian Philosophical Analysis*, Second edition, New Delhi: Oxford University Press, 2015.

Mendelsohn, Oliver, 'The Transformation of Authority in Rural India', *Modern Asian Studies*, Vol. 15, No. 4, 1993, pp. 805–42.

—— and Marika Vicziany, *The Untouchables: Subordination, Poverty and the State in Modern India*, Cambridge: Cambridge University Press, 1998.

Menon, Meena, *Riots and After in Mumbai: Chronicles of Truth and Reconciliation*, New Delhi: Sage Publications, 2011.

Miklian, Jason, 'The Purification Hunt: The Salwa Judum Counterinsurgency in Chhattisgarh India' in Alpa Shah and Judith Pettigrew (eds.), *Windows into a Revolution: Ethnographies of Maoism in India and Nepal*, New Delhi: Social Science Press and Orient BlackSwan, 2012.

Mishra, Ritesh, 'BSF officer killed in 6 serial blasts by Maoists in Chhattisgarh', *Hindustan Times*, 8 November 2018.

Misra, Tilottoma (ed.), *The Oxford Anthology of Writings from North-East India: Poetry and Essays*, Delhi: Oxford University Press, 2010.

——, 'Introduction' in *The Oxford Anthology of Writings from North-East India:*

*Fiction,* New Delhi: Oxford University Press, 2011.

Mohan, Deepanshu, 'Rising number of crimes against women reflects decay in India's institutions, *The Wire,* 18 April 2018.

Mohanty, Manoranjan, 'Challenges of Revolutionary Violence: The Naxalite Movement in Perspective', *Economic and Political Weekly,* Special issue on Maoist Movement in India,Vol. XLI, No. 29, 22–28 July 2006.

Mukherjee, Nirmalangshu, 'Arms Over the People: What Have the Maoists Achieved in Dandakaranya?', *Economic and Political Weekly,*Vol. XLV, No. 25, 19 June 2010,

Mukherjee, S. N., *Sir William Jones: A Study in Eighteenth-century British Attitudes to India,* Cambridge: Cambridge University Press, 1968.

Mukhim, Patricia, 'Where is this North-east?', *India International Centre Quarterly,* Vol. 32, 2005.

Mustafa, Faizan, 'SC/ST Act: Court ruling will have chilling effect on reporting crimes against Dalits', *The Wire,* 20 March 2018.

Naimisharay, Mohandas, *Apne Apne Pinjre,* New Delhi:Vani Prakashan, 2013.

Ngangom, Robin S., 'Everywhere I Go' in Tilottoma Misra (ed.), *The Oxford Anthology of Writings from North-East India: Poetry and Essays,* New Delhi: Oxford University Press, 2010.

Nongkynrih, Kynpham Sing and Robin S. Ngangom (eds.), *Anthology of Contemporary Poetry from the Northeast,* Shillong: NEHU, 2003.

Oberoi, Harjot Singh, *The Construction of Religious Boundaries,* Chicago: University of Chicago Press, 1994.

Office of the United Nations High Commissioner for Human Rights, *Report on the Situation of Human Rights in Kashmir; Developments in the Indian State of Jammu and Kashmir from June 2016 to April 2018 and General Human Rights Concerns in Azad Jammu and Kashmir and Gilgit-Baltistan,* 14 June 2018.

Oomen, T. K., *Reconciliation in Post-Godhra Gujarat: The Role of Civil Society,* New Delhi: Pearson/Longman, 2008.

Pawde, Kumud, 'The Story of My "Sanskrit"', translated by Priya Adarkar in Arjun Dangle (ed.), *The Poisoned Bread,* Hyderabad: Orient Blackswan, 2009.

Peer, Bahsharat, *Curfewed Nights,* New Delhi: Random House, 2010.

Plato, *The Apology,* translated by Benjamin Jowett, Chicago: William Benton, Encyclopedia Britannica, reprinted by Oxford University Press, 1952.

Rajagopal, Krishna Das, 'Manorama "mercilessly tortured"', *The Hindu,* 14 May 2014.

Rajagopal, Krishna, 'SC recalls verdict diluting SC/ST anti-atrocities law', *The Hindu,* 1 October 2019.

Ramanujam, Srinivasa, *Renunciation and Untouchability in India: The Notional and the Empirical in the Caste Order,* New Delhi: Routledge India, 2019.

Ramanujan, A. K., 'Is there an Indian way of thinking?' in McKim Marriott (ed.), *India through Hindu Categories,* New Delhi: Sage Publications, 1990.

Rammohun, E.N 'The Naga Insurgency-Part I', *The United Service Institution of India.*

Rao, Narasimha P.V., *Ayodhaya December 1992,* New Delhi: Penguin/Viking, 2006.

Sartre, Jean-Paul, 'Preface' in Frantz Fanon, *The Wretched of the Earth,* translated by Constance Farrington, Harmondsworth: Penguin Books, 2001.

Saxena, N. C., 'Nature and Origins of Communal Riots in India' in A. A. Engineer (ed.), *Communal Riots in Post-Independence India*, New Delhi: Sangam Books, 1984.

Schofield, Victoria, *Kashmir in Conflict: India, Pakistan and the Unending War,* New Delhi: Viva, 2010.

Seetharaman, G., 'National Register of Citizens in Assam: Issue of illegal foreigners continues to be a major political one', *Economic Times*, 14 June 2015.

Sethi, Nitin, 'As Forests Feed Growth, Tribals Given the Go-by' in Santosh Paul (ed.), *The Maoist Movement in India: Perspectives and Counterperspectives,* New Delhi: Routledge, 2013.

Shah, Ghanshyam, 'Communal riots in Gujarat: reports of a preliminary investigation', *Economic and Political Weekly*, Vol. 5, Nos. 3–5, 1970.

Shah, Zeeshan, 'Mumbai Riots 1992, Srikrishna Commission Report and Action Taken' *Indian Express*, 6 December 2017.

————, Harsh Mander, Sukhadeo Thorat, Satish Deshpande, and Amita Baviskar, *Untouchability In Rural India*, New Delhi: Sage Publications, 2006.

Shakespeare, William, *Macbeth* in Robert Maynard Hutchins (ed.), *Great Books of the Western World*, Vol. 2, Chicago: William Benton, 1952.

Shameem, Basharat, 'English Writing in Kashmir: A Literary Culture's Rise from Conflict', NewsClick, 27 March 2019, available at <http://www.newsclick.in/english-writing-kashmir-literary-cultures-rise-conflict>.

Sharma, Jyotirmaya, 'Savarkar's Justification for Himsa', Book Extract, *Outlook*, 2 October 2015.

Singh, Santosh, 'A lasting signature on Bihar's most violent years', *Indian Express*, 4 June 2012.

Singh, Tayenjam Bijoykumar, 'Kurukshetragi Peerang-Ratan Thiyam's Gift to Mothers' in Tilottoma Misra (ed.) *The Oxford Anthology of Writings from North-East India: Poetry and Essays*, New Delhi: Oxford University Press, 2010.

Singh, Tayenjam Bijoykumar, 'The Mauled Cub', in Tilottoma Misra (ed.), *The Oxford Anthology of Writings from North-East India: Fiction*, New Delhi: Oxford University Press, 2010.

Singh, Vijaita '75% of militants killed in Kashmir Valley were locals', *The Hindu*, 3 June 2019.

————, 'Peace deal on verge of being finalized say Naga groups', *The Hindu*, 11 September 2020.

Sinha, Chinki, 'Everyone's a poet of loss, memory and madness in Kashmir', *DailyO*, 17 August 2016.

Soni, Anusha, 'Supreme Court rejects PIL seeking probe into killing, exodus of Kashmiri Pandits' *India Today*, 24 July 2017.

Sundar, Nandini, 'Bastar, Maoism and Salwa Judum', *Economic and Political Weekly*, Special issue on Maoist Movement in India, Vol. XLI, No. 29, 22–28 July 2006.

Syam, Amreeta, 'Kurukshetra' in P. Lal (ed.), *Vyasa's Mahabharata: Creative Insights*, Calcutta: Writers Workshop, 1992.

Talbot, Ian and Darshan Singh Tatla (eds.), *Epicentres of Violence: Partition Voices and Memories from Amritsar*, Ranikhet: Permanent Black, 2006.

Tambiah, Stanley J., *Leveling Crowds: Ethnonationalist Conflicts and Collective Violence in South Asia*, Berkeley: University of California Press, 1997.

Teltumbde, Anand, *Khairlanji: A Strange and Bitter Crop*, New Delhi: Navayana, 2008.

———, *Republic of Caste*, New Delhi: Navayana, 2018.

Thapar, Romila, 'Imagined Religious Communities? Ancient History and the Modern Search for a Hindu Identity', *Modern Asian Studies*, Vol. 3, No. 2, 1989, pp. 60–88.

*The Mahabharata of Krishna-Dwaipayana Vyasa*, translated by Kisari Mohan Ganguly, Vol. 8, Shanti Parva, Part I, New Delhi: Munshiram Manoharlal, 1998.

Tikoo, Anmol, 'What About the Kashmiri Pandits? Thirty Years Later Make the Question Count' *The Wire*, 23 January 2020.

Tripathi, Rahul, 'The contours of the new Red map', *Indian Express*, 27 November 2020.

Tunzelmann, Alex von, *The Secret History of the End of an Empire*, London: Simon and Schuster, 2007.

UNDP Human Development Report, *The Real Wealth of Nations: Pathways to Human Development*, available at <http://www.hdr.undp.org/sites/default/files/reports/270/hdr_2010_en_complete_reprint.pdf>.

Valmiki, Omprakash, *Jhoothan: A Dalit's Life*, translated from the Hindi by Arun Prabha Mukherjee, Kolkata: Samya, 2003.

Vatsayan S. H., 'Agyeya', 'Getting Even' in Bhalla (ed.) *Stories about the Partition of India*, Vol. 1, New Delhi: Manohar Publishers, 2012.

Venkatesan, J., 'Salwa Judum is illegal says Supreme Court', *The Hindu*, 5 July 2011.

Vignesh, V., 'The great divide', *New Indian Express*, 3 June 2018.

Waheed, Mirza, *The Collaborators*, New Delhi: Penguin Books India, 2012.

Wal, Aradhna, 'Reliving a nightmare', *The Hindu*, 12 May 2014.

Wessler, Heinz Werner, 'Who am I?: On the narrativity of identity and violence in Sheila Rohekar's novel *Taviz*', *Orientalia Suecana*, Vol. 60, 2011, pp. 49–59.

White-Spunner, Barney, *Partition: The Story of Indian Independence and the Creation of Pakistan in 1947*, London: Simon and Schuster, 2017.

Yashpal, *This Is Not That Dawn* (Jhootha Sach), Anand (tr.), New Delhi: Penguin Books India, 2010.

# INDEX